HUMAN RIGHTS IN THE CONSTITUTIONAL LAW OF THE UNITED STATES

In the period since the end of the Second World War, there has emerged what never before existed: a truly global morality. Some of that morality – the morality of human rights – has become entrenched in the constitutional law of the United States. This book explicates the morality of human rights and elaborates three internationally recognized human rights that are embedded in U.S. constitutional law: the right not to be subjected to cruel, inhuman, or degrading punishment; the right to moral equality; and the right to religious and moral freedom. The implications of one or more of these rights for three great constitutional controversies – capital punishment, same-sex marriage, and abortion – are discussed in depth. Along the way, Michael J. Perry addresses the question of the proper role of the Supreme Court of the United States in adjudicating these controversies.

Michael J. Perry holds a Robert W. Woodruff Chair at Emory University, where he teaches in the law school. Previously, Perry held the Howard J. Trienens Chair in Law at Northwestern University, where he taught for fifteen years, and the University Distinguished Chair in Law at Wake Forest University. Perry has written on American constitutional law and theory; law, morality, and religion; and human rights theory in more than seventy-five articles and essays and eleven books, including *The Political Morality of Liberal Democracy*; *The Idea of Human Rights*; *We the People: The Fourteenth Amendment and the Supreme Court*; *Under God? Religious Faith and Liberal Democracy*; *Toward a Theory of Human Rights: Religion, Law, Courts*; and *Constitutional Rights, Moral Controversy, and the Supreme Court*.

Human Rights in the Constitutional Law of the United States

Michael J. Perry

Emory University School of Law

CAMBRIDGE
UNIVERSITY PRESS

CAMBRIDGE UNIVERSITY PRESS
Cambridge, New York, Melbourne, Madrid, Cape Town,
Singapore, São Paulo, Delhi, Mexico City

Cambridge University Press
32 Avenue of the Americas, New York, NY 10013-2473, USA

www.cambridge.org
Information on this title: www.cambridge.org/9781107666085

First published 2013

Printed in the United States of America

A catalog record for this publication is available from the British Library.

Library of Congress Cataloging in Publication Data

Perry, Michael J.
Human rights in the constitutional law of the United States / Michael J. Perry.
    pages cm
Includes index.
ISBN 978-1-107-03836-3 (hardback)
1. Civil rights – United States.   2. Constitutional law – United States.   3. Human rights –
United States.   4. Human rights.   I. Title.
KF4749.P47   2013
342.7308′5–dc23   2013007042

ISBN 978-1-107-03836-3 Hardback
ISBN 978-1-107-66608-5 Paperback

For Sarah, Daniel, and Gabriel, the loves of my life

CONTENTS

ABOUT THE AUTHOR

Michael J. Perry specializes in three areas: Constitutional Law, Human Rights, and Law and Religion. He is the author of twelve books and more than seventy-five articles and essays. The titles of Perry's books reflect his particular interests: *The Constitution, the Courts, and Human Rights* (Yale, 1982); *Morality, Politics, and Law* (Oxford, 1988); *Love and Power: The Role of Religion and Morality in American Politics* (Oxford, 1991); *The Constitution in the Courts: Law or Politics?* (Oxford, 1994); *Religion in Politics: Constitutional and Moral Perspectives* (Oxford, 1997); *The Idea of Human Rights: Four Inquiries* (Oxford, 1998); *We the People: The Fourteenth Amendment and the Supreme Court* (Oxford, 1999); *Under God? Religious Faith and Liberal Democracy* (Cambridge, 2003); *Toward a Theory of Human Rights: Religion, Law, Courts* (Cambridge, 2007); *Constitutional Rights, Moral Controversy, and the Supreme Court* (Cambridge, 2009); *The Political Morality of Liberal Democracy* (Cambridge, 2010); and *Human Rights in the Constitutional Law of the United States* (Cambridge, 2013).

Since 2003, Perry has held a Robert W. Woodruff University Chair at Emory University, where he teaches in the law school. A Woodruff Chair is the highest honor Emory University bestows on a member of its faculty.

Before coming to Emory, Perry was the inaugural occupant of the Howard J. Trienens Chair in Law at Northwestern University (1990–97), where he taught for fifteen years (1982–97). He then held the University Distinguished Chair in Law at Wake Forest University (1997–2003). Perry began his teaching career at the Ohio State University College of Law (1975–82) and has taught as a visiting professor at several law schools: Yale (1978–9), Tulane (spring semester, 1987), New York Law School (spring semester, 1990), the University of Tokyo

United States. My aim in Part I of this book is to provide that basic understanding. I begin, in Chapter 1, by sketching the internationalization of human rights: the growing international recognition and protection, in the period since the end of the Second World War, of certain rights as human rights. Then, in Chapter 2, I explain what it means to say, in the context of the internationalization of human rights, that a right is a "human right." Finally, in Chapter 3, I discuss the normative ground of human rights: the fundamental imperative, articulated in the very first article of the foundational human rights document of our time – the Universal Declaration of Human Rights (1948) – that governments "act towards all human beings in a spirit of brotherhood."

With Part I behind us, we are ready to turn, in Part II, to the constitutional morality of the United States. The three international human rights with which I am concerned in this book – each of which, as I explain in due course, is entrenched in the constitutional law of the United States and is therefore part of the constitutional morality of the United States – are the right not to be subjected to "cruel and unusual" punishment, the right to moral equality, and the right to religious and moral freedom. (At the beginning of Part II, I identify the conditions whose satisfaction warrants our concluding that a right is entrenched in the constitutional law of the United States.) I elaborate each of those three rights in Part II, and I pursue three inquiries:

- Does punishing a criminal by killing him or her violate the right not to be subjected to "cruel and unusual" punishment?
- Does excluding same-sex couples from civil marriage violate the right to moral equality or the right to religious and moral freedom?
- Does criminalizing abortion violate the right to moral equality or the right to religious and moral freedom?

I also pursue, in Part II, a fourth inquiry: In exercising judicial review *of a certain sort* – judicial review to determine whether a law (or other public policy) claimed to violate a right that is part of the constitutional morality of the United States does in fact violate the right – should the Supreme Court of the United States inquire whether *in its own judgment* the law violates the right? Or, instead, should the Court proceed deferentially, inquiring only whether *the lawmakers' judgment* that the law does *not* violate the right is a reasonable one? In short, how large or small a role should the Court play in protecting (enforcing) the constitutional morality of the United States?

I HAVE LONG BEEN ENGAGED BY, and have before written about, questions such as those I address in this book: questions about the implications of constitutionally entrenched human rights – and the question about the proper role of the Supreme Court in adjudicating such questions. (The title of my first book, published over thirty years ago, in 1982: *The Constitution, the Courts, and Human Rights*.) Indeed, I have before written about each of the three constitutional controversies at the heart of this book: capital punishment, same-sex marriage, and abortion. Because I am not satisfied with my earlier efforts, I revisit the controversies here.

ACKNOWLEDGEMENTS

I am grateful, for his counsel, to my editor at Cambridge University Press, John Berger, and, for their helpful comments, to the readers for the Cambridge University Press. For extensive written comments on the penultimate draft of this book, I am grateful to Daniel Conkle, Indiana University (Bloomington) College of Law. For helpful comments as I was preparing the final draft, I am grateful to Jason Mazzone, University of Illinois College of Law, and to Rafael Domingo Osle, University of Navarra (Spain) School of Law. For discussion of issues concerning capital punishment as I was drafting Chapter 4, I am grateful both to Cathleen Kaveny, University of Notre Dame School of Law and Department of Theology, and to John Stinneford, University of Florida College of Law. For discussion of issues concerning abortion as I was drafting Chapter 9, I am grateful to Gerry Whyte, Trinity College (Dublin) Faculty of Law. Finally, I am indebted to my students – both my students at Emory Law and my students at University of San Diego School of Law, where I taught for three consecutive fall semesters during the time I was drafting this book. My students are, for me, indispensable conversation partners.

I was privileged to discuss the material in Chapter 7, on the right to religious and moral freedom, and in Chapter 8, on same-sex marriage, in several venues. I am grateful, for their helpful comments, to the discussants in each of those venues: in March 2011, a one-week intrasession course at University of Dayton School of Law, co-taught with Richard Saphire; in May 2011, a symposium at Bar Ilan University, Tel Aviv, Israel, on Religious Law and State's Affairs; in September 2011, two faculty workshops at Washington University in St. Louis, one at the School of Law, the other at the John C. Danforth Center on Religion and Politics; in October 2011, a conference at Yale Divinity School on Same-Sex Marriage and the Catholic Church: Voices from Law, Religion, and the Pews; in November 2011, a faculty workshop at Pepperdine University School of Law; in March 2012, the Overton and Lavona Currie Lecture in Law and Religion at Emory University School of Law; in September 2012, a conference at the Fondazione Studium Generale Marcianum, Venice, Italy, hosted by the Alta Scuola Società Economia Teologia, on Political Representation in a Plural Society: People, Religion and Parties between East and West; in November 2012, the Stanford Interdisciplinary Conference on Conscience at Stanford University; and in February 2013, a lecture in the 2012–13 Lecture Series sponsored by the Buechner Institute, King College, Bristol, Tennessee.

An earlier version of Chapter 3, on the normative ground of human rights, appeared both in Charles Taliaferro, Victoria S. Harrison, and Stewart Goetz, eds., *The Routledge Companion to Theism* (2013) and in Mark Goodale, ed., *Human Rights at the Crossroads* (2013). An earlier version of material in Chapters 7 and 8, on the right to religious and moral freedom (Chapter 7) and the implications of the right for the controversy over same-sex marriage (Chapter 8), appeared in *Journal of State and Religion* (2012); a somewhat later version of the material appeared in J. Patrick Hornbeck II and Michael Norko, eds., *More Than a Monologue: Sexual Diversity and the Catholic Church, Volume 2: Inquiry, Thought, and Expression* (2013).

Part I   **THE MORALITY OF HUMAN RIGHTS**

1915 to 1923, the Ottoman Turks, who were Muslim, committed genocide against the Armenian minority, who were Christian.[3]
Not counting deaths inflicted in battle, the Soviet Union's Joseph
Stalin was responsible for the deaths of over forty-two million people (1929–53); China's Mao Zedong, over thirty-seven million (1923–
76); and Germany's Adolph Hitler, over twenty million (1933–45),
including over ten million Slavs and about five and a half million
Jews.[4]

One need only mention these places to recall some more recent
atrocities: Cambodia (1975–9), Bosnia (1992–5), Rwanda (1994),
and, in the early years of the twenty-first century, the Darfur region of
Sudan.[5]

several: murder, starvation, exhaustion, exposure, disease, and a plummeting birth rate.
See 225–34. As Hochschild observes, this was "a death toll of Holocaust dimensions," 4.
The holocaust in the Congo was not an isolated event. See, e.g., Giles Foden, "Rehearsal
for Genocide," *New York Times Book Review*, Apr. 20, 2003; Ross A. Slotten, "AIDS in
Namibia," 41 *Social Science Medicine* 277 (1995): "In 1884, Namibia formally became
a German colony and was known as German South West Africa. During the time of
annexation, the Herero and Nama peoples were the largest tribes, inhabiting the most
desirable land, which the Germans gradually expropriated between 1893 and 1903. This
expropriation led to many battles, culminating in the intentional genocide of 60% of the
population. To this day, the Hereros and Namas have not recovered their original numerical
strength."

[3] See Israel W. Charney, ed., *Encyclopedia of Genocide* 61–105 (1999). See also Peter
Balakian, *The Burning Tigris: The Armenian Genocide and America's Response* (2003).

[4] See Charney, *Encyclopedia of Genocide*, 29 (Table 5) and 439: "[The Nazi] genocides
likely cost the lives of about 16,300,000 people: nearly 5,300,000 Jews, 260,000 Gypsies,
10,500,000 Slavs, and 220,000 homosexuals, as well as another 10,000 handicapped
Germans." See also Ian Kershaw, "Afterthought: Some Reflections on Genocide, Religion,
and Modernity," in Omer Bartov and Phyllis Mack, eds., *In God's Name: Genocide and
Religion in the Twentieth Century* 377 (2001): "The Nazi genocide against the Jews – the
Holocaust, as it now called – is estimated to have resulted in the murder of about five
and a half million Jews in Nazi-occupied Europe, around half the number targeted in the
notorious Wannsee Conference of January 1942."

In *Bloodlands: Europe between Hitler and Stalin* (2010), historian Timothy Snyder
writes: "Today there is widespread agreement that the mass killing of the twentieth
century is of the greatest moral significance for the twenty-first. How striking, then,
that there is no history of the bloodlands" (xix). Thanks to Snyder's extensive, sear-
ing account, we now have that history. For an informative review of Snyder's book, see
Anne Applebaum, "The Worst of the Madness," *New York Review of Books*, Nov. 11,
2010.

[5] For a narrative of the failures of the United States to respond to genocides, see Samantha
Power, *"A Problem from Hell": America and the Age of Genocide* (2002).

Sadly, there is so much more.[6] For an exhaustive and exhausting account of the grim – indeed, horrific – details, one can consult the two-volume *Encyclopedia of Genocide*, which reports:

> In total, during the first eighty-eight years of [the twentieth] century, almost 170 million men, women, and children were shot, beaten, tortured, knifed, burned, starved, frozen, crushed, or worked to death; buried alive, drowned, hanged, bombed, or killed in any other of the myriad other ways governments have inflicted deaths on unarmed, helpless citizens and foreigners. Depending on whether one used high or more conservative estimates, the dead could conceivably be more than 360 million people. It is as though our species has been devastated by a modern Black Plague.[7]

The twentieth century was not only a dark and bloody time, however. Beginning in the middle of the twentieth century, a growing number of countries around the world responded to the savage horrors of the twentieth century by recognizing certain rights as human rights and enshrining them in constitutions and/or treaties, thereby rendering the moral landscape of the twentieth century a touch less bleak.[8]

The first major event in the internationalization of human rights took place on June 26, 1945, shortly before the end of the Second

---

[6] See, e.g., Mark Danner, *The Massacre at El Mozote: A Parable of the Cold War* (1994); Iris Chang, *The Rape of Nanking: The Forgotten Holocaust of World War II* (1997); Philip Dray, *At the Hands of Persons Unknown: The Lynching of Black America* viii (2002): "Through 1944, when lynchings first began to decline strongly, [the Tuskegee Institute] recorded 3,417 lynchings of blacks . . . Not until 1952 did a year pass without a single recorded lynching." See generally Jonathan Glover, *Humanity: A Moral History of the Twentieth Century* (1999).

[7] Charney, *Encyclopedia of Genocide*, 28. On genocide in particular, see Roger W. Smith, "American Self-Interest and the Response to Genocide," *Chronicle of Higher Education*, July 30, 2004: "[G]enocide – intentional acts to eliminate in whole, or in substantial part, a specific human population – has claimed the lives of some 60 million people in the 20th century, 16 million of them since 1945, when the watchword was 'Never again.' Genocide has, in fact, been so frequent, the number of victims so extensive, and serious attempts to prevent it so few, that many scholars have described the 20th century as 'the age of genocide.'" See generally Daniel Jonah Goldhagen, *Worse than War: Genocide, Eliminationism, and the Ongoing Assault on Humanity* (2009).

[8] For a brief account of the "historical antecedents" of international human rights, see Thomas Buergenthal, Dinah Shelton, and David P. Stewart, *International Human Rights* 1–28 (4th ed. 2009).

World War:[9] the signing of the Charter of the United Nations, which entered into force four months later, on October 24. These are the salient Charter provisions for present purposes:

- The Preamble: "We the peoples of the United Nations [are] determined . . . to reaffirm faith in fundamental human rights, in the dignity and worth of the human person, in the equal rights of men and women and of nations large and small."
- Article 1(3): "The purposes of the United Nations are . . . to achieve international cooperation . . . in promoting and encouraging respect for human rights and for fundamental freedoms for all without distinction as to race, sex, language, or religion."
- Article 13(1): "The General Assembly shall initiate studies and make recommendations for the purpose of . . . assisting in the realization of human rights and fundamental freedoms for all without distinction as to race, sex, language, or religion."
- Article 55(3): "With a view to the creation of conditions of stability and well-being which are necessary for peaceful and friendly relations among nations based on respect for the principle of equal rights and self-determination of peoples, the United Nations shall promote . . . universal respect for, and observance of, human rights and fundamental freedoms for all without distinction as to race, sex, language, or religion."
- Article 56: All Members pledge themselves to take joint and separate action in cooperation with the [United Nations] for achievement of the purposes set forth in Article 55.
- Article 62(2): "[The Economic and Social Council] may make recommendations for the purpose of promoting respect for, and observance of, human rights and fundamental freedoms for all."
- Article 68: "The Economic and Social Council shall set up commissions . . . for the promotion of human rights."

---

[9] Although the European phase of the Second World War ended in May 1945, the Pacific phase continued into the summer. In August 1945, the United States inaugurated nuclear warfare by dropping two atomic bombs on Japan: the first ("Little Boy") on Hiroshima, on August 6; the second ("Fat Man") on Nagasaki, on August 9.

the treaty, when a number of countries – specified in the text of the treaty – become parties to the treaty.) As of December 2012, there were 167 parties to the ICCPR, including, as of 1992, the United States; 114 parties to the (First) Optional Protocol to the ICCPR; and 160 parties to the ICESCR. In 1989, the UN General Assembly adopted the Second Optional Protocol to the ICCPR, "aiming at the abolition of the death penalty"; in 1991, the protocol entered into force; as of December 2012, there were 75 parties to the protocol.

At the website of the Office of the United Nations High Commissioner for Human Rights, there is a list of five documents under the heading "The International Bill of Human Rights," namely, the UDHR and the four treaties referenced in the preceding paragraph: the ICCPR, the (First) Optional Protocol to the ICCPR, the Second Optional Protocol to the ICCPR, and the ICESCR. The ICCPR and the ICESCR are called "covenants" – rather than "conventions," which is the standard title for the other UN-sponsored human rights treaties – to mark their singular importance, along with the UDHR, as the foundational documents of international human rights.

The treaties listed under the heading "The International Bill of Human Rights" are not the only, or even the earliest, international human rights treaties. Here, in the order in which they were adopted by the UN General Assembly, is a list of the other principal such treaties now in force, along with their optional protocols now in force and the names of the bodies responsible for monitoring compliance with the treaties. The year each treaty or protocol entered into force is indicated parenthetically, as is the number of state parties to each treaty and protocol as of December 2012.

- Convention on the Prevention and Punishment of the Crime of Genocide (1951; 142 parties, including, as of 1988, the United States); no monitoring body.
- International Convention on the Elimination of All Forms of Racial Discrimination (1969; 175 parties, including, as of 1994, the United States); Committee on the Elimination of Racial Discrimination.
- Convention on the Elimination of All Forms of Discrimination against Women (1981; 187 parties, but not the United States); Optional Protocol to the Convention on the Elimination of All Forms

of Discrimination against Women (2000; 104 parties, but not the United States); Committee on the Elimination of Discrimination against Women.

- Convention against Torture and Other Cruel, Inhuman or Degrading Treatment or Punishment (1987; 153 parties, including, as of 1994, the United States); Optional Protocol to the Convention against Torture and Other Cruel, Inhuman or Degrading Treatment or Punishment (2006; 65 parties, but not the United States); Committee against Torture.
- Convention on the Rights of the Child (1990; 193 parties, but not the United States[17]); Optional Protocol to the Convention on the Rights of the Child on the involvement of children in armed conflict (2002; 150 parties, including, as of 2002, the United States); Optional Protocol to the Convention on the Rights of the Child on the sale of children, child prostitution, and child pornography (2002; 162 parties, including, as of 2002, the United States); Committee on the Rights of the Child.
- International Convention on the Protection of the Rights of All Migrant Workers and Members of Their Families (2003; 46 parties, but not the United States); Committee on Migrant Workers.
- Convention on the Rights of Persons with Disabilities (2008; 127 parties, but not the United States); Optional Protocol to the Convention on the Rights of Person with Disabilities (2008; 76 parties, but not the United States); Committee on the Rights of Persons with Disabilities.
- International Convention for the Protection of All Persons from Enforced Disappearance (2010; 37 parties, but not the United States); Committee on Enforced Disappearances.[18]

---

[17] The Convention on the Rights of the Child has more parties than any other UN-sponsored human rights treaty. Only the United States and Somalia are not parties. On the Convention, see Ursula Kilkelly, "The CRC at 21: Assessing the Legal Impact," 62 *Northern Ireland Legal Quarterly* 143 (2011).

[18] For a recent argument that the UDHR "and subsequent documents building on the UDHR's mandate have not had identifiable impact on the structures of violence and misery that continue to plague humanity," see Ibrahim J. Gassama, "A World Made of Violence and Misery: Human Rights as a Failed Project of Liberal Internationalism," 37

To appreciate fully the breadth of the internationalization of human rights in the second half of the twentieth century, it is important to understand that the UN Human Rights System is not the only human rights system. There are four transnational – or, as they are often called, regional – human rights systems: European, Inter-American, African, and Arab.[19]

Moreover, if the legal system of a country articulates and enforces human rights, that legal system is, in part, a human rights system. Because the legal system of Canada, for example, articulates and enforces human rights, the Canadian legal system is, in part, a human rights system. (Canada's Charter of Rights and Freedoms, which is part of the Canadian Constitution, articulates many human rights, which are judicially enforced.) And, indeed, the legal system of virtually every country in the world articulates and enforces, or purports

---

Brooklyn Journal of International Law 407 (2012). (The quoted language appears at 408). Gassama writes (456):

> Whatever measure of success they may claim has been in areas far from those who most need the promises of the UDHR and its progenies. The numerous covenants, conventions, treaties, agreements, protocols, resolutions, and other similar indicia of accomplishments by lawyers and diplomats and activists have not prevented recurring genocide, crimes against humanity, ethnic cleansing, widespread torture, famine, trafficking, and the like from happening. A world of abject poverty, millions of people dying from preventable ills, environmental exploitation and destruction, and unfettered violence remain a well-tolerated part of our global order.

[19] Of the four, the European and the Inter-American systems are the most developed. The newest of the four – the Arab human rights system – is the least developed. For a succinct introduction to the regional human rights systems, see Buergenthal et al., *International Human Rights*, 160–373. For a lengthy study, see Dinah Shelton, ed., *Regional Protection of Human Rights* (2008). For an excellent set of materials on the most developed of the four regional systems, see Mark W. Janis, Richard S. Kay, and Anthony W. Bradley, eds., *European Human Rights Law: Text and Materials* (3rd ed. 2008).

Will there soon be a fifth regional human rights system? See Yuval Ginbar, "Human Rights in ASEAN – Setting Sail or Treading Water?," 10 *Human Rights Law Review* 504 (2010); Diane A. Desierto, "ASEAN's Constitutionalization of International Law: Challenges to Evolution under the New ASEAN Charter," 49 *Columbia Journal of Transnational Law* 268 (2010–11); Yung-Ming Yen, "The Formation of the ASEAN Intergovernmental Commission on Human Rights: A Protracted Journey," 10 *Journal of Human Rights* 353 (2011). "ASEAN" is the Association of Southeast Asian Nations.

to enforce, human rights: "Human rights are enshrined in the constitutions of virtually every one of [the world's] states – old states and new; religious, secular, and atheist; Western and Eastern; democratic, authoritarian, and totalitarian; market economy, socialist, and mixed; rich and poor, developing, developed, and less developed."[20]

[20] Louis Henkin, *The Age of Rights* ix (1990). As a practical matter, however, that a right is enshrined in a constitution too often means little if anything. See David S. Law and Mila Versteeg, "Sham Constitutions," 101 *California Law Review* (2013). Cf. Benedikt Goderis and Mila Versteeg, "Human Rights Violations after 9/11 and the Role of Constitutional Constraints," 41 *Journal of Legal Studies* 131 (2012).

It is a promising development that over one hundred countries have established what are known as National Human Rights Institutions (NHRIs): administrative institutions whose responsibilities include monitoring, and making recommendations with respect to, the human rights situation in the country, including the country's compliance (or not) with its international commitments, and receiving and investigating complaints from individuals and groups that their human rights have been, or are being, violated. On NHRIs and their recent growth, see the essays collected in Ryan Goodman and Thomas Pegram, eds., *Human Rights, State Compliance, and Social Change: Assessing National Human Rights Institutions* (2012). See also Rachel Murray, "The Role of National Human Rights Institutions," in Mashood A. Baderin and Manisuli Senyonjo, eds., *International Human Rights Law: Six Decades after the UDHR and Beyond* 304 (2010); Thomas Pegram, "Diffusion across Political Systems: The Global Spread of National Human Rights Institutions," 32 *Human Rights Quarterly* 729 (2010).

2 WHAT IS A "HUMAN RIGHT"?

Notwithstanding their European origins, . . . [i]n Asia, Africa, and South America, [human rights now] constitute the only language in which the opponents and victims of murderous regimes and civil wars can raise their voices against violence, repression, and persecution, against injuries to their human dignity.

– Jürgen Habermas[1]

Again, my aim in Part I of this book is to provide a basic understanding of the morality of human rights, in preparation for our exploration, in Part II, of certain aspects of the constitutional morality of the United States. Toward that end, a clarification of what Jürgen Habermas, in the passage just quoted, calls the "language" of human rights is in order.[2] In this chapter, I explain what it means, in the context of the internationalization of human rights, to say that a right is a "human right," and I then explain what sort of right a human right is: legal? moral? both?

WHEN WE READ ANY HUMAN RIGHTS INSTRUMENT, be it international, regional, or national, we see that the substantive provisions of the instrument – as distinct from the procedural provisions, which concern such things as monitoring bodies and reporting requirements – state rules of conduct. More precisely, the substantive provisions state rules of conduct *mainly for government*, both rules that direct government *not* to do something *to* human beings and rules

---

[1] Jürgen Habermas, *Religion and Rationality: Essays on Reason, God, and Modernity* 153–4 (Eduardo Mendieta, ed., 2002).

[2] Cf. Lloyd Weinreb, "Natural Law and Rights," in Robert P. George, ed., *Natural Law Theory: Contemporary Essays* 278, 281 (1992): "[D]espite their ubiquity in our discourse, it is unclear just what a right is."

that direct government *to do* something *for* human beings. As Habermas emphasizes, the language (vocabulary, terminology) of "human rights" has become the principal language in which such rules are articulated and discussed. Moreover, the language of "rights" entails the language of "duties": To say that A has a "right" that B not do X to A is to say that B has a "duty" not to do X to A; to say that A has a "right" that B do Y for A is to say that B has a "duty" to do Y for A.

In the language of "rights" and "duties," those whose conduct is governed by a rule are duty-bearers with respect to the rule, and those to whom the duty-bearers are not to do something or for whom the duty-bearers are to do something are rights-holders. To say that someone, A, "has" a particular right is a way of saying that there is a particular rule of conduct according to which A is a rights-holder. And to say that someone, B, has "violated" a particular right of A's is to say that there is a particular rule of conduct according to which A is a rights-holder and B is a duty-bearer and that B has done to A what according to the rule the duty-bearers are not to do to the rights-holders, or that B has not done for A what according to the rule the duty-bearers are to do for the rights-holders.

However, to say that there is a particular right – a particular rule of conduct – is *not* to say what authority, if any, the right/rule has. In saying that there is a particular right, one may claim that the right is: (1) legislated (so to speak) by God, (2) warranted by "reason," (3) protected in the legal system of one's country, (4) listed in a treaty to which one's country is a party, and so on. The claim that a particular right/rule has this or that authority – that, for example, the right/rule is warranted by "reason" – is contestable and indeed may be false.

As the various international human rights treaties – all of which I listed in the preceding chapter – illustrate:

- In the case of all international human rights, the duty-bearers include government actors.
- In the case of most international human rights, the duty-bearers include only government actors.
- In the case of some international human rights, the duty-bearers include nongovernment ("private") actors as well as government actors.

- In the case of most international human rights, the rights-holders include all human beings (i.e., all *born* human beings[3]).
- In the case of some international human rights, however, the rights-holders include not *all* human beings but only *some*.

Article 37 of the Convention on the Rights of the Child (CRC), which is the most widely ratified international human rights treaty,[4] is an example of an international human right according to which the rights-holders are not all human beings but only some: Article 37 requires governments to "ensure that: (a) ... Neither capital punishment nor life imprisonment without possibility of release shall be imposed for offences committed by persons below eighteen years of age." Article 38 of the CRC is another example: Article 38 requires governments to "refrain from recruiting any person who has not attained the age of fifteen years into their armed forces."

As Articles 37 and 38 of the CRC reflect, that government may justifiably do something to some human beings does not entail that government may justifiably do the same thing to all human beings; that government may justifiably recruit adults into the military does not entail that it may justifiably recruit children. Similarly, that government may justifiably decline to do something for some human beings – for example, able-bodied persons – does not entail that that it may justifiably decline to do the same thing for human beings who are disabled. One of the most recent international human rights treaties to enter into force (2008) is the Convention on the Rights of Persons with Disabilities.[5]

In what sense is a right according to which the rights-holders are not all human beings but only some – for example, children – truly a *human* right? The Universal Declaration of Human Rights (UDHR) states, in Article 1, that "[a]ll human beings ... should act towards one another

---

[3] The UDHR states, in Article 1, that "[a]ll human beings are born free and equal in dignity ... and should act towards one another in a spirit of brotherhood." See Chapter 9 (discussing abortion as a human rights issue).

[4] As of December 2012, there were 193 State Parties to the CRC: every member of the United Nations except Somalia and the United States.

[5] As of December 2012, there were 127 State Parties to the Convention on the Rights of Persons with Disabilities.

in a spirit of brotherhood." As the concept "human right" is understood in the UDHR and in all the international human rights treaties, a right is a *human* right, *even if according to the right the rights-holders are not all but only some human beings*, if the fundamental rationale for establishing and protecting the right – for example, as a treaty-based right – is that conduct that violates the right violates the imperative to "act towards all human beings in a spirit of brotherhood," which imperative is the normative ground of human rights. (I discuss the normative ground of human rights in the next chapter.) The fundamental rationale for Article 38 of the CRC is that conduct that violates Article 38 fails to act "in a spirit of brotherhood" toward some human beings: children.

ARE HUMAN RIGHTS LEGAL RIGHTS? A particular right – including a particular human right – is a legal right in a particular country, *in a meaningfully practical sense of "legal,"* if and only if the right is generally enforceable in that country. So, a particular right – for example, the right to freedom of religion – may be a legal right in one country (e.g., Canada) but not in another (e.g., Saudi Arabia).

We discussed the UDHR in the preceding chapter. It bears emphasis that the fact that a right is listed in the UDHR does not mean that the right is a legal right anywhere, because that a right is listed in the UDHR does not mean that the right is enforceable anywhere. Indeed, as Eleanor Roosevelt stated, immediately preceding the UN General Assembly's adoption of the UDHR:

> In giving our approval to the [UDHR] today, it is of primary importance that we keep clearly in mind the basic character of the document. It is not a treaty; it is not an international agreement. It is not and does not purport to be a statement of law or of legal obligation. It is a declaration of basic principles of human rights and freedoms, to be stamped with the approval of the General Assembly by a formal vote of its members, and to serve as a common standard of achievement for all nations.[6]

---

[6] XIX The Department of State Bulletin 751 (1948).

On "customary international law" and the debate among international lawyers about whether the rights listed in the UDHR, or some of them, have achieved the status of customary international law, see Richard B. Lillich, Hurst Hannum, H. James Anaya, and Dinah Shelton, eds., *International Human Rights: Problems of Law, Policy, and Practice*

As it happens, "the Universal Declaration of Human Rights has served as a model for constitution makers. Countless constitutions written since 1948 contain guarantees that either mirror or draw upon the Declaration."[7]

As I just explained, not every human right – not every right internationally recognized as a human right – is a legal right in every country. Indeed, and sadly, although many human rights are legal rights in many countries, no human rights are legal rights in some countries. (Happily, the number of such countries is diminishing, albeit slowly.) Nonetheless, is every human right a moral right? More precisely, is every putative human right a putative moral right?

Recall that as the concept "human right" is understood in the UDHR and in all the international human rights treaties, a right is a *human* right if the fundamental rationale for establishing and protecting the right is that conduct that violates the right violates the "act towards all human beings in a spirit of brotherhood" imperative. Given that understanding of "human right," and assuming that the category "moral right" includes whatever else it includes,[8] rights whose fundamental rationale is that conduct that violates the right violates the "act towards all human beings in a spirit of brotherhood" imperative, every human right is a moral right.

Some have insisted, however, that "moral" rights are not really rights, that the only genuine rights are legal rights, that so-called "moral" rights are phony (counterfeit, *faux*, pseudo-) rights. Consider, in that regard, Jeremy Bentham's famous dismissal of the language of "natural" rights:

> [1.] Of a natural right who has any idea? I, for my part, have none: a natural right is a round square, – an incorporeal body. What a legal

---

146–61 (2006). See also Thomas Buergenthal, Dinah Shelton, and David P. Stewart, *International Human Rights* 41–6 (4th ed. 2009).

[7] A.E. Dick Howard, "A Traveler from an Antique Land: The Modern Renaissance of Comparative Constitutionalism," 50 *Virginia Journal of International Law* 3, 18 (2009) (citing Hurst Hannum, "The Status of the Universal Declaration of Human Rights in National and International Law," 25 *Georgia Journal of International and Comparative Law* 287, 313 (1995–96)).

[8] There is no consensus about the concept "morality." See, e.g., Jean Porter, "Christian Ethics and the Concept of Morality: An Historical Inquiry," 26 *J. Society of Christian Ethics* 3 (2006); Paul Bloomfield, ed., *Morality and Self-Interest* (2008); Joel J. Kupperman, "Why Ethical Philosophy Needs to be Comparative," 85 *Philosophy* 185 (2010).

right is I know. I know how it was made. I know what it means when
made. To me a right and a legal right are the same thing . . . Right
and law are correlative terms: as much so as son and father. Right
is with me the child of law: from different operations of the law
result different sorts of rights.[9]

[2.] *Right*, the substantive *right*, is the child of law: from *real* laws
come *real* rights, but from laws of nature, fancied and invented by
poets, rhetoricians, and dealers in moral and intellectual poisons
come *imaginary* rights, a bastard brood of monsters, "gorgons and
chimeras dire."[10]

[3.] *Natural rights* is simple nonsense: natural and imprescriptible
rights, rhetorical nonsense – nonsense upon stilts.[11]

According to Amartya Sen, "[Bentham's] suspicion remains very alive
today, and despite the persistent use of the idea of human rights in
practical affairs, there are many who see the idea of human rights
[understood as *moral* rights] as no more than 'bawling upon paper,' to
use another of Bentham's barbed portrayals of natural rights claims."[12]

The fundamental difference between legal rights and moral rights
concerns the enforceability of the rights. Legal rights are, as such,
enforceable. Social rights too – rights that, although they do not have
the status of law in a particular community, are nonetheless widely
regarded by members of the community as authoritative for the community – are, as such, enforceable; members of the community enforce
them by shaming those who violate the rights, or by shunning them.
In what way, if any, are moral rights – that is, moral rights as such, and
not as social or as legal rights – enforceable?

For one who believes that God enforces (true) moral rights, by punishing or otherwise holding accountable those who violate the rights,
moral rights too are enforceable. But for one who is not a theist – or
for a theist who does not believe that God is in the business of holding
accountable those who violate true moral rights – moral rights are not,

---

[9] Jeremy Bentham, "Supply Without Burthen or Escheat Vice Taxation," in Jeremy Waldron, ed., *Nonsense Upon Stilts: Bentham, Burke and Marx on the Rights of Man* 70, 72–73
(1987).

[10] Jeremy Bentham, "Anarchical Fallacies," ibid., 46, 69.

[11] Ibid., 53.

[12] Amartya Sen, "Elements of a Theory of Human Rights," 32 *Philosophy and Public Affairs*
315, 316 (2004).

as such, enforceable. And for some for whom moral rights are not, as such, enforceable, moral rights are not really "rights" at all. Consider, for example, Raymond Geuss: "[E]ssential to the existence of a set of 'rights' [is] that there be some specifiable and more or less effective mechanism for enforcing them."[13] Alasdair MacIntyre makes a similar point: "[W]henever [there is] good reason for describing transactions in [the language of rights], it is always in virtue of the existence ... of some particular set of institutional arrangements requiring description in those terms, and the rights in question therefore will always be institutionally conferred, institutionally recognized and institutionally enforced rights."[14]

Given what Bentham, Geuss, MacIntrye, and others have emphasized, why not just abandon the arguably misleading language of "moral" rights? What is gained, if anything, by using that language?

> [T]he ancients and the medievals did not have the notion of a right – was their moral life stunted in some way as a result? Did they lack the tools for dealing with certain aspects of the moral enterprise? Among them moral questions were dealt with in terms of what is [morally] right and wrong, what is in accordance with or required by the natural law, what people ought to do or are obliged to do, but not in terms of what someone has a right to, or has a right to do.[15]

Again, what, if anything, is gained by using the language of "moral" rights? Here is John Finnis's answer, in *Natural Law and Natural Rights*:

> [T]he modern vocabulary and grammar of [moral] rights is [an] instrument for reporting and asserting the requirements of other implications of a relationship of justice from the point of view of the

---

[13] Raymond Geuss, *History and Illusion in Politics* 143 (2001). For a critique of Geuss's position, see John Tasioulas, "The Moral Reality of Human Rights," in Thomas Pogge, ed., *Freedom from Poverty as a Human Right: Who Owes What to the Very Poor?* 75, 79–88 (2007).

[14] Quoted in Nicholas Wolterstorff, *Justice: Rights and Wrongs* 32 (2008).

[15] Theodore M. Benditt, *Rights* 3 (1982). John Finnis and James Griffin make much the same point: "[I]t is salutary to bear in mind that the modern emphasis on the power of the right-holder, and the consequent systematic bifurcation between 'right' (including 'liberty') and 'duty,' is something that sophisticated lawyers were able to do without for the whole life of classical Roman law." John Finnis, *Natural Law and Natural Rights* 209–10 (1980). "Ethics ... could do without the discourse of [human] rights and still say all that is necessary to it." James Griffin, *On Human Rights* 94 (2008).

person(s) who benefit(s) from that relationship. It provides a way of talking about "what is just" from a special angle: the viewpoint of the "other(s)" to whom something (including, inter alia, freedom of choice) is owed or due, and who would be wronged if denied that something . . . The modern language of rights provides a supple and potentially precise instrument for sorting out and expressing the demands of justice.[16]

James Griffin makes a similar but more focused point, in *On Human Rights*: not about the usefulness of moral-rights talk generally but about the usefulness of a particular kind of moral-rights talk, namely, human-rights talk:

> [T]he discourse [of human rights] has distinct merits. It focuses and gives prominence to obligations that arise, not from social status or special talents and skills, but from the dignity of human status itself. The dignity of human status itself is not the only, or the most, important moral status that human beings have. The case for singling it out is largely practical. Ring-fencing this particular status gives it prominence, ease of transmission, enhanced effectiveness in our social life, and indeed in our moral life, and so on.[17]

For better or worse, the language of rights – especially the language of human rights – is now a common feature of moral discourse throughout the world, and is likely to remain so. Indeed, the language of human rights has become the moral lingua franca. (Look again at the Habermas quote at the beginning of this chapter.) It is difficult to see that there is anything of consequence to be gained by refusing to make peace with that state of affairs.

---

[16] Finnis, *Natural Law*, 210. Immediately after emphasizing the usefulness of moral-rights talk, John Finnis cautions that such talk "is often, though not inevitably or irremediably, a hindrance to clear thought when the question is: What are the demands of justice?" Ibid. For a critique of rights-talk that hinders "clear thought" about "the demands of justice," see Mary Ann Glendon, *Rights Talk: The Impoverishment of Political Discourse* (1991). It bears emphasis that Professor Glendon's critique of *some* rights-talk is not a critique of *all* rights-talk; for Glendon's embrace of talk about international human rights, see Mary Ann Glendon, *A World Made New: Eleanor Roosevelt and the Universal Declaration of Human Rights* (2001).

[17] Griffin, *On Human Rights*, 94.

3 THE NORMATIVE GROUND OF HUMAN RIGHTS

All human beings are born free and equal in dignity and rights. They are endowed with reason and conscience and should act towards one another in a spirit of brotherhood.

– Article 1, Universal Declaration of Human Rights

The fundamental imperative articulated in the foundational human rights document of our time – the Universal Declaration of Human Rights (UDHR) – directs "all human beings" to "act towards one another in a spirit of brotherhood."[1] Johannes Morsink recounts that Rene Cassin, the French delegate, in drafting Article 1 as he did,

> had wanted to stress "the fundamental principle of the unity of the human race" because Hitler had "started by asserting the inequality of men before attacking their liberties." Later on, Cassin reiterated the point that "the authors of that Article had wished to indicate the unity of the human race regardless of frontiers, as opposed to theories like those of Hitler." When someone in the third committee observed that these principles were too well known and did not need to be stated again, Cassin quickly responded that the argument "was invalid in light of recent events. Within the preceding years," he said, "millions of men had lost their lives, precisely because those principles had been ruthlessly flouted." He thought it "was essential that the UN should again proclaim to mankind

---

[1] Because the term "brotherhood" has a masculine resonance, as Diane Amann has emphasized to me, it is useful to remember that the UDHR was drafted and adopted in 1948. Is "fraternité" better? The French version of Article 1 – which is the version in which Article 1 was originally drafted – states: "Tous les êtres humains naissent libres et égaux en dignité et en droits. Ils sont doués de raison et de conscience et doivent agir les uns envers les autres dans un esprit de fraternité."

those principles which had come so close to extinction and should refute the abominable doctrine of fascism."[2]

I explained in the preceding chapter that, as the concept "human right" is understood in the UDHR and in all the international human rights treaties, a right is a *human* right if the fundamental rationale for establishing and protecting the right is that conduct that violates the right violates the "act towards all human beings in a spirit of brotherhood" imperative. That imperative is the normative ground of human rights (NGHR) in the sense that the human rights listed in the UDHR and in the various international human rights treaties are specifications of what, in the judgment of those who drafted the documents, the imperative forbids (or requires) in particular contexts. For example, the right, articulated in Article 5 of the UDHR and elsewhere, not to be subjected to "cruel, inhuman or degrading" punishment is a specification of what the imperative forbids in the context of punishment. Of course, a claim that the imperative – the NGHR – forbids (or requires) X is contestable and may be controversial.

In this, the final chapter of Part I, I address a fundamental question about the NGHR – and thereby conclude my effort, in Part I, to provide a basic understanding of the morality of human rights in preparation for our exploration, in Part II, of certain aspects of the constitutional morality of the United States. The question: What reason or reasons do we have to want governments – not just our own government but every government – to "act towards all human beings in a spirit of brotherhood"?

Before the Second World War – as I noted in Chapter 1 – it was no part of the proper business of the government of one country, insofar as international law was concerned, how the government of any other country treated its citizens: "Until World War II, most legal scholars and governments affirmed the general proposition, albeit not in so many words, that international law did not impede the natural right of

---

[2] Johannes Morsink, *The Universal Declaration of Human Rights: Origins, Drafting, and Intent* 38–9 (1999) (citations omitted).

each equal sovereign to be monstrous to his or her subjects."[3] Today, by contrast, it is a matter of international concern – as the UDHR; multiple human rights treaties, regional as well as international; and the recent emergence of the International Criminal Court all make abundantly clear – that no government treat its citizens, or any other human beings with whom it deals, "monstrously."

We obviously have good reason to concern ourselves with how our own government treats us, its citizens. But what reason or reasons warrant our concern that no government abuse its citizens or others with whom it deals; what reason or reasons warrant our trying to get every government to treat its citizens and others with whom it deals "in a spirit of brotherhood"? In particular, what reason or reasons do we have for trying to get certain rights – certain rights *against government*, against *every* government – established and protected?

Let us consider three responses, beginning with a response artic-ulated – the principal response articulated – in the three main com-ponents of the International Bill of Human Rights: the UDHR, the International Covenant on Civil and Political Rights (ICCPR), and the International Covenant on Economic, Social, and Cultural Rights (ICESCR).

"INHERENT DIGNITY" AND INVIOLABILITY

The UDHR refers, in its preamble, to "the inherent dignity . . . of all members of the human family" and states, in Article 1, that "[a]ll human beings are born free and equal in dignity . . . and should act towards one another in a spirit of brotherhood." The ICCPR and the ICESCR each refer, in their preambles, to "the inherent dignity . . . of all members of the human family" and to "the inherent dignity of the human person" – from which, both covenants declare, "the equal and inalienable rights of all members of the human family . . . derive."

[3] Tom J. Farer and Felice Gaer, "The UN and Human Rights: At the End of the Begin-ning," in Adam Roberts and Benedict Kingsbury, eds., *United Nations, Divided World* 240 (2nd ed., 1993).

Moreover, in 1986, the UN General Assembly adopted a resolution – A/RES/41/120, titled "Setting International Standards in the Field of Human Rights" – according to which international human rights treaties should not designate a right as a human right unless the right is, inter alia, "of fundamental character and derive[s] from the inherent dignity and worth of the human person." In 1993, the UN-sponsored World Conference on Human Rights adopted the Vienna Declaration and Programme of Action, which includes this language in its preamble: "Recognizing and affirming that all human rights derive from the dignity and worth inherent in the human person."

The passages quoted in the preceding paragraph constitute this twofold claim: *Each and every (born) human being (1) has equal inherent dignity and (2) is inviolable: not to be violated.*

The *Oxford English Dictionary* gives this as the principal definition of "dignity": "The quality of being worthy or honourable; worthiness, worth, nobleness, excellence." That every human being has "inherent" dignity is the International Bill's way of stating that the dignity that every human being has, he or she has not as a member of one or another group (racial, ethnic, national, religious, etc.), not as a man or a woman, not as someone who has done or achieved something, and so on, but simply as a human being. To say that every human being has "equal" inherent dignity is to say that no human being has more – or less – inherent dignity than another human being: "All human beings are . . . equal in dignity." Hereafter, when I say "inherent dignity," I mean "equal inherent dignity."

That every human being is inviolable – not to be violated – is to say that we should never violate any human being; instead, we should always respect every human being; that is, we always "should act towards one another in a spirit of brotherhood." We *violate* a human being, in the relevant sense of "violate," when we fail to "act towards [him or her] in a spirit of brotherhood." We *respect* a human being when we do "act towards [him or her] in a spirit of brotherhood."

According to the passages quoted above, human rights "derive" from the inherent dignity and inviolability of every human being. What is the "derivation"?

Because we should never violate human beings but instead should always respect them, we should do what we reasonably can, all things considered, both to prevent certain hurtful things from being done to human beings, whether to all human beings or just to some (e.g., children), and to require that certain helpful things be done for human beings, whether for all human beings or just for some (e.g., the disabled). Therefore, and in particular, we should do what we reasonably can to get certain rights – certain rules of conduct – established and protected. If we refuse to do what we reasonably can (all things considered) both to prevent certain hurtful things from being done to human beings and to require that certain helpful things be done for human beings, then we do not respect those human beings – we do not "act towards [them] in a spirit of brotherhood" – but, instead, we violate them.

What rights should we – "all human beings" – do what we reasonably can to get established and protected? That is: What hurtful things should we do what we reasonably can to prevent from being done to human beings? What helpful things should we do what we reasonably can to require be done for human beings?

In the context of the UDHR and human rights treaties, both international and regional, the fundamental concern is rights *against government*.[4] In that context, the answer to the question posed in the preceding paragraph is: those hurtful things the doing of which by government, and those helpful things the not doing of which by government, we judge to be failures by government to act toward its citizens and/or others with whom it deals "in a spirit of brotherhood."

The large majority of the nations of the world agree about what many of the "doings" and "not doings" by government are that constitute failures by government to act toward its citizens and/or others with whom it deals "in a spirit of brotherhood." The large majority of nations also agree, therefore, about what many of the rights are – rights against government – that should be established and protected: the rights listed in the UDHR and in those human rights treaties to which the large majority of nations is party.

---

[4] Some rights against government are indirectly rights against nongovernmental (nonstate) actors: the rights that require government to protect human beings from one or another kind of abusive action by nongovernmental actors. See Monica Hakimi, "State Bystander Responsibility," 21 *European Journal of International Law* 314 (2010).

THESE THREE LINKED PASSAGES are prologue to an important, challenging inquiry about the twofold claim that every human being has inherent dignity and is inviolable:

- "The masses blink and say: 'We are all equal. – Man is but man, before God – we are all equal.' Before God! But now this God has died." – Friedrich Nietzsche[5]
- "Nietzsche's thought[:] there is not only no God, but no metaphysical order of any kind." – Bernard Williams[6]
- "Few contemporary moral philosophers ... have really joined battle with Nietzsche about morality. By and large we have just gone on taking moral judgments for granted as if nothing had happened. We, the philosopher watchdogs, have mostly failed to bark." – Philippa Foot[7]

The dignity and inviolability claims cohere well with some religious worldviews. (As Charles Taylor has explained: "[The] affirmation of universal human rights [that characterizes] modern liberal political culture [represents an] authentic development ... of the gospel."[8]) But do they also cohere, well or otherwise, with any secular worldview: either any worldview that denies, as Nietzsche denied, or even any worldview that is agnostic about, the existence of a "transcendent" reality, as distinct from the reality that is or could

---

[5] This passage – quoted in George Parkin Grant, *English Speaking Justice* 77 (1985) – appears in Nietzsche's *Thus Spoke Zarathustra*, Part IV ("On the Higher Man"), near the end of section 1.

[6] Bernard Williams, "Republican and Galilean," *New York Review of Books*, Nov. 8, 1990, 45, 48 (reviewing Charles Taylor, *Sources of the Self: The Making of Modern Identity* (1989)). Cf. John M. Rist, *Real Ethics: Rethinking the Foundations of Morality* 2 (2002): "[Plato] came to believe that if morality, as more than 'enlightened' self-interest, is to be rationally justifiable, it must be established on metaphysical foundations."

[7] Phillippa Foot, *Natural Goodness* 103 (2001).

[8] Charles Taylor, *A Catholic Modernity?*, 16 (1999). Taylor hastens to add "that modern culture, in breaking with the structures and beliefs of Christendom, also carried certain facets of Christian life further than they ever were taken or could have been taken within Christendom. In relation to the earlier forms of Christian culture, we have to face the humbling realization that the breakout was a necessary condition of the development." For Taylor's development of the point, with particular reference to modern liberal political culture's affirmation of universal human rights, see pp. 18–19.

be the object of natural scientific inquiry?[9] Put another way: Are secular worldviews and the dignity and inviolability claims like oil and water? Do the claims "mix" with a worldview such as Bertrand Russell's?

> That man is the product of causes which had no prevision of the end they were achieving; that his origin, his growth, his hopes and fears, his loves and his beliefs, are but the outcome of accidental collocations of atoms; that no fire, no heroism, no intensity of thought and feeling, can preserve an individual life beyond the grave; that all the labor of the ages, all the devotion, all the inspiration, all the noonday brightness of human genius, are destined to extinction in the vast death of the solar system, and that the whole temple of man's achievement must inevitably be buried beneath the debris of a universe in ruins – all these things, if not quite beyond dispute, are yet so certain that no philosophy which rejects them can hope to stand. Only within the scaffolding of these truths, only on the firm foundation of unyielding despair, can the soul's habitation henceforth be safely built.[10]

Let us address two difficult questions, the first of which is this: *If every human being has inherent dignity, why does every human being have it?*

The claim that every human being has inherent dignity is controversial: Not everyone believes that every human being has inherent dignity. Moreover, even among those who *do* believe it, not everyone

---

[9] On the idea of the "transcendent," see Charles Taylor, *A Secular Age* (2007); Michael Warner, Jonathan VanAntwerpen, and Craig Calhoun, eds., *Varieties of Secularism in a Secular Age* (2010).

[10] Bertrand Russell, *Mysticism and Logic* 47–8 (1917). Russell's position brings to mind one of Nietzsche's sayings:

> Man a little, eccentric species of animal, which – fortunately – has its day; all on earth a mere moment, an incident, an exception without consequences, something of no importance to the general character of the earth; the earth itself, like every star, a hiatus between two nothingnesses, an event without plan, reason, will, self-consciousness, the worst kind of necessity, stupid necessity – Something in us rebels against this view; the serpent vanity says to us: "all that must be false, for it arouses indignation – Could all that not be merely appearance? And man, in spite of all, as Kant says – "

Friedrich Nietzsche, *The Will to Power* 169 (Walter Kaufmann and R.J. Hollingdale, trs., and Walter Kaufmann, ed., 1967).

gives the same answer to this question: Why – in virtue of what – does every human being have inherent dignity?

A religious believer may give one or another religious answer.[11] For example, a religious believer may say: "Every human being is created in the image of God." Or he or she may say: "Every human being is sacred: speaking analogically, every human being is a beloved child of God and a sister/brother to oneself."[12]

---

[11] Among countless examples, two from the nineteenth century are, for me, unforgettable. First, William Gladstone:

> [P]erhaps the litmus test of whether the reader is in any sense a liberal or not is Gladstone's foreign-policy speeches. In [one such speech,] taken from the late 1870s, around the time of the Midlothian campaign, [Gladstone] reminded his listeners that "the sanctity of life in the hill villages of Afghanistan among the winter snows, is as inviolable in the eye of almighty God as can be your own... that the law of mutual love is not limited by the shores of this island, is not limited by the boundaries of Christian civilization; that it passes over the whole surface of the earth, and embraces the meanest along with the greatest in its unmeasured scope." By all means smile at the oratory. But anyone who sneers at the underlying message is not a liberal in any sense of that word worth preserving.

Samuel Brittan, "Making Common Cause: How Liberals Differ, and What They Ought To Agree On," *Times Literary Supplement*, Sept. 20, 1996, 3–4. Second, and a little earlier than Gladstone, Herman Melville:

> But this august dignity I treat of, is not the dignity of kings and robes, but that abounding dignity that has no robed investiture. Thou shalt see it shining in the arm that wields a pick or drives a spike; that democratic dignity which, on all hands, radiates without end from God Himself! The great God absolute! The centre and circumference of all democracy! His omnipresence, our divine equality!

Herman Melville, *Moby Dick* 126 (Penguin Classics, 1992).

[12] See Michael J. Perry, *Toward a Theory of Human Rights: Religion, Law, Courts* 7–13 (2007); for a slightly revised version, see Michael J. Perry, *The Political Morality of Liberal Democracy* 29–44 (2010). See also Charles E. Curran, *Catholic Social Teaching: A Historical and Ethical Analysis 1891–Present* 132 (2002): "Human dignity comes from God's free gift; it does not depend on human effort, work, or accomplishments. All human beings have a fundamental, equal dignity because all share the generous gift of creation and redemption from God... Consequently, all human beings have the same fundamental dignity, whether they are brown, black, red, or white; rich or poor, young or old; male or female; healthy or sick." As philosopher Hilary Putnam has noted, the moral image central to what Putnam calls the Jerusalem-based religions "stresse[s] equality and also fraternity, as in the metaphor of the whole human race as One Family, of all women and men as sisters and brothers." Hilary Putnam, *The Many Faces of Realism* 60–1 (1987). In an essay on "The Spirituality of The Talmud," Ben Zion Bokser and Baruch M. Bokser state: "From this conception of man's place in the universe comes the sense of the supreme sanctity of all human life. 'He who destroys one person has dealt a blow

A nonbeliever, by contrast, may give one or another secular (non-religious) answer, such as: "Every human being, or virtually every human being, has, or at a later stage of life will have, the wondrous human capacities to love, to reason, to imagine, and the like." Consider, for example, philosopher James Griffin: "Human life is different from the life of other animals. We human beings have a conception of ourselves and of our past and future. We reflect and assess. We form pictures of what a good life would be – often, it is true, only on a small scale, but occasionally also on a large scale. And we try to realize these pictures. This is what we mean by a distinctively *human* existence – distinctive so far as we know . . . Human rights can be seen as protections of our human standing or . . . our personhood."[13]

Of course, any religious answer to "*Why* does every human being have inherent dignity?" will be controversial, not only as between religious believers and nonbelievers, but also as among religious believers of different stripes. But every secular answer with which I am familiar is controversial too, not only as between religious believers and nonbelievers, but also as among secular thinkers of different stripes.

Moreover, it is open to serious question whether any secular worldview has the resources needed to warrant the claim that *all* human beings – even infants and the severely mentally disabled – have inherent dignity.[14] And, indeed, according to Griffin, neither infants nor

---

at the entire universe, and he who sustains or saves one person has sustained the whole world.'" Ben Zion Bokser and Baruch M. Bokser, "Introduction: The Spirituality of the Talmud," *The Talmud: Selected Writings* 7 (1989). They continue (30–1):

> The sanctity of life is not a function of national origin, religious affiliation, or social status. In the sight of God, the humble citizen is the equal of the person who occupies the highest office. As one talmudist put it: "Heaven and earth I call to witness, whether it be an Israelite or pagan, man or woman, slave or maidservant, according to the work of every human being doth the Holy Spirit rest upon him" . . . As the rabbis put it: "We are obligated to feed non-Jews residing among us even as we feed Jews; we are obligated to visit their sick even as we visit the Jewish sick; we are obligated to attend to the burial of their dead even as we attend to the burial of the Jewish dead."

13   James Griffin, *On Human Rights* 32–33 (2008).
14   See Raimond Gaita, *A Common Humanity: Thinking About Love and Truth and Justice* (2000); Perry, *Toward a Theory of Human Rights*, 14–29; Michael J. Perry, "Morality and Normativity," 13 *Legal Theory* 211 (2008); Perry, *The Political Morality of Liberal Democracy*, 45–57; Nicholas Wolterstorff, *Justice: Rights and Wrongs* (2007); Nicholas Wolterstorff, "Can Human Rights Survive Secularization?," 54 *Villanova Law Review*

the severely mentally disabled have human rights – neither infants nor the severely mentally disabled are holders of human rights – because infants and the severely mentally disabled do not have a conception of themselves and of their pasts and futures, they do not reflect and assess, and they do not form pictures of what a good life would be.[15]

Now, the second of the two questions: *If* every human being is inviolable, *why* is every human being inviolable?

Again, the fundamental warrant for the international human rights articulated in the International Bill of Human Rights and elsewhere begins with a twofold claim. The first claim – the dignity claim – is about the status of every (born) human being: *Every human being has inherent dignity.* The second claim – the inviolability claim – is about the normative force that status – the inherent dignity that every human being has – has for us: *Every human being is inviolable: not to be violated.* According to the inviolability claim, we should never violate any human being; instead, we should always respect every human being. In the words of the UDHR, we "should act towards one another in a spirit of brotherhood."

The inviolability claim, like the dignity claim, is controversial. Just as not everyone believes that every human being has inherent dignity, not everyone believes that every human being is inviolable, and, indeed, it may be the case that one does not believe that every human being is inviolable *because* one does not believe that every human being has inherent dignity. But even if we assume for the sake of discussion that every human being has inherent dignity, why should we think – why should we conclude – that we should never violate any human being? Why should we think, that is, that we should live our lives so as never to violate any human being? We can imagine someone saying – and indeed we don't have to try very hard to imagine someone saying: "Okay, I'll assume that every human being has inherent dignity. So what? What

---

411 (2009); John Dobard, "The Inheritance of Excellence: On the Uses, Justification, and Problem of Human Dignity" (2010), http://ssrn.com/abstract=1580548. But cf. Ari Kohen, *In Defense of Human Rights: A Non-Religious Grounding in a Pluralistic World* (2007).

[15] For critical commentary on this aspect of Griffin's position, see Mark Platts, "The Languages of Rights and of Human Rights," 85 *Philosophy* 319 (2010). See also Rowan Cruft, "Two Approaches to Human Rights," 60 *Philosophical Quarterly* 176, 178–9 (2009).

is that to me? Why should I care?" It is not enough to say, in response: "Because every human being has inherent dignity." It is not obvious, even if we assume that every human being has inherent dignity, why we should conclude that we should never violate any human being. One or more premises are missing. The (assumed) truth of the dignity claim does not entail the truth of the inviolability claim.

A religious believer may give one or another religious answer. An adherent to one of the Jerusalem-based religions (which is how philosopher Hilary Putnam has referred to Judaism, Christianity, and Islam[16]) may say something to this effect: "The perfection for which God created us, the true happiness (*eudaimonia*) that is our ultimate end, consists, in part, in discerning – in our hearts, so to speak, if not also in our minds – the Other (i.e., every "other," every human being) as sacred – as a beloved child of God and a sister/brother to oneself – and in loving the Other. To love the Other – love not in the sense of *eros* or *philia* but of *agape* – is never to violate but always to respect the Other."[17] Such an answer presupposes what is surely true: that we human beings – most of us, at least – are committed to achieving our true happiness, even though we may and usually do disagree with one another – sometimes radically so – about what our true happiness consists in.[18]

The question, again, is why, even assuming that every human being has inherent dignity, we should think that we should never violate any human being but instead should always respect every human being. Even if one rejects any religious answer as implausible, as, of course, anyone will who rejects any and all religious worldviews as implausible, the question remains whether there is any satisfactory secular answer to the question – any satisfactory secular equivalent of or alternative to a religious answer. That a proposition coheres with – that it

---

[16] See n. 12.

[17] For an elaboration of such an answer, including the idea of love as *agape*, see Perry, *Toward a Theory of Human Rights*, 7–13; for a slightly revised version, see Perry, *The Political Morality of Liberal Democracy*, 29–44.

[18] Not everyone conventionally regarded as "religious" or "spiritual" is a theist. Most Buddhists, for example, are not theists. Cf. Laura Kittel, "Healing Heart and Mind: The Pursuit of Human Rights in Engaged Buddhism as Exemplified by Aung San Suu Kyi and the Dalai Lama," 15 *International Journal of Human Rights* 905 (2011); Sallie B. King, "Buddhism and Human Rights," in John Witte Jr. and M. Christian Green, eds., *Religion and Human Rights* 103 (2012).

"makes sense," that it is "intelligible," in the context of – a religious worldview does not entail that the proposition also coheres with any secular worldview. The inviolability claim – according to which we, every one of us, should live our lives so as never to violate *any* human being but always to respect *every* human being – coheres with some religious worldviews. It is open to serious question, however, whether the claim coheres with any secular worldview. As Charles Taylor has put the point:

> The logic of the subtraction story is something like this: Once we slough off our concern with serving God, or attending to any other transcendent reality, what we're left with is human good, and that is what modern societies are concerned with. But this radically under-describes what I'm calling modern humanism. That I am left with only human concerns doesn't tell me to take universal human welfare as my goal; nor does it tell me that freedom is important, or fulfillment, or equality. Just being confined to human goods could just as well find expression in my concerning myself exclusively with my own material welfare, or that of my family or immediate milieu. The, in fact, very exigent demands of universal justice and benevolence which characterize modern humanism can't be explained just by the subtraction of earlier goals and allegiances.[19]

THAT THE INTERNATIONAL BILL OF HUMAN RIGHTS is silent – that it is agnostic, so to speak – both about *why* every human being has inherent dignity and about *why* we should never violate any human being is not surprising, given the plurality of religious and nonreligious views that existed among those who bequeathed us the International Bill. Catholic philosopher Jacques Maritain reported:

> [A]t one of the meetings of a UNESCO National Commission where human rights were being discussed, someone expressed astonishment that certain champions of violently opposed ideologies had agreed on a list of those rights. "Yes," they said, "we agree

---

[19] Charles Taylor, "Closed World Structures," in Mark A. Wrathall, ed., *Religion after Metaphysics* 47, 61 (2003). Cf. Richard Joyce, *The Myth of Morality* (2001); Richard Joyce, "Morality, Schmorality," in Paul Bloomfield, ed., *Morality and Self-Interest* 51 (2008).

about the rights *but on condition that no one asks us why.*" That "why" is where the argument begins.[20]

However, there was agreement among those who drafted the UDHR not just about "the rights" but also about the fundamental justification of – the fundamental warrant for – the rights, namely, that every human being has inherent dignity and we should never violate any human being. Again, the UDHR explicitly refers to "the inherent dignity . . . of all members of the human family" and states that "[a]ll human beings are born free and equal in dignity and rights . . . and should act towards one another in a spirit of brotherhood." So, the comment quoted by Maritain should have been stated thus: "Yes, we agree not only about the rights but also about the fundamental warrant for the rights. But our agreement is no deeper than that: We do not agree about *why* every human being has inherent dignity or about *why* we should never violate any human being."

THE ALTRUISTIC PERSPECTIVE

Again, what reason or reasons warrant our concern that no government abuse its citizens or others with whom it deals; what reason or reasons warrant our trying to get every government to treat its citizens and others with whom it deals "in a spirit of brotherhood"? In particular, what reason or reasons do we have for trying to get certain rights – certain rights *against government,* against *every* government – established and protected?

Let us now consider a second response, one that, unlike the first response, depends neither on any religious premises nor on any secular philosophical premises.

Imagine a statement along these lines:

I detest and oppose states of affairs in which human beings – *any human beings, not just ourselves and those for whom we happen to*

---

[20] Jacques Maritain, "Introduction," in *UNESCO, Human Rights: Comments and Interpretation* 9 (1949). See Mary Ann Glendon, *A World Made New: Eleanor Roosevelt and the Universal Declaration of Human Rights* 73–8 (2001).

have special affection, such as family, friends, and fellow country-men – suffer grievously in consequence of laws and other policies that are misguided or worse. I detest and oppose such states of affairs, because I detest and oppose such suffering. And so I work to build a world in which such suffering is, over time, diminished.

Is such an orientation in the world – which for present purposes we may call altruism – sufficiently widespread, robust, and durable to keep human rights "afloat," as poet and Nobel laureate Czeslaw Milosz put it, "if the [religious] bottom is taken out"?

What has been surprising in the post-Cold War period are those beautiful and deeply moving words pronounced with veneration in places like Prague and Warsaw, words which pertain to the old repertory of the rights of man and the dignity of the person.

I wonder at this phenomenon because maybe underneath there is an abyss. After all, those ideas had their foundation in religion, and I am not over-optimistic as to the survival of religion in a scientific-technological civilization. Notions that seemed buried forever have suddenly been resurrected. But how long can they stay afloat if the bottom is taken out?[21]

---

[21] Czeslaw Milosz, "The Religious Imagination at 2000," *New Perspectives Quarterly*, Fall 1997: 32. Consider, in connection with Milosz's worry, this statement by Jurgen Habermas (who is not a religious believer):

> Among the modern societies, only those that are able to introduce into the secular domain the essential contents of their religious traditions which point beyond the merely human realm will also be able to rescue the substance of the human.

Jürgen Habermas, quoted in Michael Reder and Josef Schmidt, SJ, "Habermas and Religion," in Jürgen Habermas et al., *An Awareness of What Is Missing: Faith and Reason in a Post-Secular Age* 5 (2010). Cf. Jürgen Habermas, *Time of Transitions* 150–51 (2006):

> Christianity has functioned for the normative self-understanding of modernity as more than a mere precursor or a catalyst. Equalitarian universalism, from which sprang the ideas of freedom and social solidarity, of an autonomous conduct of life and emancipation, of the individual morality of conscience, human rights, and democracy, is the direct heir to the Judaic ethic of justice and the Christian ethic of love. This legacy, substantially unchanged, has been the object of continual critical appropriation and reinterpretation. To this day, there is no alternative to it. And in light of the current challenges of the postnational constellation, we continue to draw on the substance of this heritage. Everything else is just idle postmodern talk.

Whatever the answer to the question that precedes the Milosz quote, I can discern nothing in our historical experience to suggest that altruism – which may be wedded to religious faith[22] but certainly need not be[23] – is any less widespread, robust, and durable a basis for keeping human rights "afloat" than religion has been.[24]

With altruism now in view, look again at the UDHR's reference, in its preamble, to "the inherent dignity ... of all members of the human family" and its statement, in Article 1, that "[a]ll human beings are born free and equal in dignity ... and should act towards one another in a spirit of brotherhood." Although that language obviously can be read as asserting a truth about human beings – that they have inherent dignity – must it be so read? Can't it also be read simply as expressing – in what Hilary Putnam has called "the metaphor of the whole human race as One Family, of all women and men as sisters and brothers"[25] – what Kristen Renwick Monroe has called "the altruistic perspective":

> [I]t is the [altruistic] perspective itself that constitutes the heart of altruism. Without this particular perspective, there are no altruists ... [The perspective] consists of a common perception, held by all altruists, that they are strongly linked to others through a shared humanity. This self-perception constitutes such a central core to altruists' identity that it leaves them with no choice in their

---

[22] Cf. Jack Mahoney, SJ, "Evolution, Altruism, and the Image of God," 71 *Theological Studies* 677 (2010).

[23] See Kristen Renwick Monroe, *The Heart of Altruism: Perceptions of a Common Humanity* (1996).

[24] See Omer Bartov and Phyllis Mack, "Introduction," in Omer Bartov and Phyllis Mack, eds., *In God's Name: Genocide and Religion in the Twentieth Century* 1 (2001): "[R]eligion has played an important role in several outbreaks of genocide since World War I." See also:

> Violence and religion have been closely associated in a variety of intricate, often contradictory ways, since the earliest periods of human civilization. Institutionalized religions have practiced violence against both their adherents and their real or imagined opponents. Conversely, religions have also been known to limit social and political violence and to provide spiritual and material comfort to its victims. Religious faith can thus generate contradictory attitudes, either motivating aggression or restraining it. Individual perpetrators and victims of violence can seek in religious institutions and personal faith both a rationale for atrocity, a justification to resist violence, or a means to come to terms with the legacy of destruction by integrating it into a wider historical or theological context.

[25] See n. 12.

behavior toward others. They are John Donne's people. All life concerns them. Any death diminishes them. Because they are a part of mankind.[26]

Even if the answer to the question posed in the preceding paragraph – the question whether the Article 1 language can be read simply as expressing "the altruistic perspective" – is yes, the problem of "justification" persists: the justification of the altruistic perspective. Consider, for example, what Leszek Kolakowski wrote: "When Pierre Bayle argued that morality does not depend on religion, he was speaking mainly of psychological independence; he pointed out that atheists are capable of achieving the highest moral standards . . . and of putting to shame most of the faithful Christians. That is obviously true as far as it goes, but this matter-of-fact argument leaves the question of validity intact."[27] Consider, too, the words of John Rist: "Although a 'moral saint' may exist without realist (and therefore religious) beliefs, yet his stance as a moral saint cannot be justified without recourse to realism."[28]

To the demand for justification, the altruist – especially the altruist who is neither religiously nor philosophically engaged – may respond:

> Again, I detest and oppose states of affairs in which any human beings suffer grievously in consequence of laws and other policies that are misguided or worse. You ask what "justifies" my altruism – if indeed anything justifies it. But for me that sensibility is where "I have reached bedrock and my spade is turned."[[29]] This is simply how I am oriented in the world – and how I am deeply content to be oriented. Moreover, given the deliverances of evolutionary biology, I believe that there is no more fitting way – no more deeply

---

[26] Monroe, *The Heart of Altruism*, 216. See also Kristen Renwick Monroe, "Explicating Altruism," in Stephen G. Post et al., eds., *Altruism and Altruistic Love: Science, Philosophy, and Religion in Dialogue* 106 (2002); Kristen Renwick Monroe, *Ethics in an Age of Terror: Identity and Moral Choice* (2012).

[27] Leszek Kolakowski, *Religion, If There Is No God: On God, the Devil, Sin, and Other Worries of the So-Called Philosophy of Religion* 191 (1982).

[28] Rist, *Real Ethics*, 267.

[29] "I have reached bedrock and my spade is turned. Then I am inclined to say: 'This is simply what I do.'" Ludwig Wittgenstein, *Philosophical Investigations* 217 (1953).

satisfying way – for a human being to be oriented in the world.[30]
In any event, there is much to be done, and life is short. So I work
to build a world in which such suffering is, over time, diminished.
And I work to build that world with anyone who will work with me,
whatever their particular perspective or motivation.[31]

SELF-INTEREST

Now consider, as a third and final response to the question we are
addressing in this chapter, self-interest – self-interest generously conceived, as concern not only for one's own well-being but also for the
well-being of others for whom one cares, such as family and friends.[32]

The Charter of the United Nations states, in Article 55(3), that
"[w]ith a view to the creation of conditions of stability and well-being
which are necessary for peaceful and friendly relations among nations

---

[30] See Frans de Waal, *Primates and Philosophers: How Morality Evolved* 15 (2006) (based on
de Waal's 2004 Tanner Lectures at Princeton):

> The evolutionary origin of this inclination is no mystery. All species that rely
> on cooperation – from elephants to wolves and people – show group loyalty
> and helping tendencies. These tendencies evolved in the context of a close-knit
> social life in which they benefited relatives and companions able to repay the
> favor. The impulse to help was therefore never totally without survival value to
> the ones showing that impulse. But, as so often, the impulse became divorced
> from the consequences that shaped its evolution. This permitted its expression
> even when payoffs were unlikely, such as when strangers were beneficiaries.
> This brings animal altruism much closer to that of humans than usually thought,
> and explains the call for the contemporary removal of ethics from the hands of
> philosophers.

See also Frans de Waal, "Putting the Altruism Back into Altruism: The Evolution of
Empathy," 59 *Annual Review of Psychology* 279 (2008); Frans de Waal, *The Age of Empathy*
(2009); Frans de Waal, "Morals without God?," *New York Times*, Oct. 17, 2010. For
an important discussion of what experimental psychology has (and has not) revealed
about the possibility of altruism, see Stephen Stich, John M. Doris, and Erica Roedder,
"Altruism," in John M. Doris, ed., *The Moral Psychology Handbook* 147 (2010).

[31] That the altruist is not interested in "justifying" the altruistic perspective does not mean
that the altruist is not interested in growing and nurturing, among as many human beings
as possible, the altruistic perspective. See Richard Rorty, "Human Rights, Rationality,
and Sentimentality," in Susan Hurley and Stephen Shute, eds., *On Human Rights: The
1993 Oxford Amnesty Lectures* 111 (1993).

[32] If one cares sufficiently deeply for all human beings, the "self-interest" response becomes
"the altruistic perspective" response.

based on respect for the principle of equal rights and self-determination of peoples, the United Nations shall promote . . . universal respect for, and observance of, human rights and fundamental freedoms for all without distinction as to race, sex, language, or religion." The UDHR, the ICCPR, and the ICESCR all state, in their preambles, that "recognition of the inherent dignity and of the equal and inalienable rights of all members of the human family is the foundation of . . . peace in the world." The Vienna Declaration and Programme of Action, adopted in 1993 by the World Conference on Human Rights, states in paragraph 6 that "[t]he efforts of the United Nations system towards the universal respect for, and observance of, human rights and fundamental freedom for all, contribute to the stability and well-being necessary for peaceful and friendly relations among nations, and to improved conditions for peace and security . . . in conformity with the Charter of the United Nations."

In 1993, at the World Conference on Human Rights, U.S. Secretary of State Warren Christopher argued that "[a] world of democracies would be a safer world."

> States that respect human rights and operate on democratic principles tend to be the world's most peaceful and stable. On the other hand, the worst violators of human rights tend to be the world's aggressors and proliferators. These states export threats to global security, whether in the shape of terrorism, massive refugee flows, or environmental pollution. Denying human rights not only lays waste to human lives; it creates instability that travels across borders.[33]

In 2002, William Schulz, at the time the Executive Director of Amnesty International USA, echoed Christopher's argument – and, not surprisingly, invoked the example of 9/11:

> [R]espect for human rights both in the United States and abroad has implications for our welfare far beyond the maintenance of our ethical integrity. Ignoring the fates of human rights victims almost anywhere invariably makes the world – our world – a more

---

[33] Warren Christopher, "Democracy and Human Rights: Where America Stands," 4 *U.S. Department of State Dispatch* 441, 442 (1993).

dangerous place. If we learned nothing else from the horrific events of September 11, [2001,] perhaps we learned that.[34]

SUMMARY

Again: We obviously have good reason to concern ourselves with how our own government treats us, its citizens. But what reason or reasons warrant our concern that no government abuse its citizens or others with whom it deals; what reason or reasons warrant our trying to get every government to treat its citizens and others with whom it deals "in a spirit of brotherhood"? In particular, what reason or reasons do we have for trying to get certain rights – certain rights *against government*, against *every* government – established and protected?

We have considered three responses: (1) the claim, which for some is a religiously based claim, that every human being has inherent dignity and is inviolable; (2) the altruistic perspective; and (3) self-interest.

Not all three responses work for everyone.[35] Indeed, there are some for whom none of the responses work, some who have no reason to take seriously the NGHR. But there are also some for whom all three responses work – some for whom each response is, by itself, adequate: those who are in the grip of the altruistic perspective; and who would be in the grip of that perspective – who would be altruists – even if they did not affirm, but who as it happens do affirm, perhaps on religious grounds, that every human being has inherent dignity and

---

[34] Schultz elaborates the argument in his book *In Our Own Best Interests: How Defending Human Rights Benefits Us All* (2002). The quoted language appears on p. xix. See also William W. Burke-White, "Human Rights and National Security: The Strategic Connection," 17 *Harvard Human Rights Journal* 249 (2004); Alison Brysk, *Global Good Samaritans: Human Rights as Foreign Policy* (2009); Alison Brysk, "Doing Well by Doing Good," in *Human Rights and Human Welfare Roundtable: "Human Rights and Foreign Policy,"* August 2010, http://www.du.edu/korbel/hrhw/roundtable/index.html; Dohrman W. Byers, "The Morality of Human Rights: A Secular Ground," 26 *Journal of Law and Religion* 1 (2010–11).

[35] See, e.g., Richard B. Bilder, "Human Rights and U.S. Foreign Policy: Short-Term Prospects," 14 *Virginia Journal of International Law* 597, 608 (1974): "[Self-interested rationales are] hard to prove and not fully persuasive. Despite considerable effort, it has been difficult to construct a wholly convincing 'selfish' rationale for major U.S. national commitments to promote the human rights of foreigners."

is inviolable; and who, moreover, believe that even by itself self-interest (generously conceived) warrants our concern that every government act towards its citizens and others "in a spirit of brotherhood."

APPENDIX

Another Fundamental Question about the Normative Ground of Human Rights

I have just addressed the question of whether we should want – what reason or reasons we have, if any, to want – governments to "act towards all human beings in a spirit of brotherhood." There are two other fundamental questions about the NGHR I want to address in this book:

- Should we want governments *always* to "act towards all human beings in a spirit of brotherhood," *no matter what the consequences?*
- In the NGHR, does "all" human beings mean *all* human beings, *even unborn human beings?*

I address the first of those two questions in this appendix. Why in this appendix and not in the chapter itself? Because my response to the question focuses on a topic – interrogational torture – that is marginal to the principal subject matter of this book. I leave it to the reader to decide whether to engage that topic with me or to skip ahead to the next chapter. I address the second of the two questions in Chapter 9, because my response to the question focuses on a topic – abortion – to which Chapter 9 is devoted.

Again, the question for this appendix: Should we want governments *always* to "act towards all human beings in a spirit of brotherhood," *no matter what the consequences?*

I explained in the preceding chapter that as the concept "human right" is understood in the UDHR and in all the international human rights treaties, a right is a *human* right if the fundamental rationale for establishing and protecting the right is that conduct that violates the right violates the NGHR: the fundamental imperative to act towards all human beings "in a spirit of brotherhood." The NGHR requires that governments not act toward any human being inhumanely. International human rights are specifications – contestable and sometimes controversial specifications – of what governments must do or refrain from doing, in particular contexts, lest they act towards the rights-bearers inhumanely. So, for example, the right whose implications for capital punishment we consider in the next chapter – the right not to be subjected to "cruel, inhuman or degrading" punishment, which is articulated in Article 5 of the UDHR, in Article 7 of the ICCPR, and in several other human rights treaties and national constitutions (see below) – is a specification of what governments must refrain from doing in the context of punishment lest they act toward a criminal inhumanely. The right we are now about to consider – the right not to be tortured – is a specification of what governments must refrain from doing lest they act toward a human being inhumanely.

A more precise rendering of the question now before us: Should we want governments *never* to violate the NGHR – should we want governments *never* to act toward any human being inhumanely – *no matter what the consequences*? The particular version of that question on which I focus in the remainder of this appendix: Should we want governments *never* to subject a human being to torture, *no matter what the likely consequences of not subjecting him (or her) to torture*? The latter question is a version of the former question because torturing a human being is an instance – indeed, a paradigmatic instance – of treating a human being inhumanely.

THE RIGHT NOT TO BE TORTURED is widely regarded as one of the most fundamental human rights. Both Article 5 of the UDHR and Article 7 of the ICCPR state in relevant part that "[n]o one shall be subjected to torture." Article 1(1) of the Convention against Torture and Other Cruel, Inhuman or Degrading Treatment or Punishment, which was adopted by the UN General Assembly in 1984 and entered into force in 1987, states:

> The term "torture" means any act by which severe pain or suffering, whether physical or mental, is intentionally inflicted by or at the instigation of a public official on a person for such purposes as obtaining from him or a third person information or

confession, punishing him for an act he has committed or is suspected of having committed, or intimidating him or other persons. It does not include pain or suffering arising only from, inherent in or incidental to, lawful sanctions to the extent consistent with the Standard Minimum Rules for the Treatment of Prisoners.

As of December 2012, there were 153 State Parties to the Convention against Torture (CAT), including, as of 1994, the United States. The following human right provisions – in addition to the two provisions quoted above: Article 5 of the UDHR and Article 7 of the ICCPR – illustrate how widely regarded as a fundamental human right is the right not to be subjected to torture:

• Article 3 of the European Convention for the Protection of Human Rights and Fundamental Freedoms (1953): "No one shall be subjected to torture or to inhuman or degrading treatment or punishment."
• Article 5(2) of the American Convention on Human Rights (1978): "No one shall be subjected to torture or to cruel, inhuman, or degrading punishment or treatment."[36]
• Article 5 of the African Charter on Human and People's Rights (1986): "Every individual shall have the right to the respect of the dignity inherent in a human being and to the recognition of his legal status. All forms of exploitation and degradation of man particularly slavery, slave trade, torture, cruel, inhuman or degrading punishment and treatment shall be prohibited."

Consider too the following constitutional provisions, each of which entered into force in the period since the end of World War II:

• Article 36 of the Japanese Constitution (1946): "The infliction of torture by any public officer and cruel punishments are absolutely forbidden."
• Article 12 of the Canadian Charter of Rights and Freedoms, which is part of the Canadian Constitution (1982): "Everyone has the right not to be subjected to any cruel and unusual treatment or punishment."

---

[36] The United States is not a party to the American Convention on Human Rights.

- Article 12(1) of the South African Constitution (1997): "Everyone has the right to freedom and security of the person, which includes the right . . . not to be tortured in any way; and not to be treated or punished in a cruel, inhuman or degrading way."

I am concerned here not with torture as punishment but only with interrogational torture, by which I mean, as the CAT states: "any act by which severe pain or suffering, whether physical or mental, is intentionally inflicted by or at the instigation of a public official on a person for the purpose of obtaining from him or a third person information." For the purpose of obtaining information, that is, that the torturers hope will or might benefit one or more persons *other than the person(s) being tortured*. When we talk about subjecting someone to interrogational "torture," we are not talking about inflicting severe pain on someone for the purpose of benefiting the person on whom the severe pain is being inflicted.

An important distinction with respect to international human rights is the distinction between rights that are derogable and those that are nonderogable. Article 4 of the ICCPR states, in relevant part:

> In time of public emergency which threatens the life of the nation and the existence of which is officially proclaimed, the States Parties to the present Covenant may take measures derogating from their obligations under the present Covenant to the extent strictly required by the exigencies of the situation, provided that such measures are not inconsistent with their other obligations under international law and do not involve discrimination solely on the ground of race, colour, sex, language, religion or social origin.[37]

Article 4 immediately goes on to list certain rights as nonderogable: rights that parties to the ICCPR must respect without regard to whether

---

[37] On the derogability of international human rights, see Emilie Marie Hafner-Burton, Laurence R. Helfer, and Christopher J. Fariss, "Emergency and Escape: Derogation from Human Rights Treaties," *International Organization* (2011); Eric Neumayer, "Do Governments Mean Business When They Derogate? Human Rights Violations during Declared States of Emergency" (2011), http://ssrn.com/abstract=1654001.

it is a "time of [officially proclaimed] public emergency which threatens the life of the nation."[38]

One of the rights Article 4 lists as nonderogable: the right not to be subjected to interrogational torture. Article 2(2) of the CAT emphasizes the nonderogability of the right by stating that "[n]o exceptional circumstances whatsoever, whether a state of war or a threat of war, internal political instability or any other public emergency, may be invoked as a justification of torture." Is it optimal, all things considered, that Article 4 of the ICCPR and Article 2(2) of the CAT make the right against interrogational torture nonderogable?

Can there be in extremis circumstances – such as a "time of public emergency which threatens the life of the nation" – such that a government's subjecting a human being to interrogational torture would not be, or arguably would not be, for the government to do what no government is ever warranted in doing? That question, in one or another version, has been much debated in recent years. Some answer in the negative, some in the affirmative.

Some insist that there can never be circumstances, no matter how extreme, such that a government would be warranted in subjecting a human being to interrogational torture. They argue that for any government to torture any human being for any reason is, no matter what the circumstances, for the government to act in a gravely immoral way, and this, they argue, no government is ever warranted in doing.

Others allow for the possibility of circumstances in which a government's subjecting a human being to interrogational torture would be warranted. They argue that if in subjecting a human being to

---

[38] The distinction between derogable and nonderogable human rights should not be confused with different but related distinction between conditional and unconditional (absolute) human rights. It is a part of the specification of some human rights that they are conditional: they forbid (or require) government to do something *unless certain conditions are satisfied*. For example, Article 18 of the ICCPR, which protects religious and moral freedom, allows government to ban or otherwise impede a practice covered by the right if certain conditions are satisfied: "Freedom to manifest one's religion or beliefs may be subject only to such limitations as are prescribed by law and are necessary to protect public safety, order, health, or morals or the fundamental rights and freedoms of others." It is a part of the specification of some other human rights, by contrast, such as the right not to be subjected to "cruel, inhuman or degrading" punishment, that they are unconditional: they forbid (or require) government to do something, *period*.

interrogational torture a government is acting "lest the heavens fall," the government cannot reasonably be adjudged to be acting in a gravely immoral way. Legal philosopher Charles Fried has written that if the circumstances are sufficiently extreme, "it seems fanatical to maintain the absoluteness of the judgment, to do right even if the heavens will in fact fall."[39]

Whether "maintain[ing] the absoluteness of the judgment" is "fanatical," an unconditional opposition to interrogational torture is difficult to defend – impossibly difficult to defend successfully, in my judgment[40] – except on the basis of what Catholic legal philosopher John Finnis has called "faith in divine providence":

> There are hard cases, as everybody knows. The prospect of loss of human good (of persons), of damage apparently avertable by violating the moral absolutes, can seem indubitable and be felt as overwhelming. But these are cases in which we do not see the relevant parts of the scheme of providence – a scheme of which we never, in this life, see the whole or even much . . . In these cases, then, the moral absolutes call for a refusal to dishonor the basic human good at stake in our choice; they call us to leave providence to settle the "balance" of human goods, a balance which we would

---

[39] Charles Fried, *Right and Wrong* 10 (1977): "We can imagine extreme cases where killing an innocent person may save a whole nation. In such cases it seems fanatical to maintain the absoluteness of the judgment, to do right even if the heavens will in fact fall." See also Michael Moore, "Torture and the Balance of Evils," 23 *Israel Law Review* 280, 328 (1989): "It just isn't true that one should allow a nuclear war rather than killing or torturing an innocent person. It isn't even true that one should allow the destruction of a sizable city by a terrorist nuclear device rather than kill or torture an innocent person. To prevent such extraordinary harms extreme action seems to me to be justified." Jeremy Waldron criticizes Moore in "What are Moral Absolutes Like?," (2011), http://ssrn.com/abstract=1906850, 38–42.

Has Charles Fried had a conversion experience? See Charles Fried and Gregory Fried, "Torture Apologists Stain Triumph over bin Laden," *Washington Post*, May 6, 2011, where Fried criticizes the "making [of] exceptions to moral imperatives that should remain exceptionless – like Lincoln's absolute condemnation of torture . . . These things must never be done."

[40] For thoughtful discussions, see, e.g., F.M. Kamm, "Torture: During and After Action," in F.M. Kamm, *Ethics for Enemies: Terror, Torture, and War* 3 (2011); John A. Humbach, "The Possibility of Moral Absolutes: Some Thoughts in Response to Jeremy Waldron on Torture" (2011), http://ssrn.com/abstract=1943779. Cf. Michael J. Perry, "Are Human Rights Absolute?," in Michael J. Perry, *The Idea of Human Rights: Four Inquiries* 97 (1998).

merely deceive ourselves if we supposed we could truly see and settle for ourselves . . .

In short: To deny the truth of moral absolutes by arguing that they block the reasonable and responsible of greater amounts of pre-moral human good is incoherent with faith in divine providence . . . To respect the moral absolutes which are made known to us by God through reason and faith is to cooperate with God, who has practical knowledge of everything without limit. And to cooperate thus with God is to *take everything into account . . . in the only way we can.*[41]

Many of us, however, lack Finnis's "faith in divine providence."[42]

---

[41] John Finnis, *Moral Absolutes: Tradition, Revision, and Truth* 12, 20 (1991).

[42] It is not the case that religious believers are generally unconditionally opposed to interrogational torture. Evangelical Christian scholar David Gushee has lamented "the formation of a sizable and apparently permanent American Christian constituency for torture." David P. Gushee, "The Contemporary U.S. Torture Debate in Christian Historical Perspective," 39 *Journal of Religious Ethics* 589, 595–6 (2011). On the implications of Christian teaching for torture, see, in addition to the article by David Gushee, Jeremy Waldron, "What Can Christian Teaching Add to the Debate about Torture?," 63 *Theology Today* 330 (2006); Jean Porter, "Torture and Christian Conscience: A Response to Jeremy Waldron," 61 *Scottish Journal of Theology* 340 (2008).

Given what happened in Europe before and during World War II, it is scarcely surprising that many Israelis lack Finnis's "faith in divine providence." In a case that was before the Israeli Supreme Court in the 1990s, involving the use of physical force in the interrogation of a Palestinian detainee believed to have "extremely vital information whose immediate extraction would help save lives and prevent severe terror attacks in Israel," the government attorney argued that the physical force in question was "moderate" but that in any event "[n]o enlightened nation would agree that hundreds of people should lose their lives because of a rule saying torture is forbidden under any circumstances."

Justices Aharon Barak, Mishael Cheshin, and Eliahu Mazza joined the debate, pressing [the Israeli human-rights lawyer, Andre] Rosenthal to declare whether he agreed that torture was justifiable if it could lead investigators to a bomb about to explode. When Mr. Rosenthal demurred from full agreement, Justice Cheshin turned angrily on him: "That's the most immoral and extreme position I've ever heard in my life," he said. "A thousand people are about to be killed, and you propose that we don't do anything."

Later, after the court granted the government's request to lift an injunction on the use of the physical force in question, Mr. Rosenthal explained "that what he and other human-rights lawyers had been seeking was not so much a ban on force, but a review by the court of the limits of the law, and making public the criteria for using force." Serge Schmemann, "Israel Allows Use of Physical Force in Arab's Interrogation," *New York Times*, Nov. 16, 1996. See Supreme Court of Israel, "Judgment Concerning the Legality of the General Security Service's Interrogation Methods (September 6, 1999)," in Sanford Levinson, ed., *Torture: A Collection* 165 (2004); Miriam Gur-Arye, "Can the War against Terror

I want to move past the question about the morality vel non of interrogational torture; I have nothing to add to the seemingly interminable debate surrounding that question that has not already been well and passionately said in recent years – in the context of 9/11, the controversies over waterboarding and rendition, and such – by thoughtful, articulate partisans in the debate. I want to consider a different question: Even if we assume, for the sake of discussion, that that there *can* be circumstances so extreme that in subjecting a human being to interrogational torture a government would not be acting immorally, does it nonetheless make sense – is it nonetheless optimal – for human rights instruments and national laws to do what the ICCPR and the CAT both do: make the right against interrogational torture nonderogable?[43]

There are two main reasons – which together are conclusive, in my judgment – for answering in the affirmative:

1. If in banning interrogational torture a country's lawmakers or the drafters of human rights treaties were to create an exception for interrogational torture in certain specified circumstances, they would thereby create an environment in which episodes that fit this profile would very likely be more numerous than they would otherwise be: *the use of interrogational torture by government officials in circumstances that fall short of the extremity of the specified circumstances.* This is so because, as experience teaches, including some quite recent experience, there would be a tendency on the part of some government officials to exploit the exception – to drive a truck through it, so to speak.[44] In their study of the "Laws of Torture in Israel and Beyond, 1987–2009," two Israeli scholars report:

Justify the Use of Force in Interrogations? Reflections in Light of the Israeli Experience," in Levinson, *Torture*, 183; Itamar Mann and Omer Shatz, "The Necessity Procedure: Laws of Torture in Israel and Beyond," 6 *Unbound* 59 (2010).

[43] I first addressed that question in "Are Human Rights Absolute?"

[44] See Yuval Ginbar, *Why Not Torture Terrorists?*, (2010), reviewed by Ruth Blakeley, 4 *International Journal of Human Rights* 644 (2011). See also John T. Parry, "Escalation and Necessity: Defining Torture at Home and Abroad," in Levinson, *Torture*, 145; David D. Cole, "The Sacrificial Yoo: Accounting for Torture in the OPR Report," 4 *Journal of National Security Law and Policy* 455 (2010); Ruth Blakeley, "Dirty Hands, Clean Conscience? The CIA Inspector General's Investigation of 'Enhanced Interrogation Techniques' in the War on Terror and the Torture Debate," 10 *Journal of Human Rights* 544 (2011).

[E]mpirical evidence suggests that movement towards legitimizing torture perpetuates a growing zone of independence and impunity in security services, above and beyond
what is allowed by law. Harsh torture techniques that have
been recognized but limited in various ways have tended
to "migrate" across theatres of war and spread virally.
Every step toward legitimation opens up new frontiers for
"hypocrisy" and for exceeding the already permissive limitations enumerated by the law. This dynamic is tightly bound
with the fact that contemporary torture is always psychological. No less than obtaining information through the use of
physical pain, it extracts information by relying on the victim's imagination of the unknown method that may come
next, lurking behind the corner of its own legal limitations.[45]

2. If in banning interrogational torture the lawmakers and treaty
drafters were to refuse to create an exception for interrogational
torture in any circumstances, however extreme, they would not
thereby prevent government officials from resorting to interrogational torture in truly extreme circumstances; rather, they would
only create an environment in which one could reasonably hope
that episodes that fit this profile would less numerous than they
would otherwise be: *the use of interrogational torture by government
officials in less than truly extreme circumstances.* As James Griffin
has put the point: "Nations solemnly, some perhaps even sincerely,
swear never to torture, but I know of no modern nation, faced with
a serious threat of terrorism, that has not then tortured."[46] It is not

---

[45] Mann and Shatz, "The Necessity Procedure," 108. (With respect to Mann and
Shatz's claim that "contemporary torture is always psychological," see David Luban
and Henry Shue, "Mental Torture: A Critique of Erasures in U.S. Law" (2011),
http://ssrn.com/abstract=1797806.) Cf. Darrell Cole, "Torture and Just War," 40 *Journal of Religious Ethics* 26, 39–40 (2012) (arguing "that states cannot be trusted with the
power of legalized torture").

[46] James Griffin, "What Should We Do about Torture?," in N. Ann Davis, Richard Keshen,
and Jeff McMahan, eds., *Ethics and Humanity: Themes from the Philosophy of Jonathan
Glover* 3, 11 (2010). Griffin continues:

It is chastening that the number of nations where torture is now practices on a
regular basis is 132, while the number of nations that have ratified the [CAT] is
130. There must be a large overlap between these two classes. Oona Hathaway
has done an empirical study of the practices of more than 160 nations over the
course of forty years, one of the conclusions of which is that: "not only does
it appear that the [CAT] does not always have the intended effect of reducing
torture in the countries that ratify, but, in some cases, the opposite might even

only naïve to think that exceptions would not be exploited; it is also naïve to think that an exceptionless ban on interrogational torture would prevent government officials from resorting to such torture if the officials judged the circumstances to be sufficiently extreme. I concur, therefore, in Griffin's answer to the question that is the title of his essay: "What Should We Do about Torture?" "[W]e cannot do better," concludes Griffin,

> than to work for . . . an absolute prohibition of torture; much stricter training of police, military, and intelligence agents; much more energetic rooting out and more severe punishment of torturers and those who order or condone torture; and re-education of the public. *We could then only hope that anyone who, despite all these changes, resorts to torture has correctly identified a particular exception.* This will not, of course, prevent unjustifiable or inexcusable torture, but no permissible social arrangements will produce full compliance with any prohibition.[47]

Now, let us return to the question about torture that I posed above: Should we want governments *never* to subject a human being to interrogational torture, *no matter what the likely consequences of not subjecting him (or her) to such torture*? I have said in this appendix that it is difficult to defend – except on the basis of "faith in divine providence" – the proposition that governments should never subject a human being to interrogational torture. If I am right about that, then it is difficult to defend the proposition that governments should never violate the NGHR, that they should never act towards a human being inhumanely. In some imaginable and sufficiently extreme circumstances, government officials may have to choose between (a) acting inhumanely to one human being, A, by subjecting A to interrogational torture, and (b) not acting to save, or to try to save, one or more other human beings from grievous suffering and/or death – a kidnapped child, for example – by not subjecting A to interrogational torture.[48]

---

be true." (11–12, quoting Oona A. Hathaway, "The Promise and the Limits of the International Law of Torture," in Levinson, *Torture*, 201)

[47] Griffin, "What Should We Do about Torture?," 17 (emphasis added).
[48] I concur in what Richard Posner says, including what he says about the kidnapped child, in "Torture, Terrorism, and Interrogation," in Levinson, *Torture*.

As I have explained in this appendix, however, even if in some imaginable and sufficiently extreme circumstances it is morally permissible – even, perhaps, morally obligatory[49] – for government officials to subject a human being to interrogational torture, there are conclusive reasons for lawmakers and treaty-drafters to make bans on torture exceptionless. It is optimal, all things considered, that laws and treaties do just what both Article 4 of the ICCPR and Article 2(2) of the CAT do: make the right against torture, even interrogational torture, nonderogable. There are conclusive reasons, that is, for laws and treaties to require that governments *never* violate the NGHR – that they *never* treat any human being inhumanely – even if we assume that it is *not* the case, as a moral matter, that governments should never violate the NGHR.[50]

---

[49] Cf. Posner, "Torture, Terrorism, and Interrogation," 295: "No one who doubts . . . that if the stakes are high enough torture is permissible . . . should be in a position of responsibility." (Passages rearranged.)

[50] Under an exceptionless ban on interrogational torture – a criminal ban – how should the law deal with someone who violates the ban but who fits the profile James Griffin sketched in the passage I quoted in the text three paragraphs back: someone who "has correctly identified a particular exception"? (Perhaps he was trying to save the life of a kidnapped child.) I recommend that the reader interested in thinking about that important question begin by reading these two essays: "The Prohibition on Torture and the Limits of the Law" by Owen Gross and "Torture, Terrorism, and Interrogation" by Richard Posner. Both essays are included in *Torture: A Collection*, edited by Sanford Levinson and published in 2004.

Part II THE CONSTITUTIONAL MORALITY OF THE UNITED STATES

I said in the introduction to this book that a basic understanding of the morality of human rights – which I sought to provide in Part I – greatly enhances our understanding of the constitutional morality of the United States. In particular, and as the chapters that follow illustrate, a basic understanding of the morality of human rights greatly enhances our understanding of the three rights to which we are now about to turn, each of which is part of the constitutional morality of the United States; each of which, that is, is both internationally recognized as a human right and entrenched in the constitutional law of the United States: the right not to be subjected to "cruel and unusual" punishment, the right to moral equality, and the right to religious and moral freedom.

Before we proceed further, a clarification is in order. A right is "entrenched in the constitutional law of the United States," in the sense in which I mean, if either of two conditions is satisfied. Let R stand for a particular right. These are the two conditions:

First: R is entrenched in the constitutional law of the United States if constitutional enactors entrenched R in the constitutional law of the United States; if other, later enactors did not entrench a different right – a right that supersedes R – in the constitutional law of the United States; and if no right that supersedes R has become constitutional bedrock. (On constitutional bedrock, see the next paragraph.) By constitutional "enactors," I mean what Richard Kay means:

> By enactors, I mean the human beings whose approval gave the Constitution the force of law. In the case of the original establishment of the United States Constitution that means the people comprising the majorities in the nine state conventions whose ratification preceded the Constitution entering into force. With respect

to the amendments that means the people comprising the majorities in the houses of Congress proposing the amendments and in the ratifying legislatures of the necessary three-quarters of the states.[1]

Second: R is entrenched in the constitutional law of the United States if R is a bedrock feature of the constitutional law of the United States, in this sense: R has become, in the words of Robert Bork, "so embedded in the life of the nation, so accepted by the society, so fundamental to the private and public expectations of individuals and institutions," that the Supreme Court of the United States should and almost certainly will continue to deem R constitutionally authoritative even if it is open to serious question whether enactors ever entrenched R in the constitutional law of the United States.[2] As Michael McConnell has put the point: "[M]any decisions, even some that were questionable or controversial when rendered, have become part of the fabric of American life; it is inconceivable that they would now be overruled ... This overwhelming public acceptance constitutes a mode of popular ratification."[3]

The three rights to which we now turn are, each of them, as I explain in due course, entrenched in the constitutional law of the United States.

[1] Richard S. Kay, "Original Intention and Public Meaning in Constitutional Interpretation," 103 Northwestern University Law Review 703, 709 n. 28 (2009).
[2] Robert Bork, *The Tempting of America: The Political Seduction of the Law* 158 (1989).
[3] Michael W. McConnell, "Active Liberty: A Progressive Alternative to Textualism and Originalism?," 119 *Harvard Law Review* 2387, 2417 (2006). See Akhil Reed Amar, *America's Unwritten Constitution: The Precedents and Principles We Live By* 239 (2012).

4   CAPITAL PUNISHMENT

The right not to be subjected by government to any punishment (or other treatment) that is "cruel, inhuman or degrading" is internationally recognized as a human right. A version of that right is entrenched in the constitutional law of the United States – and is therefore part of the constitutional morality of the United States: the right not to be subjected by government, federal or state, to any punishment that is "cruel and unusual."

That the right not to be subjected by government to "cruel, inhuman or degrading" punishment is internationally recognized as a human right could not be clearer:

- Article 5 of the Universal Declaration of Human Rights (1948): "No one shall be subjected to torture or to cruel, inhuman or degrading treatment or punishment."
- Article 7 of the International Covenant on Civil and Political Rights (1976): "No one shall be subjected to torture or to cruel, inhuman or degrading treatment or punishment." As of December 2012, there were 167 State Parties to the International Covenant, including, as of 1992, the United States.[1]

---

[1] In ratifying the International Covenant on Civil and Political Rights, the United States stated that it "reserves the right, subject to its Constitutional constraints, to impose capital punishment on any person (other than a pregnant woman) duly convicted under existing or future laws permitting the imposition of capital punishment, including such punishment for crimes committed by persons below eighteen years of age." The United States also stated that it "considers itself bound by article 7 to the extent that 'cruel, inhuman or degrading treatment or punishment' means the cruel and unusual treatment or punishment prohibited by the Fifth, Eighth, and/or Fourteenth Amendments to the Constitution of the United States."

- Article 3 of the European Convention for the Protection of Human Rights and Fundamental Freedoms (1953): "No one shall be subjected to torture or to inhuman or degrading treatment or punishment."
- Article 5(2) of the American Convention on Human Rights (1978): "No one shall be subjected to torture or to cruel, inhuman, or degrading punishment or treatment."[2]
- Article 5 of the African Charter on Human and People's Rights (1986): "Every individual shall have the right to the respect of the dignity inherent in a human being and to the recognition of his legal status. All forms of exploitation and degradation of man particularly slavery, slave trade, torture, cruel, inhuman or degrading punishment and treatment shall be prohibited."[3]

I explained in Chapter 2 that, as the concept "human right" is understood in the Universal Declaration of Human Rights and in all the international human rights treaties, a right is a *human* right if the fundamental rationale for establishing and protecting the right – for example, as a treaty-based right – is that conduct that violates the right violates the normative ground of human rights (NGHR): "Act towards all human beings in a spirit of brotherhood." Particular human rights are specifications of what the NGHR requires in particular contexts; the right not to be subjected to "cruel, inhuman or degrading" punishment is a specification of what the NGHR requires in the context of punishment. The ban on punishments that are "cruel, inhuman or degrading" is a ban on punishments that cross the line, so to speak: punishments so extreme that they violate the NGHR. To

---

[2] The United States is not a party to the American Convention on Human Rights.

[3] Consider too the following constitutional provisions, each of which entered into force in the period since the end of the Second World War:

- Article 36 of the Japanese Constitution (1946): "The infliction of torture by any public officer and cruel punishments are absolutely forbidden."
- Article 12 of the Canadian Charter of Rights and Freedoms, which is part of the Canadian Constitution (1982): "Everyone has the right not to be subjected to any cruel and unusual treatment or punishment."
- Article 12(1) of the South African Constitution (1997): "Everyone has the right to freedom and security of the person, which includes the right... not to be tortured in any way; and not to be treated or punished in a cruel, inhuman or degrading way."

inquire whether a punishment is "cruel, inhuman or degrading" within the meaning of the Universal Declaration and the other human rights instruments quoted above is essentially to inquire whether capital punishment crosses the line by failing to treat the criminal "in a spirit of brotherhood."

There is no reason to think that the phrase "cruel, inhuman or degrading," although articulated in the disjunctive ("A, B, *or* C"), presupposes – and there is good reason for us not to presuppose – an administrable distinction among "cruel," "inhuman," and "degrading."

- Can a punishment be "cruel" but neither "inhuman" nor "degrading"? No: A "cruel" punishment is also "inhuman," because it is "inhuman" (inhumane) to subject one to a "cruel" punishment; similarly, a "cruel" punishment is also "degrading," because it is "degrading" to subject one to a "cruel" punishment.
- Can a punishment be "inhuman" but neither "cruel" nor "degrading"? No: An "inhuman" punishment is also "cruel," because it is "cruel" to subject one to an "inhuman" punishment; similarly, an "inhuman" punishment is also "degrading," because it is "degrading" to subject one to an "inhuman" punishment.
- Can a punishment be "degrading" but neither "cruel" nor "inhuman"? No: A "degrading" punishment is also "cruel," because it is "cruel" to subject one to a "degrading" punishment; similarly, a "degrading" punishment is also "inhuman," because it is "inhuman" to subject one to a "degrading" punishment.

So, in inquiring whether a punishment is "cruel, inhuman or degrading," the terms "cruel," "inhuman," and "degrading" are functionally equivalent and therefore interchangeable. We may ask, therefore, simply whether a punishment is "cruel."

I said that to inquire whether a punishment is "cruel" ("cruel, inhuman or degrading") within the meaning of the Universal Declaration and the other human rights instruments quoted above is essentially to inquire whether capital punishment crosses the line by failing to treat the criminal "in a spirit of brotherhood." Similarly, in inquiring whether capital punishment fails to treat the criminal "in a spirit of brotherhood," I mean: Is capital punishment "cruel, inhuman or degrading"? I am skeptical that there are any punishments that fail to treat the criminal "in a spirit of brotherhood" but are not "cruel, inhuman or degrading." In any event, my assumption in this chapter is that if capital punishment fails to treat the criminal "in a spirit of brotherhood," it is because capital punishment is "cruel, inhuman or degrading."

In the United States, a majority of citizens self-identify as Christian, and for some of them, at least, we may fairly assume that if they were confronted by the question whether a punishment fails to treat the criminal "in a spirit of brotherhood," they would translate the question into the Christian vocabulary of "love" and ask whether the punishment falls short of the ideal embodied in Jesus' "new" commandment, reported in John 13:34, to "love one another ... just as I have loved you."[4] The "love" in Jesus' counsel to "love one another" is not *eros* or *philia*, but *agape*, which "discloses to us the full humanity of others. To become properly aware of that full humanity is to become incapable of treating it with contempt, cruelty, or indifference. The full awareness of others' humanity that love involves is an essentially motivating perception."[5] The "one another" in Jesus' counsel is radically inclusive: "You have heard how it was said, You will love your neighbor and hate your enemy. But I say this to you, love your enemies and pray for those who persecute you; so that you may be children of your Father in heaven, for he causes his sun to rise on the bad as well as the good, and sends down rain to fall on the upright and the wicked

---

[4] See also John 15:12, 17. In the language of second of the two great commandments, to ask whether a punishment fails to treat the criminal "in a spirit of brotherhood" is to ask whether the punishment fails to treat the criminal "lovingly." According to the Gospel, there are two great commandments: "But when the Pharisees heard that he had silenced the Sadducees they got together and, to put him to the test, one of them put a further question, 'Master, which is the greatest commandment of the Law?' Jesus said to him, 'You must love the Lord your God with all your heart, with all your soul, and with all your mind. This is the greatest and the first commandment. The second resembles it: You must love your neighbor as yourself. On these two commandments hang the whole Law, and the Prophets too." (Matthew 22:34–40. See also Mark 12:28–34; Luke 10:25–28.) On the translation of the second great commandment: "[W]hereas 'Thou shalt love thy neighbor as thyself' represents the Greek of the Septuagint (Leviticus 19:18) and of the New Testament, the Hebrew from which the former is derived means rather 'You shall treat your neighbor lovingly, for he is like yourself.'" J. L. Mackie, *Ethics: Inventing Right and Wrong* 243 (1977).

[5] Timothy Chappell, "Book Review," 111 *Mind* 411, 412 (2002).

alike . . . You must therefore set no bounds to your love, just as your heavenly Father sets none to his." (Matthew 5:43–48)[6] As philosopher Raimond Gaita has emphasized, "the language of love . . . compels us to affirm that even . . . the most radical evil-doers . . . are fully our fellow human beings."[7]

Some of the reasons that have been given in support of the abolition of capital punishment have nothing to do with the possibility that capital punishment is cruel. The two principal such reasons:

- In the United States, capital punishment is imposed in a racially discriminatory and/or freakishly arbitrary manner.[8]

---

[6] Other relevant Gospel passages include, in Luke, the Parable of the Good Samaritan (Luke 10:29–37) and, in Matthew, the Parable of the Last Judgment (Matthew 25:31–46).

[7] Raimond Gaita, A Common Humanity: Thinking about Love and Truth and Justice xviii–xix (2000). Graham Greene wrote that "[w]hen you visualized a man or a woman carefully, you could always begin to feel pity . . . When you saw the corners of the eyes, the shape of the mouth, how the hair grew, it was impossible to hate. Hate was just a failure of imagination." Graham Greene, *The Power and the Glory* 131 (Penguin, 1940). The poet Denise Levertov wrote somewhere – perhaps in *The Poet in the World* (1973) – that "[m]an's capacity for evil . . . is less a positive capacity . . . than a failure to develop man's most fundamental human function, the imagination, to its fullness, and consequently a failure to develop compassion."

[8] See John Paul Stevens, "On the Death Sentence," *New York Review of Books*, Dec. 23, 2010 (reviewing David Garland, *Peculiar Institution: America's Death Penalty in the Age of Abolition* (2010)):

> In 1987, the Court held in *McCleskey v. Kemp* that it did not violate the Constitution for a state to administer a criminal justice system under which murderers of victims of one race received death sentences much more frequently than murderers of victims of another race. The case involved a study by Iowa law professor David Baldus and his colleagues demonstrating that in Georgia murderers of white victims were eleven times more likely to be sentenced to death than were murderers of black victims. Controlling for race-neutral factors and focusing solely on decisions by prosecutors about whether to seek the death penalty, Justice Blackmun observed in dissent, the effect of race remained "readily identifiable" and "statistically significant" across a sample of 2,484 cases.

Justice Stevens then observes "[t]hat the murder of black victims is treated as less culpable than the murder of white victims provides a haunting reminder of once-prevalent Southern lynchings." See also David R. Dow, "Death Penalty, Still Racist and Arbitrary," *New York Times*, July 9, 2011; Campbell Robertson, "Bias Law Used to Move a Man Off Death Row," *New York Times*, April 20, 2012. The *New York Times* reported that "[m]inority service members are more than twice as likely than whites – after accounting for the crimes' circumstances and the victims' race – to be sentenced to death, according to a forthcoming study co-written by David Baldus, an eminent death-penalty scholar, who died in June." Editorial, "The Military and the Death Penalty," *New York Times*, Aug. 31, 2011.

- Capital punishment is sometimes imposed on – it sometimes kills – persons who are factually innocent.[9]

> Apart from the fact that it is imposed in a racially discriminatory manner, capital punishment is imposed in an "utterly arbitrary" manner. See Lincoln Caplan, "The Random Horror of the Death Penalty," *New York Times*, Jan. 8, 2012, reporting on a study "conducted by John Donohue, a Stanford law professor, . . . analyz[ing] all murder cases in Connecticut over a 34-year period and [finding] that inmates on death row are indistinguishable from equally violent offenders who escape that penalty. [The study] shows that the process in Connecticut – similar to that in other death-penalty states – is utterly arbitrary and discriminatory." The principal basis of the arbitrariness is "geographic disparity"; in Waterbury, Connecticut, for example, "a death-eligible killer was at least seven times as likely to be sentenced to death as in the rest of the state."

[9] See Lawrence C. Marshall, "The Innocence Revolution and the Death Penalty," 1 *Ohio State J. Criminal Law* 573 (2004); "Wrongful Convictions Symposium," 52 *Drake Law Review* 587–738 (2004); Adam Liptak, "Study Suspects Thousands of False Convictions," *New York Times*, April 19, 2004; Thom Brooks, "Retribution and Capital Punishment," in Mark D. White, ed., *Retributivism: Essays on Theory and Policy* 232 (2011). But see Charles Lane, "End of Innocence: The Death Penalty's Self-Defeating Foes," *New Republic*, Nov. 11, 2010, 10. Cf. Nicholas D. Kristof, "Framed for Murder?," *New York Times*, Dec. 9, 2010 (discussing *Cooper* v. *Brown*, U.S. Court of Appeals for the Ninth Circuit, No. 05–99004W, May 11, 2009).

In response to the possibility of executing the innocent, "[a] commission appointed by [then-Massachusetts] Gov. Mitt Romney has come up with what it considers the first virtually foolproof formula for [ensuring that no innocent person is executed], and Mr. Romney is expected to use the plan to try to bring back capital punishment to the state, where it was abolished two decades ago." Pam Belluck, "State Panel Suggests Death Penalty Safeguards," *New York Times*, May 3, 2004. By contrast, the prestigious American Law Institute, which devised the framework for the modern system of capital punishment, recently abandoned the whole project "in light of the current intractable institutional and structural obstacles to ensuring a minimally adequate system for administering capital punishment."

> [W]hat [U.S. Supreme Court] Justice Harry A. Blackmun called the American "machinery of death" is broken. Cops fudge the truth. They coerce false testimony. Court-appointed lawyers sleep through trials. They miss deadlines. They fail to put on exculpatory evidence. Juries believe every word uttered by "expert" witnesses who opine on defendants they have never met. Jurors evade responsibility by hiding behind the other jurors. Judges evade responsibility by hiding behind jury verdicts, and appeals courts hide behind the trial courts. The [U.S.] Supreme Court can hide from a case by refusing to take it. Elected judges, particularly in Texas, must deliver convictions. Federal judges named to the federal bench because they are pals with a senator overlook deeply flawed trials . . . "Prosecutors and judges kowtow to family members of murder victims who demand an eye for an eye, and the lonely lawyer declaiming about proper procedures is a shouting lunatic in the asylum."

Dahlia Lithwick, "Death and Texas," *New York Times Book Review*, Feb. 14, 2010: 10. See also Adam Liptak, "Group Gives Up Death Penalty Work," *New York Times*, Jan. 4, 2010 (reporting on the decision by the American Law Institute to abandon the project of trying to reform the system of capital punishment "in light of the current intractable institutional

In this chapter, however, I am interested only in this reason, which presupposes neither that capital punishment is racially discriminatory nor that it kills some who are innocent:

- Capital punishment imposed on anyone, including a mentally competent adult who, after a fair trial, has been found guilty of having committed a depraved crime, is cruel (within the meaning of the internationally recognized human right not to be subjected to cruel punishment).

I am not interested here in the much less controversial claim that capital punishment imposed on a child, or on a mentally handicapped adult, is cruel. In this chapter, when I say capital punishment, I mean, unless I indicate otherwise, capital punishment that fits this profile: imposed on a mentally competent adult who, after a fair trial, has been found guilty of having committed a depraved crime.[10] Is capital punishment, thus understood, cruel?

Some punishments – burning at the stake, drawing and quartering, disemboweling, and so on – are conspicuously cruel. Indeed, some punishments constitute torture, which the several human rights provisions quoted above specifically ban. The nations of the world are virtually unanimous in agreeing that punishing a criminal *by torturing him* violates the criminal's right not to be subjected to cruel punishment. According to Article 1(2) of the Declaration on the Protection of All Persons from Being Subjected to Torture and Other Cruel, Inhuman or Degrading Treatment or Punishment, "[t]orture constitutes an aggravated and deliberate form of cruel, inhuman or degrading treatment or punishment."

---

and structural obstacles to ensuring a minimally adequate system for administering capital punishment"); Carol S. Steiker and Jordan M. Steiker, "No More Tinkering: The American Law Institute and the Death Penalty Provisions of the Model Penal Code," 89 *Texas Law Review* 353 (2010); Carol S. Steiker and Jordan S. Steiker, "Part II: Report to the ALI Concerning Capital Punishment," 89 *Texas Law Review* 367 (2010).

[10] For recent accounts of truly horrible crimes, see Garland, *Peculiar Institution*, 1–8; Cathleen Kaveny, "A Horrific Crime: But Is Execution the Answer?," *Commonweal*, May 17, 2010. Cf. William Glaberson, "Harrowing Cheshire Case Still Haunts Jurors," *New York Times*, Jan. 2, 2010.

Does punishing a criminal *by executing him* also violate his right not to be subjected to cruel punishment?[11] Does punishment-by-execution violate the imperative to treat *all* human beings "in a spirit of brotherhood"?

The legitimate aims of criminal punishment are widely regarded to be incapacitation, retribution, deterrence, and/or rehabilitation.[12] Can capital punishment be defended against the charge of cruelty on the basis of one or more of those four aims?

Punishing a criminal by killing him or her is obviously not aimed at rehabilitation.[13] Nor is it aimed at incapacitation: Most persons convicted of having committed a capital crime are not executed; the relative few who are executed are not executed because it is believed that they, unlike the ones who are not executed, cannot otherwise be incapacitated; rather, they are executed because it is believed that given what they did, execution is warranted. It bears mention, in that regard, that section 2267 of the *Catechism of the Catholic Church* (2nd ed., 1997) states, in relevant part: "Today, ... as a consequence of the possibilities which the state has for effectively preventing crime, by rendering one who has committed an offense incapable of doing harm – without definitively taking away from him the possibility of redeeming himself – the cases in which the execution of the offender is an absolute necessity 'are very rare, if not practically non-existent.'"[14] Putting aside both rehabilitation and incapacitation leaves us with retribution and deterrence.

---

[11] To punish a criminal by executing him or her is not necessarily to torture him or her. Cf. Stevens, "On the Death Sentence": "Changes designed to avoid the needless infliction of pain have [turned w]hat was once a frightening spectacle [into what] now resembles painless administration of preoperative anesthesia in the presence of few witnesses. American officials do not enjoy executions; 'they seem, in short, embarrassed, as if caught in a transgression.'"

[12] See, e.g., *Graham v. Florida*, 130 S.Ct. 2011 (2010); *Ewing v. Florida*, 538 U.S. 11, 25 (2003).

[13] That some criminals repent while awaiting their day of execution – a wait that today can span many years – does not entail that capital punishment is aimed at, or that it plausibly could be aimed at, rehabilitation. For a discussion of rehabilitation in the context of capital punishment, see Meghan J. Ryan, "Death and Rehabilitation" (2012), http://ssrn.com/abstract=2128175.

[14] The words "are very rare, if not practically non-existent" are borrowed from Pope John Paul II's encyclical *Evangelium Vitae* (1995).

The aim of retribution must not be confused with the aim of vengeance. The human appetite for vengeance is both familiar – all too familiar – and understandable. (Who among us lacks that appetite?) But vengeance, unlike retribution, is not a legitimate aim of punishment. Whereas vengeance is about "getting even," retribution is about imposing a punishment that adequately reflects the gravity of what the criminal did, which includes to whom he or she did it, how he or she did it, and why he or she did it. Imposing an adequately severe punishment serves an important pedagogical function for all the members of the community, not just for the criminal him- or herself. It is essential to the ongoing moral life of the community – which includes respecting the victims, indirect as well as direct, of crime – that the punishment imposed not communicate that the crime is less grave than it is. A punishment that marks the crime as less grave than it is is corrosive to the ongoing moral life of the community; it sends the wrong message – to the perpetrator, to the victims, both direct and indirect, and to all the other members of the community. Retribution can and sometimes does warrant subjecting a criminal to a severe punishment: Imposing a severe punishment may be, in context and all things considered, an essential way of saying "This crime is especially grave."[15]

But that retribution can and sometimes does warrant subjecting a criminal to a severe punishment does not entail that government may do to the criminal whatever he or she did to his or her victim; it does not entail, for example, that government may rape or otherwise torture the criminal. A punishment crosses the line if it is "cruel, inhuman or degrading" – if, that is, imposition of the punishment constitutes a failure by government to treat the criminal "in a spirit of brotherhood."

---

[15] To the extent retribution is elaborated in terms of moral culpability (blameworthiness), retribution is an increasingly, and deeply, problematic warrant for criminal punishment. See, e.g., Joshua Greene and Jonathan Cohen, "For Law, Neuroscience Changes Nothing and Everything," in Semir Zeki and Oliver Goodenough, eds., *Law and the Brain* 207 (2006); David Eagleman, "The Brain on Trial," *The Atlantic*, July/August 2011. For a skeptical but in my judgment unavailing response to Greene and Cohen, see Michael S. Pardo and Dennis Patterson, "Neuroscience, Normativity, and Retributivism," in Thomas Nadelhoffer, ed., *The Future of Punishment* (forthcoming). For a recent discussion of retributivism, see the essays in Mark D. White, ed., *Retributivism: Essays on Theory and Policy* (2011).

The same point applies to deterrence. As I explain in Appendix A to this chapter, there is ample reason to doubt that capital punishment has a greater deterrent effect than life in prison without the possibility of parole. But even if in some locales – in some countries and/or in some states in the United States – capital punishment does have at least a somewhat greater deterrent effect, it does not follow that to punish a criminal by killing him is to treat the criminal "in a spirit of brotherhood": That a more severe punishment has a greater deterrent effect than a less severe one does not entail that the more severe punishment is not too severe, that is does not cross the line, that it does not violate the imperative to treat the criminal "in a spirit of brotherhood." Even assuming, contra the best available evidence (see Appendix A), that in some locales capital punishment has at least a somewhat greater deterrent effect, the question remains: Does punishing a criminal by killing him or her treat the criminal "in a spirit of brotherhood"?

In the period since the end of the Second World War, the judgment has become increasingly widespread, as we will see, that it is *not* to treat a criminal "in the spirit of brotherhood" – in the vocabulary of Christianity, it is not to treat a criminal "lovingly" – to punish a criminal by killing him or her, thereby denying to him or her, inter alia, the opportunity both to live a life of ongoing, deepening repentance and to achieve the kind of redemption that such repentance makes possible.[16] It is noteworthy, in that regard, that the *Catechism of the Catholic Church*, which was published in 1997 – and which reflects

---

[16] Recall what the Elder, Father Zossima, says in Dostoevsky's *The Brothers Karamazov*:

> Do not be afraid of anything, never be afraid, and do not grieve. Just let repentance not slacken in you, and God will forgive you everything. There is not and cannot be in the whole world such a sin that the Lord will not forgive one who truly repents of it. A man even cannot commit so great a sin as would exhaust God's boundless love. How could there be a sin that exceeds God's love? Only take care that you repent without ceasing, and chase away fear altogether. Believe that God loves you so as you cannot conceive of it; even with your sin and in your sin he loves you. And there is more joy in heaven over one repentant sinner than over ten righteous men – that was said long ago. Go, then, and do not be afraid. Do not be upset with people, do not take offense at their wrongs. Forgive the dead man in your heart for all the harm he did you; be reconciled with him truly. If you are repentant, it means that you love. And if you love, you already belong to God... With love everything is bought, everything is saved. If even I, a sinful man, just like you, was moved to tenderness and felt pity for you, how much more will God be. Love is such a priceless treasure that you can but the

the influence of Pope John Paul II, who famously opposed capital punishment[17] – teaches that it is immoral to "tak[e] away from [a criminal] the possibility of redeeming himself" if it is not absolutely necessary for a society to do so in order to protect itself from him.[18]

We find intimations of the judgment articulated at the beginning of the preceding paragraph in the writings of two North African philosophers, one born in the twentieth century, the other in the fourth: the famously atheist Albert Camus (1913–60) and the famously theist Augustine of Hippo (354–430). Camus wrote that "[w]e know enough to say that this or that major criminal deserves hard labor for life. But we do not know enough to decree that he should be shorn of his future – in other words, of the chance we all have of making amends."[19] Jeffrie Murphy tells us that "[i]n [the following] letter to Marcellinus, the special delegate of the Emperor Honorius to settle the dispute between Catholics and Donatists, Augustine is concerned with the punishment to be administered for what must have, to him, seemed the most vicious of crimes: the murder of one Catholic priest and the mutilation of another by members of a radical Donatist faction."

> I have been a prey to the deepest anxiety for fear your Highness might perhaps decree that they be sentenced to the utmost penalty of the law, by suffering a punishment in proportion to their deeds. Therefore, in this letter, I beg you by the faith which you have in Christ and by the mercy of the same Lord Christ, not to do this, not to let it be done under any circumstances. For although we [bishops] can refuse to be held responsible for the death of men who were not manifestly presented for trial on charge of ours,

---

whole world with it, and redeem not only your own but other people's sins. Go, and do not be afraid.

Fyodor Dostoevsky, *The Brothers Karamazov*, 52 (1880; Richard Pevear and Larissa Volokhonsky, trs., 1990). Cf. Robert Smith and G. Ben Cohen, "Redemption Song: *Graham v. Florida* and the Evolving Eighth Amendment Jurisprudence," 108 *Michigan Law Review First Impressions* 86 (2010), also available at http://ssrn.com/abstract=1791130.

[17] See E. Christian Brugger, *Capital Punishment and Roman Catholic Moral Tradition* (2003). John Paul's opposition to capital punishment is now the official teaching of the Roman Catholic Church. See, e.g., the statement of the Catholic bishops of Ohio quoted in the text accompanying n. 53.

[18] See text accompanying n. 14.

[19] Albert Camus, "Reflections on the Guillotine," in *Albert Camus, Resistance, Rebellion, and Death* 230 (Justin O'Brien, tr., 1974).

but on the indictment of officers whose duty it is to safeguard the public peace, we yet do not wish that the martyrdom of the servants of God should be avenged by similar suffering, as if by way of retaliation... We do not object to wicked men being deprived of their freedom to do wrong, but we wish it to go just that far, so that, without losing their life or being maimed in any part of their body, they may be restrained by the law from their mad frenzy, guided into the way of peace and sanity, and assigned to some useful work to replace their criminal activities. It is true, this is called a penalty, but who can fail to see that it should be called a benefit rather than a chastisement when violence and cruelty are held in check, but the remedy of repentance is not withheld?[20]

Again, the judgment has become increasingly widespread, in the period since the end of the Second World War, that to punish a criminal by killing him is not to treat the criminal "in a spirit of brotherhood." Consider the following developments, and note the trajectory of the developments.

Neither the Universal Declaration of Human Rights, which was adopted by the UN General Assembly in 1948, nor the International Covenant on Civil and Political Rights, which was adopted in 1966 and entered into force in 1976, bans capital punishment. (The International Covenant does state, in Article 6(2), that "[i]n countries which have not abolished the death penalty, sentence of death may be imposed only for the most serious crimes in accordance with the law in force at the time of the commission of the crime." It also states, in Article 6(5), that "[s]entence of death shall not be imposed for crimes committed by persons below eighteen years of age and shall not be carried out on pregnant women.") In 1989, however, the General Assembly adopted the Second Optional Protocol to the International Covenant on Civil and Political Rights, which entered into force in 1991. Article 1 provides: "1. No one within the jurisdiction of a State Party to the present Protocol shall be executed. 2. Each State Party shall take all necessary measures to abolish the death penalty within its jurisdiction." Article 2 permits a State, at the time it becomes a party to the Protocol, to reserve for itself the right to apply "the death penalty in

---

[20] Jeffrie G. Murphy, *Getting Even: Forgiveness and Its Limits* 109–10 (2003).

time of war pursuant to a conviction for a most serious crime of a military nature performed during wartime." Although a party to the International Covenant, the United States is not a party to the Second Optional Protocol. As of December 2012, there were 75 State Parties to the Second Optional Protocol, including Argentina, Australia, Austria, Belgium, Bosnia and Herzogovina, Brazil, Canada, Chile, Croatia, Czech Republic, Denmark, Finland, France, Germany, Greece, Hungary, Ireland, Italy, Mexico, Netherlands, New Zealand, Norway, Poland, Portugal, Serbia, Slovakia, Slovenia, South Africa, Spain, Sweden, Switzerland, Turkey, and the United Kingdom of Great Britain and Northern Ireland. Of the 73 State Parties, only five – Brazil, Chile, Cyprus, Greece, and Spain – entered a reservation under Article 2; Cyprus and Spain subsequently withdrew their reservations.[21]

When it entered into force in 1950, the European Convention for the Protection of Human Rights and Fundamental Freedoms did not ban capital punishment; to the contrary, Article 2(1) of the European Convention stated that "[n]o one shall be deprived of his life intentionally save in the execution of a sentence of a court following his conviction for a crime for which this penalty is provided by law." In 1982, however, the Council of Europe adopted Protocol No. 6 to the European Convention, Article 1 of which states: "The death penalty shall be abolished. No one shall be subjected to such penalty or executed." Article 2 states: "A State may make provision in its law for the death penalty in respect of acts committed in time of war or of imminent threat of war." Then, in 2002, the Council of Europe went even further by adopting Protocol No. 13: "Noting that Protocol No. 6 to the Convention . . . does not exclude the death penalty in respect of acts committed in time of war or of imminent threat of war; [b]eing resolved to take the final step in order to abolish the death penalty in all circumstances . . . The death penalty shall be abolished. No one shall be condemned to such penalty or executed."

In 2000, the European Union adopted the Charter of Fundamental Rights, Article 2 of which states: "1. Everyone has the right to life.

[21] See Eric Neumayer, "Death Penalty Abolition and the Ratification of the Second Optional Protocol," 12 *International Journal of Human Rights* 3 (2008).

2. No one shall be condemned to the death penalty, or executed." One scholar reported has reported that "[t]oday, all [twenty-seven] members of the European Union have abolished the death penalty. Abolition has been made a prerequisite for EU membership, giving Eastern and Central European nations strong incentives to prohibit the practice. In principle and in practice, Western European governments are unequivocally opposed to capital punishment."[22]

The Protocol to the American Convention on Human Rights to Abolish the Death Penalty, adopted by the General Assembly of the Organization of American States in 1990, provides for the total abolition of the death penalty but allows a state "to reserve the right to apply the death penalty in wartime in accordance with international law, for extremely serious crimes of a military nature," if the state makes a reservation to that effect at the time it ratifies the Protocol." As of December 2012, there were thirteen State Parties to the protocol, only two of which – Brazil and Chile – have made a "wartime" reservation. The United States is a party neither to the American Convention nor to the protocol.

AS I NOTED AT THE BEGINNING OF THIS CHAPTER, a version of the internationally recognized human right not to be subjected to "cruel, inhuman or degrading" punishment is entrenched in the constitutional law of the United States: the right of every human being not to be subjected to "cruel and unusual" punishment. The latter right, like the former, is a right against government generally: It is a bedrock feature of the constitutional law of the United States – it is constitutional bedrock – that the latter right, which at one time applied only to the federal government, now applies to state government as well.[23]

---

[22] Kathryn F. King, "The Death Penalty, Extradition, and the War against Terrorism: U.S. Responses to European opinion about Capital Punishment," 9 *Buffalo Human Rights Law Review* 161, 171 (2003).

[23] The U.S. Supreme Court's justification for the rule that the Eighth Amendment applies to state government: The Fourteenth Amendment (1868) made some provisions of the Bill of Rights (1791), including the Eighth Amendment – provisions that prior to the Fourteenth Amendment had been applicable only to the federal government – applicable to state government as well. The first case in which the Court ruled that the Eighth Amendment is applicable to state government: *Robinson v. California*, 370 U.S. 660 (1962).

The Eighth Amendment to the Constitution of the United States declares: "Excessive bail shall not be required, nor excessive fines imposed, nor cruel and unusual punishments inflicted." In several cases since 1977, the Supreme Court of the United States has ruled that Cruel and Unusual Punishments Clause (CUPC) of the Eighth Amendment forbids government to impose capital punishment on a person if his crime (a) did not involve a homicide[24] or (b) did involve a homicide but at least one of these three conditions obtains: (i) he did "not himself kill, attempt to kill, or intend that a killing take place";[25] (ii) he is mentally disabled;[26] or (iii) he was seventeen or younger when he committed the crime.[27] Should we go further than a majority of the Supreme Court has yet been willing to go and conclude that the CUPC forbids government to impose capital punishment on *any* person, *even a mentally competent adult, no matter what his crime*?

To answer that question – indeed, to answer the question whether in going as far as it has gone, the Court has already gone too far – we must answer this question: When is a punishment "cruel and unusual" within the meaning of the constitutional right not to be subjected to "cruel and unusual" punishment. No answer to that question has become constitutional bedrock. Therefore, we must inquire when a punishment is "cruel and unusual" within the meaning of the right that was entrenched in the constitutional law of the United States by the enactors of the Eighth Amendment.[28] But precisely what right did they entrench? Answering that question requires that we answer

---

Whether the Fourteenth Amendment did in fact make some Bill of Rights provisions applicable to state government, however – more precisely, whether the enactors of the Fourteenth Amendment meant the Amendment to make some Bill of Rights provisions applicable to state government – has long been the subject of historical controversy. For a recent discussion of the controversy, see Suja A. Thomas, "Nonincorporation," 88 *Notre Dame Law Review* (2012–13). Nonetheless, it is now constitutional bedrock that some Bill of Rights provisions, including the Eighth Amendment, are applicable to state government.

[24] See *Kennedy* v. *Louisiana*, 554 U.S. 407 (2008): "[I]n cases of crimes against individuals," capital punishment is excessive "for crimes that [do not] take the life of the victim." See also *Coker* v. *Georgia*, 433 U.S. 584 (1977) (plurality op'n).

[25] *Enmund* v. *Florida*, 458 U.S. 782, 797 (1982).

[26] *Atkins* v. *Virginia*, 536 U.S. 304 (2002).

[27] *Roper* v. *Simmons*, 543 U.S. 551 (2005).

[28] I explained at the beginning of Part II what I mean by constitutional "enactors."

this question: What did the Eighth Amendment's enactors understand "cruel and unusual" to mean?[29]

In an important recent article, John Stinneford carefully examines both the seventeenth-century English antecedents of the Eighth Amendment and the late eighteenth-century American context in which the Eighth Amendment was drafted and ratified. He concludes that as understood by the Eighth Amendment's enactors, the word "cruel" in the CUPC refers not only to barbaric punishments but also to excessive punishments.[30] If Stinneford is right, as I believe he is, then history supports the Supreme Court's rulings that the CUPC bans punishments that even if not "cruel" in the sense of barbaric are nonetheless "cruel" in the sense of excessive;[31] that is, the CUPC bans punishments that are excessive if they are also "unusual."

Stinneford then argues that as understood by the Eighth Amendment's enactors, the word "unusual" in the CUPC means only "contrary to long usage."[32] However, Stinneford's historical narrative does not lead me to doubt that that as understood by the enactors, "unusual" in the CUPC means simply what "unusual" commonly meant at the time the Eighth Amendment was added to the Constitution (1789–91).[33] According to Samuel Johnson's *A Dictionary of the English Language*, first published in 1756, "unusual" meant: "Not common; not

---

[29] For those who believe that the Fourteenth Amendment made the Eighth Amendment applicable to the states (see n. 23): There is no reason to think that the Fourteenth Amendment's enactors understood/meant "cruel and unusual" differently from the way the Eighth Amendment's enactors understood/meant it.

[30] John F. Stinneford, "Rethinking Proportionality under the Cruel and Unusual Punishments Clause," 97 *Virginia Law Review* 899, 926–61 (2011).

[31] Although the Supreme Court has sometimes determined whether a punishment is excessive by measuring it in relation to the aim of deterrence as well as in relation to the aim of retribution, Stinneford argues that history supports the proposition that for Eighth Amendment purposes, whether a punishment is excessive should be determined by measuring it solely in relation to the aim of retribution. See Stinneford, "Rethinking Proportionality," 962–8.

[32] See ibid. at 968–72. See also John F. Stinneford, "The Original Meaning of 'Unusual': The Eighth Amendment as a Bar to Cruel Innovation," 102 *Northwestern University Law Review* 1739 (2008).

[33] Cf. *Trop* v. *Dulles*, 356 U.S. 86, 100 n. 32 (1958): "If the word 'unusual' is to have any meaning apart from the word 'cruel,' . . . the meaning should be the ordinary one, signifying something different from that which is generally done."

frequent; rare."[34] Stinneford's historical narrative does support *this* proposition: The principal way of determining whether a punishment was "unusual" was to look to see whether the punishment was "contrary to long usage." But that the principal way of determining whether a punishment was "unusual" was to look to see whether the punishment was "contrary to long usage" does not entail that as understood by the Eighth Amendment's enactors, "unusual" in the CUPC means only "contrary to long usage."[35]

Moreover, it is deeply counterintuitive that as understood by the Eighth Amendment's enactors, "unusual" in the CUPC means only "contrary to long usage." If one is concerned, as the Eighth Amendment's enactors were concerned, about the possibility of government's imposing "cruel" punishments – barbaric or otherwise excessive punishments – and so one wants, as they did, to ban such punishments, why would one countenance only an inquiry into whether a punishment is "contrary to long usage"? Why wouldn't one countenance as well an inquiry into whether with the passage of time a punishment not

---

[34] Volume 2, page 503. Johnson's dictionary was "the standard authority at the time when the Constitution was drawn up in 1787." Andrew O' Hagan, "Word Wizard," *New York Review of Books*, Apr. 27, 2006 (quoting and reviewing Henry Hitchings, *Defining the World: The Extraordinary Story of Dr. Johnson's Dictionary* (2006)). Johnson's dictionary "is a beautiful read, and its influence is unending . . . Without it, English-speakers would not be English-speakers as we think of them."

[35] Stinneford writes: "The historical evidence shows that the framers and early interpreters of the Eighth Amendment's Cruel and Unusual Punishments Clause understood it to prohibit punishments that were excessive in light of prior practice." Stinneford, "Rethinking Proportionality," 942. But even so, the historical evidence does not support the proposition that they understood the CUPC to prohibit *only* punishments that are excessive in light of prior practice – in particular, that they understood the CUPC *not* to prohibit, *not* to cover, punishments that are excessive in light of contemporary practice. According to Stinneford (947):

> Although one function of [the CUPC] was to prevent Congress from approving the use of torture, proponents of the Cruel and Unusual Punishments Clause also wanted to prevent the imposition of retroactive punishments and (most relevant for our purposes) excessive punishments. There is no evidence that any of the framers understood the Cruel and Unusual Punishments Clause to prohibit *only* barbaric methods of punishment.

> We may say, analogously, that although one function of the CUPC was to prohibit punishments that are excessive in light of prior practice, there is no evidence that they understood the CUPC to prohibit *only* such punishments – that they understood it *not* to prohibit punishments that are excessive in light of contemporary practice.

"contrary to long usage" has nonetheless become "uncommon; infrequent; rare"? After all, that a punishment has become "uncommon; infrequent; rare" is not less probative of whether a punishment is excessive than whether the punishment is "contrary to long usage." Stinneford's principal concern in his article is with the excessiveness of some new punishments, and that's fine; I don't begrudge Stinneford his principal concern.[36] But there is no good reason for us not to be concerned as well with – *or for us to assume that as understood by the Eighth Amendment's enactors, the Amendment is indifferent to* – the excessiveness of some old punishments: punishments whose excessiveness is evidenced by the punishments' having become "uncommon; infrequent; rare."

If Stinneford is right about the meaning of "unusual" in the CUPC, then history does not support the Supreme Court's inquiring, as it sometimes does in Eighth Amendment cases, whether a punishment, even if not unusual in the past, is unusual *now*.[37] But Stinneford is wrong, in my judgment, about the meaning of "unusual" in the CUPC. According to Stinneford's version of "unusual," the CUPC bans only barbaric and otherwise excessive punishments that are "contrary to long usage." But according to what I judge to be the accurate version of "unusual," the CUPC bans excessive punishments – even those not "contrary to long usage" – if the excessiveness is evidenced by the fact that the punishments are unusual *now*. In deciding whether, as

---

[36]   See ibid., 969–70:

> The core purpose of the Cruel and Unusual Punishments Clause is to protect against sudden, drastic increases in the harshness of punishment. The government has a pronounced tendency to react to perceived crises by ratcheting up the harshness of punishments. Such crises occur in a variety of circumstances. Sometimes a person commits a crime in an outrageous manner, provoking an outcry for extreme punishment. Sometimes the government "has it in for" a political enemy or a member of a disfavored group and inflicts cruel punishments out of animosity or prejudice. And sometimes there is a societal moral panic. A moral panic occurs when a given problem suddenly appears to be beyond the capacity of government to control via traditional means. When this occurs, enormous pressure is placed upon the legislature to do something to show that it is in control. The Cruel and Unusual Punishments Clause is meant to prevent the government from responding to such situations by drastically increasing punishments beyond their traditional bounds.

[37]   See, e.g., *Atkins* v. *Virginia*, 536 U.S. 304 (2002); *Roper* v. *Simmons*, 543 U.S. 551 (2005).

claimed, a punishment violates the CUPC of the Eighth Amendment, the Court is correct to ask whether the punishment is *(a) excessive and (b) evidenced as such by the fact that it is unusual* (i.e., in the Samuel Johnsonian sense of "not common; not frequent; rare").[38]

Is capital punishment excessive – and in that sense "cruel"? Yes, if punishing a criminal by killing him crosses the line by failing to treat the criminal "in a spirit of brotherhood." The point can be put in the language of "dignity," which for some may be a more familiar language: Yes, if punishing a criminal by killing him crosses the line by failing to respect the criminal's dignity. Over a half century ago, in a plurality opinion, Chief Justice Earl Warren stated, in words that have since been endorsed in many majority opinions:[39] "The basic concept underlying the Eighth Amendment is nothing less than the dignity of man. While the State has the power to punish, the Amendment stands to assure that this power be exercised within the limits of civilized standards."[40]

Let me pause to clarify the relationship between the claim that punishing a criminal by killing him fails to treat the criminal "in a spirit of brotherhood" and the claim that punishing a criminal by killing him fails to respect the criminal's dignity. As I explained in Chapter 3, many persons who affirm the "in a spirit of brotherhood" imperative – or a verbally different but functionally equivalent imperative, such as the imperative to treat every human being "lovingly"[41] – believe that every human being, even the most heinous criminal, has a "dignity" that is the principal warrant for – the principal ground of – the imperative. When such a person claims that a law or other policy fails to respect A's dignity, he or

---

[38] I think my position is more plausible than Stinneford's, and Stinneford thinks his is more plausible than mine. If we were to conclude, however, that both positions have roughly equal plausibility – and that no third position has greater plausibility – which position should we then affirm? Mine. Why? Because the Eighth Amendment right would be morally superior to what it otherwise would be, in this important sense: The Eighth Amendment right not to be subjected to "cruel and unusual" punishment would be in closer alignment with the human right – the right internationally recognized as a human right – not to be subjected to "cruel, inhuman or degrading" punishment. Is there a more attractive default standard than this: bringing our fundamental law into closer alignment with one or more rights internationally recognized as human rights?

[39] See, e.g., *Atkins* v. *Virginia*, 536 U.S. 304, 311 (2002).

[40] *Trop* v. *Dulles*, 356 U.S. 86, 100 (1958).

[41] See n. 4.

she is expressing the conclusion, albeit in a language – "dignity" language – that presupposes his or her belief about the principal ground of the imperative, that the policy fails to treat A as the imperative requires (e.g., "in a spirit of brotherhood"). For many other persons, however – many other persons, that is, who affirm the "in a spirit of brotherhood" imperative or a functionally equivalent imperative – "dignity" language, because it seems to them to have religious and/or metaphysical presuppositions that they reject, is deeply problematic. So it bears emphasis to such a person that the claim that a policy fails to respect A's dignity can and should be heard simply as one way of expressing – as one idiom for expressing – the conclusion that the policy fails to treat A as the imperative requires.

Does punishing a criminal by killing him or her cross the line, by failing to treat the criminal as the "in a spirit of brotherhood" imperative requires? (Or, if you prefer, by failing to respect the criminal's dignity?) That is the question we have been addressing thus far in this chapter. And, again, the judgment has become increasingly widespread, in the period since the end of the Second World War, that it *does* cross the line, that it *is* excessive, to punish a criminal by killing him or her, thereby denying to him or her the opportunity both to live a life of ongoing, deepening repentance and to achieve the kind of redemption that such repentance makes possible.[42]

Is capital punishment evidenced as excessive by the fact that capital punishment is "unusual"? That a punishment is not unusual does not entail that it is not excessive. Nonetheless, the CUPC bans punishments that are excessive only if they are also unusual. (Compare the Japanese Constitution – drafted after the Second World War by General Douglas MacArthur's staff[43] – Article 36 of which forbids "cruel" punishments without regard to whether the punishments are also "unusual": "The infliction of torture by any public officer and cruel punishments are absolutely forbidden.") Why ban punishments that are excessive only if they are also unusual? Because whether a punishment claimed to

---

[42] Cf. *Trop v. Dulles*, 356 U.S. 86, 101 (1958): "The [Eighth] Amendment must draw its meaning from the evolving standards of decency that mark the progress of a maturing society."

[43] See Kyoko Inoue, *MacArthur's Japanese Constitution* (1991).

be excessive is in truth excessive is often contestable, and the fact that a punishment is unusual is probative of whether it is in truth excessive.

Again, is capital punishment "unusual"? We know that capital punishment was not unusual in the past; the question is whether capital punishment has become unusual, whether it is unusual *now*.

Eighteen states – eighteen out of fifty – plus the District of Columbia no longer authorize capital punishment. Here is the list, ordered by the year since which capital punishment has not been authorized in the jurisdiction: Michigan (1846), Wisconsin (1853), Maine (1887), Minnesota (1911), Alaska (1957), Hawaii (1957), Vermont (1964), Iowa (1965), West Virginia (1965), North Dakota (1973), District of Columbia (1981), Massachusetts (1984), Rhode Island (1984), New York (2004), New Jersey (2007), New Mexico (2009), Illinois (2011),[44] Connecticut (2012), Maryland (2013). Thirty-two states, the federal government, and the U.S. military still authorize capital punishment. To authorize capital punishment – to maintain it on the books – is not necessarily to impose the death penalty often or at all.[45]

---

[44] See Samuel G. Freedman, "Faith Was on [Illinois] Governor's Shoulder," *New York Times*, March 25, 2011.

[45] The Supreme Court began a moratorium on capital punishment in 1972 (see *Furman* v. *Georgia*, 408 U.S. 238 (1972)) and ended it four years later (see *Gregg* v. *Georgia*, 428 U.S. 153 (1976)). "The Supreme Court's decision in *Furman* effectively declared unconstitutional the death penalty statutes then in place in 40 states and commuted the sentences of 629 death row inmates around the country. Because only Justices Brennan and Marshall asserted that the death penalty was per se unconstitutional, the opinions of Justices Stewart, White, and Douglas suggested that states could rewrite their death penalty statutes to remedy the constitutional problems." Marc L. Miller and Ronald F. Wright, *Criminal Procedures: Cases, Statutes, and Executive Materials* 184–85 (2003). In the more than thirty-five years since the moratorium ended, the following retentionist states – states that still retain capital punishment – have executed five or fewer persons (the number executed is in the parentheses): Colorado (1), Connecticut (1), Idaho (1), Kansas (0), Kentucky (3), Maryland (5), Montana (3), Nebraska (3), New Hampshire (0), Oregon (2), Pennsylvania (3), South Dakota (1), Tennessee (1), Washington (5), Wyoming (1). In the same period, the U.S. government has executed three persons and the U.S. military, none. In the ten years from January 1, 2001, to December 31, 2010, these states executed either no one or just one person: Colorado (0), Connecticut (1), Idaho (0), Kentucky (1), Montana (1), Nebraska (0), Oregon (0), Pennsylvania (0), South Dakota (1), Utah (1), Wyoming (0). See Editorial, "The Death Penalty's De Facto Abolition," *New York Times*, Oct. 15, 2011:

> From their annual high points since the penalty was reinstated 35 years ago, the number executed has *dropped by half*, and the number sentenced to death has

Still, it is not plausible to contend that in the United States at this time, capital punishment is "unusual": "not common; not frequent; rare."[46]

However, we need not – and indeed should not – confine our inquiry to the borders of the United States: Is capital punishment "unusual" among the nations of the world? Given why we're asking the question ("Is capital punishment 'unusual'?") in the first place, it would make no sense – none at all – to confine our inquiry to the United States. If every nation in the world except the United States had abolished capital punishment, wouldn't that be probative of whether capital punishment is in fact excessive and in that sense cruel, probative of whether continued reliance on capital punishment in the United States is inconsistent with the "in a spirit of brotherhood" imperative? Confining our inquiry to the United States would deprive us of the very information we need to "reality test" the judgment that capital punishment is excessive.

Misunderstanding is predictable here, so let me be clear: We should cast our net broadly not because we think that the United States should follow the moral lead of other nations. ("Perish the thought!" some will say.) Rather, we should cast our net broadly because what other nations are doing is probative – not determinative, but probative – of whether capital punishment is in fact excessive and in that sense cruel.[47] A majority of the Supreme Court understands the point:

> *dropped by almost two-thirds.* Sixteen states don't allow the penalty, and eight of the states that do have *not carried out an execution* in 12 years or more. There is more.
>
> Only one-seventh of the nation's 3,147 counties have carried out an execution since 1976. Counties with one-eighth of the American population produce two-thirds of the sentences. As a result, the death penalty is the embodiment of arbitrariness. Texas, for example, in the past generation, has executed five times as many people as Virginia, the next closest state. But the penalty is used heavily in just four of Texas's 254 counties.

[46] Benjamin Wittes has suggested determining the "unusualness" of a punishment by "set[ting] the number of states at three-quarters of the number of states in the Union, currently 38. This corresponds to the number of states required to amend the Constitution." Benjamin Wittes, "What Is 'Cruel and Unusual'?," *Policy Review*, December 2005 and January 2006.

[47] For an interesting, Habermasian argument in support of casting our net broadly, see Jessica Olive and David Gray, "A Modest Appeal for Decent Respect," 23 *Federal Sentencing Reporter* 72 (2010). Cf. Joan F. Hartman, "'Unusual' Punishment: The Domestic Effects

Our determination that the death penalty is disproportionate punishment for offenders under 18 finds confirmation in the stark reality that the United States is the only country in the world that continues to give official sanction to the juvenile death penalty. This reality does not become controlling, for the task of interpreting the Eighth Amendment remains our responsibility. Yet at least from the time of the Court's decision in *Trop v. Dulles* [1958], the Court has referred to the laws of other countries and to international authorities as instructive for its interpretation of the Eighth Amendment's prohibition of "cruel and unusual punishments."[48]

When we do cast our net broadly, we discover that capital punishment is undeniably, and increasingly, "unusual" – undeniably, and increasingly, "uncommon; infrequent; rare" – among the nations of the world. The list of "abolitionist" nations is quite long; it includes, in addition to our neighbors to the north (Canada) and to the south (Mexico), all the countries of Europe, Australia, New Zealand, and South Africa. The list of "retentionist" liberal democracies is quite small; it includes India, Japan, South Korea, and the United States.[49] In 2011, Amnesty International reported:

At the end of 2010 the global trend towards abolition of the death penalty could not have been clearer. While in the mid-1990s 40 countries on average were known to carry out executions each year, during the first years of this century executions were reported in 30 countries on average. Most recently, 25 countries reportedly executed prisoners in 2008 while 19 countries – the lowest number ever recorded by Amnesty International – did so in 2009. In 2010, 23 countries were known to have carried out executions. The number of countries that are abolitionist in law or practice has substantially increased over the past decade, rising from 108 in 2001 to 139 in recent years.

of International Norms Restricting the Application of the Death Penalty," 52 *University of Cincinnati Law Review* 655 (1983).

[48] *Roper v. Simmons*, 543 U.S. 551, *575* (2005) (citing *Trop v. Dulles*, 356 U.S. 86, 102–3 (1958)).

[49] For Amnesty International's accounting of "abolitionist" and "retentionist" countries, and of worldwide executions and death sentences in 2011, see the report excerpted in Appendix B to this chapter.

However, "[t]he fact that there is an overwhelming consensus ceases to be so impressive unless . . . each country has converged on the same conclusion for the same reason and that the same reason is also important to us."[50] Earlier in this chapter I listed several international and regional human rights instruments that call for the abolition of capital punishment. The story of the emergence of those instruments over the last several decades confirms that the convergence of a large majority of the nations of the world "on the same conclusion" – that capital punishment should be abolished – was indeed animated mainly by "the same reason," a reason that is undeniably "important to us": Punishing a criminal by killing him fails to respect the dignity, and the attendant right to life, that every human being, even the most heinous criminal, has. (As I explained above, the claim that capital punishment fails to respect the criminal's dignity is a way of expressing the conclusion that capital punishment fails to treat the criminal as the "in a spirit of brotherhood" imperative requires.) Consider these statements:

- The Protocol to the American Convention on Human Rights to Abolish the Death Penalty (1990): "[E]veryone has the inalienable right to respect for his life, a right that cannot be suspended for any reason; . . . the tendency among the American States is to be in favor of abolition of the death penalty; . . . application of the death penalty has irrevocable consequences, forecloses the correction of judicial error, and precludes any possibility of changing or rehabilitating those convicted; . . . the abolition of the death penalty helps to ensure more effective protection of the right to life; . . . an international agreement must be arrived at that will entail a progressive development of the American Convention on Human Rights; and . . . States Parties to the American Convention on Human Rights have expressed their intention to adopt an international agreement with a view to consolidating the practice of not applying the death penalty in the Americas."

---

[50] Youngjae Lee, "International Consensus as Persuasive Authority in the Eighth Amendment," 56 *University of Pennsylvania Law Review* 63, 115 (2007).

- The Second Optional Protocol to the International Covenant on Civil and Political Rights (1991): "[A]bolition of the death penalty contributes to enhancement of human dignity and progressive development of human rights" and "all measures of abolition of the death penalty should be considered as progress in the enjoyment of the right to life."
- The Charter of Fundamental Rights of the European Union (2000): "Human dignity is inviolable. It must be respected and protected . . . Everyone has the right to life. No one shall be condemned to the death penalty, or executed."
- Protocol No. 13 to the European Convention for the Protection of Human Rights and Fundamental Freedoms (2002): "[E]veryone's right to life is a basic value in a democratic society and . . . the abolition of the death penalty is essential for the protection of this right and for the full recognition of the inherent dignity of all human beings."

WHEN I WAS FIRST DRAFTING THIS CHAPTER, Notre Dame legal scholar Cathleen Kaveny, who is also a moral theologian, published a piece in *Commonweal* titled "A Horrific Crime." She wrote:

> After deliberating for four days last month, a Connecticut jury imposed the death penalty on Steven Hayes, one of two men charged with three horrific murders during a home invasion in July 2007. Joshua Komisarjevsky, his alleged accomplice, will be tried separately next spring.[51]

> Hayes and Komisarjevsky broke into the suburban home of the Petit family in the dead of the night, beat the father senseless with a baseball bat, raped the mother, and terrorized the two daughters, one seventeen years old and the other just eleven. The little girl was also raped. When morning came, the two men forced the mother to withdraw fifteen thousand dollars from the bank, promising to release the family if she complied with their demands. Despite the fact that she managed to alert the authorities, help came too late. She was murdered within an hour of the timestamp marking her

---

[51] See William Glaberson, "Death Penalty for 2nd Man in Connecticut Triple-Murder Case," *New York Times*, Dec. 9, 2011.

appearance on the grainy footage from the bank camera. Most horrible of all was the fate of the two girls. They were tied to their beds and doused with accelerant, left to burn alive after the criminals set the house ablaze. Only the smallest of cosmic mercies permitted the daughters to die of smoke inhalation before the flames reached their bodies.

When I heard the verdict, I experienced an immediate sense of relief. Since then I have been struggling to reconcile my initial reaction with my moral opposition to the death penalty.[52]

I thought, as I read Kaveny's narrative of the Connecticut case, that my appetite for vengeance is quite robust, and that the execution of criminals such as Hayes and Komisarjevsky helps to sate my appetite for vengeance. It is hard, very hard, to affirm the imperative, or, if one affirms it, to be faithful to the imperative, that we, through our governments, act toward every human being, even one who has committed a gruesomely depraved crime, "in a spirit of brotherhood." But if we aspire to be – if we are committed to be – a community constituted in part by our fidelity to that imperative, then we must abandon capital punishment; we must stop punishing criminals, *any* criminals, by killing them; capital punishment is contrary to our commitment to be such a community. As the Catholic bishops of Ohio recently emphasized in urging Governor John Kasich and state lawmakers to end the death penalty: "Life imprisonment respects the moral view that all life, *even that of the worst offender*, has value and dignity . . . Fair and effective punishment is possible without the death penalty."[53]

Listen again to Kaveny:

The hard fact is that society cannot impose a condign punishment, or an effective deterrent to these monstrous acts, without in some sense recreating and participating in the brutality of the criminals themselves. And viewed more broadly, that fact suggests how we should think about the death penalty. We need to ask

---

[52] Kaveny, "A Horrific Crime."
[53] Catholic Conference of Ohio, Press Release: "Catholic Bishops of Ohio Call upon Governor Kasich and Legislative Leaders to End the Death Penalty," Feb. 4, 2011 (emphasis added).

not [just] what it does to the criminals, but what it does to us as a society. The execution is a separate event from the crime. At the moment of execution, a criminal is helpless before the power of the state. We strap him to a gurney and snuff out his life. Can a society engage in this ritual while meaningfully advancing a commitment to the unconditional dignity of every human being?[54]

Recalling that, as I noted previously, "dignity" language – which is the language on which on which Kaveny, the Ohio bishops, the U.S. Supreme Court, and many human rights instruments rely – is, for some, deeply problematic, it bears emphasis that Kaveny's question can be articulated without relying on such language: In engaging in this ritual, are we being faithful to the imperative to act toward *all* members of the human family in what the Universal Declaration of Human Rights calls "a spirit of brotherhood"?

The judgment is not merely increasingly widespread in the period since the end of the Second World War; the judgment is, I am persuaded, correct, that punishing a criminal by killing him crosses the line: it constitutes a failure to treat the criminal "in a spirit of brotherhood"; it is "cruel, inhuman or degrading." Moreover, a powerful argument supports the conclusion that capital punishment violates the Cruel and Unusual Punishments Clause of the Eighth Amendment: No matter what the crime, punishing a criminal, even a mentally competent adult, by killing him or her is excessive – it crosses the line – and is evidenced as such by the fact that capital punishment has become demonstrably unusual.

AS I EXPLAIN IN THE NEXT CHAPTER, to conclude, as I have here, that capital punishment violates the Eighth Amendment is not necessarily to conclude that the Supreme Court of the United States should so rule. Should the Court so rule? To answer that question, we need first to answer the question that is the subject of the next chapter: the question of judicial deference.

---

[54] Kaveny, "A Horrific Crime."

APPENDIX A

Capital Punishment: A Measurably Greater Deterrent?

Is it the case that in some countries and/or states capital punishment has a measurably greater deterrent effect than the next most severe punishment: life in prison without the possibility of parole? The evidence in support of an affirmative answer is, in the words of economists John Donohue and Justin Wolfers, "surprisingly fragile."[55] Commenting in 2005 on the possibility that in the United States capital punishment has a greater deterrent effect, Donohue and Wolfers wrote:

> Our key insight is that the death penalty – at least as it has been implemented in the United States [in the last thirty years] – is applied so rarely that the number of homicides it can plausibly have caused or deterred cannot be reliably disentangled from the large year-to-year changes in the homicide rate caused by other factors. Our estimates suggest not just "reasonable doubt" about whether there is any deterrent effect of the death penalty, but profound uncertainty. We are confident that the effects are not large, but we remain unsure even of whether they are positive or negative. The difficulty is not just one of statistical significance: whether one measures positive or negative effects of the death penalty is extremely sensitive to very small changes in econometric specifications. Moreover, we are pessimistic that existing data can resolve this uncertainty.[56]

---

[55] John Donohue and Justin Wolfers, "Uses and Abuses of Empirical Evidence in the Death Penalty Debate," 58 *Stanford Law Review* 791, 794 (2005).

[56] Ibid. See also John Donohue and Justin Wolfers, "The Death Penalty: No Evidence for Deterrence," *Economists' Voice*, April 2006, www.bepress.com/ev. Other recent studies include, in chronological order: Lawrence Katz, Steven D. Levitt, and Ellen Shustorovich, "Prison Conditions, Capital Punishment, and Deterrence," 5 *American Law & Economics Review* 318 (2003); Rudolph J. Gerber, "Economic and Historical Implications for Capital Punishment Deterrence," 18 *Notre Dame Journal of Law, Ethics and Public Policy* 437 (2004); Jeffrey Fagan, *Deterrence and the Death Penalty: A Critical Review of the New Evidence, Testimony to the New York State Assembly Standing Committee* (Jan. 21, 2005), http://www.deathpenaltyinfo.org/FaganTestimony.pdf; Richard Berk, "New Claims About Executions and General Deterrence: Déjà Vu All Over Again?," 2 *Journal of Empirical Legal Studies* 303 (2005); Robert Weisberg, "The Death Penalty Meets Social Science: Deterrence and Jury Behavior Under New Scrutiny," 1 *Annual Review of Law and Social Science* 151 (2005); Jeffrey Fagan, "Death and Deterrence Redux: Science,

One study – by my colleague, economist Joanna Shepherd Bailey – concluded that in several states, capital punishment not only has no deterrent effect but, perversely, has what she calls a "brutalization effect," increasing the number of murders:

> Consider the twenty-seven states where at least one execution occurred during the sample period [1977–96]. Executions deter murder in only six states. Capital punishment, however, actually *increases* murder in thirteen states, more than twice as many as experience deterrence. In eight states, capital punishment has no effect on the murder rate. That is, executions have a deterrent effect in only twenty-two percent of states. In contrast, executions induce additional murders in forty-eight percent of states. In seventy-eight percent of states, executions do not deter murder . . .

> If deterrence is capital punishment's purpose, as is often stated by our president and others, then, in the majority of states where executions do not deter crime, executions kill convicts uselessly. Moreover, in the many states where the brutalization effect outweighs the deterrent effect, executions not only kill convicts needlessly but also induce the additional murders of many innocent people. A very rough estimate is that, all told from 1977 to 1996, executions in no-deterrence states have killed more than 5,000 innocent people, or 250 per year. Thus, in the many states that execute without a deterrent effect, policymakers should consider abandoning the death penalty. These states' executions do not deter crime. If deterrence is the goal, capital punishment in these states simply does not work. Instead, it needlessly kills both convicts and innocents.[57]

In the United States, southern states have been, and remain, especially fond of capital punishment – a phenomenon documented and explored in sociologist David Garland's recent book *Peculiar Institution:*

Alchemy and Causal Reasoning on Capital Punishment," 4 *Ohio State Journal of Criminal Law* 225 (2006–07); New Jersey Death Penalty Study Commission Report 24–26 (January 2007).

[57] Joanna M. Shepherd, "Deterrence versus Brutalization: Capital Punishment's Differing Impacts among States," 104 *Michigan Law Review* 203, 205, 206–7 (2005).

America's Death Penalty in an Age of Abolition (2010).[58] So it was interesting well beyond the borders of Alabama when, in November 2005, the *Birmingham News* published a series of six editorials discussing capital punishment and calling for its abolition in Alabama. In responding to the deterrence-based argument for capital punishment, the opening editorial in the series emphasized that "[e]ven those on the front lines of crime are skeptical about the deterrent effect of capital punishment. In a 1995 study of 386 randomly selected police chiefs, two-thirds of them said the death penalty didn't significantly reduce the number of homicides. A 1996 survey of criminology experts – past and current presidents of three criminology associations – also rejected the notion that executions deter. More than 87 percent believed that the death penalty had no deterrent effect."[59] The editors concluded, on the basis of their review of the available evidence, that there is ample "reason to doubt the death penalty's ability to deter other murders."[60]

Although, not surprisingly, the legislature of Alabama has not abolished capital punishment, the legislatures of New Jersey (in 2007), New Mexico (2009), Illinois (2011), and Connecticut (2012) have recently done so, bringing to sixteen the number of states (plus the District of Columbia) that are now "abolitionist."

In the words of a report submitted to the New Jersey legislature in January 2007, the New Jersey Death Penalty Study Commission stated that "[t]here is no compelling evidence that the . . . death penalty rationally serves a legitimate penological interest." According to the Commission, which recommended to the legislature that it abolish capital punishment, "[t]he alternative of life imprisonment in a maximum security institution without the possibility of parole would sufficiently ensure public safety and address other legitimate social and

---

[58] Cf. Franklin E. Zimring, "The Unexamined Death Penalty: Capital Punishment and Reform of the Model Penal Code," 105 *Columbia Law Review* 1396, 1409 (2005): "In some Southern states, inadequate defense and appellate lawyers and judges willing to use procedural defaults to nullify substantive legal claims have created much higher rates. For example, Virginia's, Texas's, and Missouri's rates of execution are more than thirty times those of Ohio, Pennsylvania, and California."

[59] Editorial, "No Airtight Case for Death," *Birmingham [Alabama] News*, Nov. 10, 2005, 8A.

[60] Ibid.

penological interests, including the interests of the families of murder victims."[61]

APPENDIX B

Death Sentences and Executions 2011

Amnesty International annually provides a detailed accounting of worldwide death sentences and executions in the preceding calendar year. In its March 2012 report, titled *Death Sentences and Executions 2011* and available online, Amnesty International stated:

> At least 20 countries were known to have carried out executions in 2011. Even including newly-independent South Sudan, this is a reduction from 2010, when 23 countries were reported to have implemented death sentences, and shows a steep decline against the figure recorded a decade ago, when 31 countries were known to have carried out executions.[62]

---

[61] New Jersey Death Penalty Study Commission Report 24–30 and 56–61 (January 2007). In June 2012, after I had finished drafting this appendix, one of the authors of the study I quote at the beginning of the appendix, Justin Wolfers, along with co-author (and spouse) Betsey Stevenson, both of whom are professors at the University of Pennsylvania's Wharton School, reported:

> The reality, unsatisfying and inconvenient as it may be, is that we simply don't know how capital punishment affects the homicide rate. That's the conclusion of the National Academy of Sciences, which typically plays the role of impartial arbiter in these social-science debates. Their expert panel recently concluded that existing research "is not informative about whether capital punishment decreases, increases, or has no effect on homicide rates," and that such studies "should not influence policy judgments about capital punishment."

Betsey Stevenson and Justin Wolfers, "The Death-Penalty Debate Represents a Market Failure," *Bloomberg*, June 11, 2012, http://www.bloomberg.com/news/2012-06-11/the-death-penalty-debate-represents-a-market-failure.html.

[62] In its report, Amnesty International states:

> This report only covers the judicial use of the death penalty. The figures presented in this report are the largest that can safely be drawn from Amnesty International's research, although we emphasize that the true figures in relation to some countries are significantly higher. Some states intentionally conceal death penalty proceedings; others do not keep or make available figures on the numbers of death sentences and executions.

Reported Executions in 2011
Afghanistan (2), Bangladesh (5+), Belarus (2), China (+), Egypt
(1+), Iran (360+), Iraq (68+), Malaysia (+), North Korea (30+),
Palestinian Authority (3 in Gaza), Saudi Arabia (82+), Somalia
(10: 6 by the Transitional Federal Government; 3 in Puntland; 1
in Galmudug), South Sudan (5), Sudan (7+), Syria (+), Taiwan
(5), United Arab Emirates (1), United States (43), Vietnam (5+),
Yemen (41+).

At least 676 executions were known to have been carried out
worldwide in 2011, an increase on the 2010 figure of at least 527
executions worldwide. The increase is largely due to a significant
increase in judicial killings in Iran, Iraq, and Saudi Arabia. However, the 676 figure does not include the thousands of people who
were believed to have been executed in China in 2011. Beginning
in the 2009 report, Amnesty International ceased to publish its
estimates on the use of the death penalty in China, where such
figures are considered a state secret. Amnesty International renews
its challenge to the Chinese authorities to publish figures for the
number of people sentenced to death and executed each year, to
confirm their claims that there has been a significant reduction in
the use of the death penalty in the country over the last four years.

Amnesty International has also received credible reports of a
large number of unconfirmed or even secret executions in Iran,
which would almost double the number of officially acknowledged
executions.

Official figures on the use of the death penalty in 2011 were
available only in a small number of countries. In Belarus, China,
Mongolia, and Vietnam, data on the use of the death penalty continued to be classified as a state secret. Little or no information
was available for Egypt, Eritrea, Libya, Malaysia, North Korea,
and Singapore. In Belarus, Japan, and Vietnam, prisoners were not
informed of their forthcoming execution, nor were their families
and lawyers. In Belarus and Vietnam the bodies of the executed
prisoners were not returned to their families for burial.

Where "+" is indicated after a country and it is preceded by a number, it
means that the figure Amnesty International has calculated is a minimum figure.
Where "+" is indicated after a country and is not preceded by a number, it
indicates that there were executions or death sentences (at least more than one)
in that country but it was not possible to obtain any figures. For the purposes of
calculating global and regional totals, "+" is counted as 2.

Reported Death Sentences in 2011
Afghanistan (+), Algeria (51+), Bahrain (5), Bangladesh (49+), Belarus (2), Botswana (1), Burkina Faso (3), Cameroon (+), Chad (+), China (+), Congo (Republic of) (3), Democratic Republic of Congo (+), Egypt (123+), Gambia (13), Ghana (4), Guinea (16), Guyana (3+), India (110+), Indonesia (6+), Iran (156+), Iraq (291+), Japan (10), Jordan (15+), Kenya (11+), Kuwait (17+), Lebanon (8), Liberia (1), Madagascar (+), Malawi (2), Malaysia (108+), Mali (2), Mauritania (8), Mongolia (+), Morocco/Western Sahara (5), Myanmar (33+), Nigeria (72), North Korea (+), Pakistan (313+), Palestinian Authority (5+: 4 in Gaza; 1 in West Bank), Papua New Guinea (5), Qatar (3+), Saint Lucia (1), Saudi Arabia (9+), Sierra Leone (2), Singapore (5+), Somalia (37+: 32+ by the Transitional Federal Government; 4 in Puntland; 1 in Galmudug), South Korea (1), South Sudan (1+), Sri Lanka (106), Sudan (13+), Swaziland (1), Syria (+), Taiwan (16), Tanzania (+), Thailand (40), Trinidad and Tobago (2), Uganda (5), United Arab Emirates (31+), United States (78), Viet Nam (23+), Yemen (29+), Zambia (48), Zimbabwe (1+).

At least 1,923 people were known to have been sentenced to death in 63 countries in 2011. This is the minimum figure that can be safely inferred from Amnesty International's research and represents a decrease from the 2010 figure of at least 2,024 death sentences worldwide.

At least 18,750 people were under sentence of death worldwide at the end of 2011, which is the minimum figure based on numbers Amnesty International obtained by country.

5   THE QUESTION OF JUDICIAL DEFERENCE

Assuming that the Supreme Court of the United States (SCOTUS) should play *some* role in protecting the constitutional morality of the United States, what role – how large or small a role – should it play? More precisely: In exercising judicial review *of a certain sort* – judicial review to determine whether a law (or other public policy) claimed to violate a right that is part of the constitutional morality of the United States does in fact violate the right – should SCOTUS inquire whether *in its own judgment* the law violates the right? Or, instead, should SCOTUS proceed deferentially – deferentially in relation to the lawmakers – inquiring only whether *the lawmakers' judgment* that the law does *not* violate the right is a reasonable one?

IT HAS BEEN THE SUBJECT OF RENEWED CONTROVERSY, in recent years, what role a democracy should authorize its judiciary to play in the democracy's effort to protect human rights.[1] Most democracies, in their effort to protect human rights, have entrenched some human rights in their constitutional law. Some scholars have argued,

---

[1] See, e.g., Jeremy Waldron, "The Core of the Case Against Judicial Review," 115 *Yale Law Journal* 1346 (2006); James Allan, *The Vantage of Law: Its Role in Thinking about Law, Judging, and Bills of Rights* (2011); Mark Tushnet, "Abolishing Judicial Review," 27 *Constitutional Commentary* 581 (2011).

    Jeremy Waldron's "core of the case against judicial review" – against, that is, not all judicial review but "strong-form" judicial review (see n. 7–8 and accompanying text) – has provoked much critical commentary. See, e.g., Richard H. Fallon, Jr., "The Core of an Uneasy Case *for* Judicial Review," 121 *Harvard Law Review* 1693 (2008). Fallon writes (1709, 1715):

> [T]he core of the strongest case *for* judicial review in the kind of nonpathological society with which both Waldron and I are concerned: errors that result in the underenforcement of rights are more troubling than errors that result in their overenforcement, and judicial review may provide a distinctly valuable hedge

however, that an appropriately thoroughgoing commitment to democratic lawmaking should lead a democracy to stop short of authorizing

> against errors of underenforcement. . . [A] constitutional democracy with a well-designed system of judicial review [may] produce a morally better pattern of outcomes than a political democracy without judicial review.

For another thoughtful response to Waldron, see Juan F. Gonzalez Bertomeau, "Against the Core of the Case: Structuring the Evaluation of Judicial Review," 17 *Legal Theory* 81 (2011).

Waldron writes that his "argument against [strong-form] judicial review is not unconditional but depends on certain institutional and political features of modern liberal democracies." Waldron, "The Core of the Case," 1353. He allows that judicial review may be "necessary as a protective measure against legislative pathologies relating to sex, race, or religion in particular countries." Ibid., 1352. "But even if that is so," Waldron continues, "it is worth figuring out whether that sort of defense goes to the heart of the matter, or whether it should be regarded instead as an exceptional reason to refrain from following the tendency of what, in most circumstances, would be a compelling normative argument against [strong judicial review] . . . What is needed is some general understanding, uncontaminated by the cultural, historical, and political preoccupations of each society." Ibid. See also ibid., 1406.

At one point in his essay Waldron writes: "There may be some countries – perhaps the United States – in which peculiar legislative pathologies have developed. If that is so, then Americans should confine their non-core argument for judicial review to their own exceptional circumstances." Ibid., 1386. But how "exceptional" are the United States's circumstances? Are most liberal democracies free of the pathologies to which Waldron refers? Speaking from a British perspective, Lord Scarman, in 1984, wrote: "[I]f you are going to protect people who will never have political power, at any rate in the foreseeable future (not only individuals but minority groups with their own treasured and properly treasured social customs, religion and ways of life), if they are going to be protected it won't be done in Parliament – they will never muster a majority. It's got to be done by the Courts and the Courts can do it only if they've got the proper guidelines." Lord Scarman, "Britain and the Protection of Human Rights," 15 *Cambrian Law Review* 5, 10 (1984). More recently, and speaking from a broader perspective, Mac Darrow and Philip Alston wrote that "there are ample grounds, based on experience in countries with constitutional human rights protections, to suggest that entrenchment of bills of rights can contribute significantly to the empowerment of disadvantaged groups, providing a judicial forum in which they can be heard and seek redress, in circumstances where the political process could not have been successfully mobilized to assist them." Mac Darrow and Philip Alston, "Bills of Rights in Comparative Perspective," in Philip Alston, ed., *Promoting Human Rights Through Bills of Rights: Comparative Perspectives* 465, 493 (1999). Such statements are quite common. For example, in a case in which the eleven justices of the Constitutional Court of the Republic of South Africa ruled unanimously that imposition of the death penalty was unconstitutional under the transitional 1993 constitution, the President of the Court wrote:

> The very reason for establishing the new legal order, and for vesting the power of judicial review of all legislation in the courts, was to protect the rights of minorities and others who cannot protect their rights adequately through the democratic process. Those who are entitled to claim this protection include the social outcasts and marginalized people of our society. It is only if there is a

its courts to enforce whatever human rights are constitutionally entrenched.[2] What's the point of a democracy's entrenching human rights in its constitutional law, one might wonder, if the democracy does not also authorize its courts to enforce the rights? Something Albert Venn Dicey wrote in *An Introduction to the Study of the Law of the Constitution* (1885) points to an answer: "The restrictions placed on the action of the legislature under the French constitution are not in reality laws, since they are not rules which in the last resort will be enforced by the courts. Their true character is that of maxims of political morality, which derive whatever strength they possess from being formally inscribed in the constitution, and from the resulting support of public opinion."[3] Even if they are not judicially enforced, constitutionally entrenched human rights, qua "maxims of political morality," can serve, for the lawmakers and citizens of a democracy, as shared fundamental grounds of political-moral judgment.

Whatever the merits of the argument that a democracy should not authorize its courts to enforce constitutionally entrenched human rights, the argument has ended up on the losing side of history:[4]

In 1946, only *25%* of countries had some form of judicial review explicitly entrenched in their respective constitutions; by 2006, that proportion had increased to 82%. This measure excludes

willingness to protect the worst and the weakest amongst us, that all of us can be secure that our own rights will be protected.

Quoted in Henry J. Steiner and Philip Alston, *International Human Rights in Context* 48 (2nd ed. 2000).

[2] See especially Allan, *The Vantage of Law.*

[3] Quoted in James Bradley Thayer, "The Origin and Scope of the American Doctrine of Constitutional Law," 7 *Harvard Law Review* 129, 130 (1893).

[4] Australia is a special case: With respect to federal lawmaking, there is "judicial supremacy on the structural issues of federalism and separation of powers," but "parliamentary sovereignty on matters of rights." Stephen Gardbaum, *The New Commonwealth Model of Constitutionalism: Theory and Practice* 230 (forthcoming, 2013). However, in the Australian Capital Territory (ACT), because of ACT's 2004 Human Rights Act, and in the state of Victoria, because of Victoria's 2006 Charter of Human Rights and Responsibilities, the judiciary plays a significant role in protecting human rights. For discussion, see ibid., 230–50. See also David Kinley and Christine Ernst, "Exile on Main Street: Australia's Legislative Agenda for Human Rights" (2011), http://ssrn.com/abstract=1931915. Cf. Emma Hoiberg, "A Human Rights Act for Australia: A Transfer of Power to the High Court, or a More Democratic Form of Judicial Decision-Making?," (2012), http://ssrn .com/abstract=2172707.

countries such as the United States that have adopted judicial review in the absence of an explicit constitutional mandate. Accordingly, we constructed a second variable that captures the existence of judicial review via either explicit constitutional mandate or actual practice... Not surprisingly, this combined measure of de jure and de facto judicial review shows sharp growth that roughly parallels that of the exclusively de jure measure. In 1946, only 35% of countries had either de jure or de facto judicial review; by 2006, about 87% did. The difference between the two indicators is both small and diminishing slightly over time, which means that judicial review is generally, and increasingly, established by explicit constitutional provision.[5]

As a real-world matter, then, the serious question is no longer whether a democracy that entrenches some human rights in its constitutional law – as almost all democracies have done – should also authorize its courts to enforce the rights. (Legal scholar Martin Chanock, observing South Africa's transition to democracy in the 1990s, reported that a constitutionally entrenched and judicially enforced "bill of rights was crucial... to the whole question of legitimacy of a post-apartheid regime. For its powerful symbolism would establish an arena not just for law, but would also be a definition of what is, and is not, legitimate in politics."[6]) The serious question concerns the precise role the courts should be authorized to play in a democracy – how large or small a role – in protecting constitutionally entrenched human rights.

Some legal scholars have argued that the courts should be authorized to play only a small – that is, weak – role: They should be authorized to exercise only one or another version of "weak-form" judicial review, as Mark Tushnet has dubbed it.[7] To exercise "strong-form" judicial review is to exercise what I have elsewhere called the power

---

[5] David S. Law and Mila Versteeg, "The Evolution and Ideology of Global Constitutionalism," 99 *California Law Review* 1163, 1199 (2011). Cf. Michael C. Tolley, "Judicialization of Politics in Europe: Keeping Pace with Strasburg," 11 *Journal of Human Rights* 66 (2012).

[6] Martin Chanock, "A Post-Calvinist Catechism or a Post-Communist Manifesto? Intersecting Narratives in the South Africa Bill of Rights Debate," in Philip Alston, ed., *Promoting Human Rights Through Bills of Rights: Comparative Perspectives* 392, 394 (1999).

[7] See Mark Tushnet, "The Rise of Weak-Form Judicial Review," in Tom Ginsburg and Rosalind Dixon, eds., *Comparative Constitutional Law* 321 (2011).

of judicial "ultimacy":[8] the power to have the last word when ruling that a law violates a constitutionally entrenched human right – the last word, that is, short of an extremely improbable event, namely, a successful supermajoritarian effort to amend or repeal the constitutional provision on which the court based its ruling.[9] By contrast, to exercise "weak-form" judicial review is to exercise the power of judicial "penultimacy": the power to have, not the last word, but only the penultimate word, in the sense that when ruling that a law violates a constitutionally entrenched or otherwise legally protected human right, the ruling either, as in the United Kingdom, is advisory only – after considering the ruling, the lawmakers may disregard it – or, as in Canada, may be nullified by means of ordinary legislation. There is now a large and quite interesting literature describing and evaluating systems of judicial penultimacy.[10] The heart of the case for such systems is that weak-form judicial review is not undemocratic; unlike strong-form judicial review, weak-form judicial review is consistent with legislative supremacy. As Stephen Gardbaum has noted, "[t]he essential argument . . . is that, without a significant sacrifice in rights protection, [a system of judicial penultimacy] produces a better, more democratically defensible balance of power between courts and legislatures with respect to rights."[11]

---

[8] See Michael J. Perry, "Protecting Human Rights in a Democracy: What Role for the Courts?," in Michael J. Perry, *Toward a Theory of Human Rights: Religion, Law, Courts* 87–117 (2007).

[9] National constitutions are difficult to amend, and the U.S. Constitution especially so:

> In the [United States, a constitutional] amendment is permitted only upon completion of supermajority requirements both in Congress and in the states: an amendment must be proposed, either by 2/3 of each House of Congress or by a convention called at the request of the legislatures of 2/3 of the states, and then the proposed amendment must be approved by the legislatures of or conventions in 3/4 of the states. This makes the U.S. Constitution one of the most deeply entrenched [in the world].

Vicki C. Jackson and Mark Tushnet, *Comparative Constitutional Law* 414 (1999).

[10] See especially Gardbaum, *The New Commonwealth Model of Constitutionalism.* Other informative pieces include: Janet L. Hiebert, "Governing Like Judges?," in Tom Campbell, K. D. Ewing,★ Adam Tomkins, eds., *The Legal Protection of Human Rights: Sceptical Essays* 40 (2011); Janet L. Hiebert, "Constitutional Experimentation: Rethinking How a Bill of Rights Functions," in Ginsburg and Dixon, *Comparative Constitutional Law,* 298; Tushnet, "The Rise of Weak-Form Judicial Review."

[11] Stephen Gardbaum, "Reassessing the New Commonwealth Model of Constitutionalism," 8 *International Journal of Constitutional Law* 167, 173 (2010).

> Whether in practice, as distinct from "in theory" – whether as it has actually operated – weak-form judicial review has been significantly less undemocratic than strong-form

I have elsewhere addressed the issues highlighted in the preceding several paragraphs – any judicial review? if so, strong-form judicial review? weak-form judicial review? – and have explained elsewhere why I incline in favor of a system of judicial penultimacy like Canada's.[12] For present purposes, it suffices to say that in the United States, for better or worse, it is settled – and no one seriously doubts that for the foreseeable future it will remain settled – that SCOTUS exercises strong-form judicial review; SCOTUS exercises the power of judicial ultimacy: again, the power to have (what is as a practical matter) the last word when ruling that a law (or other public policy)[13]

judicial review is a contested question. See, e.g., James Allan, "Statutory Bills of Rights: You Read Words In, You Read Words Out, You Take Parliament's Clear Intention and You Shake It All About – Doin' the Sanky Hanky Panky," in Campbell, Ewing, and Tomkins, *The Legal Protection of Human Rights*, 108, 126:

> The United Kingdom is the textbook example how weak-form judicial review under a statutory bill of rights can collapse, and has collapsed, into something functionally indistinguishable from strong-form judicial review under an entrenched, constitutionalized bill of rights. If you think the latter is objectionable on democratic, count-everyone-as-equal grounds, then it seems to me that you have very little room indeed to distinguish the former or to take a different position as regards this statutory bill of rights. If [the latter] makes you angry and morally indignant, then so should the [former as it operates under the UK] Human Rights Act.

See also Rosalind Dixon, "Weak-Form Judicial Review and American Exceptionalism," 32 *Oxford Journal of Legal Studies* 487 (2012).
  For a more sanguine (than James Allan's) view of how the UK version of weak-form review – the UK Human Rights Act – has operated thus far, see Gardbaum, *The New Commonwealth Model of Constitutionalism*, 176–229. For a well-reviewed book-length study of how the UK Human Rights Act has operated in its first decade, see Aileen Kavanaugh, *Constitutional Review under the UK Human Rights Act* (2009). For Gardbaum's view of how the Canadian version of weak-form judicial review has operated thus far, see Gardbaum, *The New Commonwealth Model of Constitutionalism*, 107–43. In New Zealand, the courts are not authorized to opine that a law violates a legally protected human right; they are authorized only to interpret laws so that they do not arguably violate such a right, insofar as such interpretations are plausible. For Gardbaum's view of how the New Zealand version of weak-form review has operated thus far, see 144–75.

[12] See Perry, "Protecting Human Rights in a Democracy." See generally Gardbaum, *The New Commonwealth Model of Constitutionalism*.

[13] Constitutional cases do not always seem to involve the question of the constitutionality of a law or other public policy; constitutional cases sometimes involve the question of the constitutionality of a government officials's (e.g., a police officer's) conduct. Nonetheless, such cases do involve – they necessarily (if implicitly) involve – the question of the constitutionality of a public policy, namely, the policy of permitting the government official to engage in the conduct at issue. If a law or other public policy forbad the official engage in the conduct at issue, the question of the constitutionality of the conduct would not need to be addressed; if, however, no public policy forbids the official to engage in the conduct,

violates a constitutionally entrenched human right. No state legislature nor even the Congress of the United States may overrule by ordinary legislation a decision by SCOTUS that a law is unconstitutional; such a decision may be overruled only (later) by SCOTUS itself or by extraordinary, supermajoritarian lawmaking, in the form of constitutional amendment.[14]

This important question arises, therefore: In exercising its great power of judicial ultimacy – in exercising strong-form judicial review – to determine whether a law violates a constitutionally entrenched human right, should SCOTUS inquire whether *in its own judgment* the law violates the right? Or, instead, should SCOTUS proceed deferentially, inquiring only whether *the lawmakers' judgment* that the law does *not* violate the right is a reasonable one?[15]

The locus classicus of the argument that SCOTUS should proceed deferentially is an article by James Bradley Thayer in an 1893 issue of the *Harvard Law Review*: "The Origin and Scope of the American Doctrine of Constitutional Law."[16] Thayer emphasized, in his article,

---

the constitutional question must be addressed. And to rule on the constitutionality of the conduct is necessarily to rule on the constitutionality of government's permitting the official to engage in the conduct.

[14] Cf. Richard A. Posner, "Review of Jeremy Waldron, *Law and Disagreement*," 100 *Columbia Law Review* 582, 592 (2000): "There is no reason to suppose that the issue [whether American-style judicial review is a good idea] should be resolved the same way in two different countries, even countries that share the same language and the same basic legal and political heritage. That depends on all sorts of empirical questions and judgmental imponderables involving the political and legal cultures of the two countries and the career path of judges and legislators in them."

[15] Mark Tushnet mistakenly writes that "[t]he U.S. system of judicial review rests on the proposition that the [constitutional] interpretation found more reasonable . . . by judges . . . prevails over reasonable interpretations found more reasonable by Congress." Tushnet, "Abolishing Judicial Review," 585. As I am about to explain, "the U.S. system of judicial review" does not preclude SCOTUS's exercising judicial review in the deferential way counseled by James Bradley Thayer. Whether SCOTUS *should* exercise judicial review as Thayer counseled, or whether it is realistic to believe that SCOTUS *will* do so, are separate questions.

[16] 7 *Harvard Law Review* 129 (1893). See generally "One Hundred Years of Judicial Review: The Thayer Centennial Symposium," 88 *Northwestern University Law Review* 1–468 (1993).

Felix Frankfurter described [James Bradley Thayer], his teacher, as "our great master of constitutional law." Thayer, said Frankfurter, "influenced Holmes, Brandeis, the Hands (Learned and Augustus) . . . and so forth. I am of the view that if I were to name one piece of writing on American Constitutional Law – a

that there is often room for a reasonable difference in judgments about whether a law claimed to violate a constitutional norm does in fact violate the norm. "[M]uch which will seem unconstitutional to one man, or body of men, may reasonably not seem so to another . . . [A] court cannot always, and for the purpose of all sorts of questions, say that there is but one right and permissible way of construing the constitution."[17] The judgment of the lawmakers whose law is in question is presumably that the law is constitutional. SCOTUS should not rule that the law is unconstitutional, argued Thayer, if the lawmakers' judgment is

> silly test maybe – I would pick an essay by James Bradley Thayer in the Harvard Law Review, consisting of 26 pages, published in October, 1893, called 'The Origin and Scope of the American Doctrine of Constitutional Law' . . . Why would I do that? Because from my point of view it's a great guide for judges and therefore, the great guide for understanding by non-judges of what the place of the judiciary is in relation to constitutional questions."

Leonard W. Levy, "Editorial Note," in Leonard W. Levy, ed., *Judicial Review and the Supreme Court: Selected Essays* 84 (1967).

> Thayer was a friend and professional colleague of Oliver Wendell Holmes, first in law practice and then at Harvard, where Thayer taught for thirty years. Louis Brandeis was a student of Thayer's, and Felix Frankfurter, who just missed Thayer at Harvard, acknowledged Thayer's substantial influence. Of Thayer's most famous essay in constitutional law, "The Origin and Scope of the American Doctrine of Constitutional Law," Holmes wrote, "I agree with it heartily and it makes explicit the point of view from which implicitly I have approached the constitutional questions upon which I have differed from some other judges."

Paul Kahn, Legitimacy and History: Self-Government in American Constitutional Theory 84 (1992).

[17] Thayer, "The Origin and Scope of the American Doctrine of Constitutional Law," 144, 150.
According to Thayer, the deferential approach is fitting when a federal court reviews, for federal constitutionality, federal action, or when a state court reviews, either for federal constitutionality or for state constitutionality, state action, but not when a federal court reviews, for federal constitutionality, state action, in which case (according to Thayer) a nondeferential approach is fitting. See ibid., 154–5. This distinction makes little sense, however. See Sanford Gabin, *Judicial Review and the Reasonable Doubt Test* 5 (1980): "[T]he reasonable doubt test should be applied not just to all national legislation but, contrary to Thayer's prescription, to all state legislation as well." Most commentators who discuss Thayer's conception of proper judicial role fail even to note the distinction. See, e.g., Alexander M. Bickel, *The Least Dangerous Branch: The Supreme Court at the Bar of Politics* 35–46 (1962); Wallace Mendelson, "The Influence of James B. Thayer upon the Work of Holmes, Brandeis, and Frankfurter," 31 *Vanderbilt Law Review* 71 (1978); but see Charles L. Black, Jr., *Decision According to Law* 34–5 (1981). Even Thayer's most prominent judicial disciple, Felix Frankfurter, failed to note the distinction – or to heed it. See *West Virginia State Board of Education* v. *Barnette*, 319 U.S. 624, 661–2, 666–7 (Frankfurter, J., dissenting) (1943).

reasonable. And the lawmakers' judgment is reasonable, according to Thayer, if rational, well-informed, and thoughtful persons could affirm the judgment: "The reasonable doubt . . . of which our judges speak is that reasonable doubt which lingers in the mind of a competent and duly instructed person who has carefully applied his faculties to the question. The rationally permissible opinion of which we have been talking is the opinion reasonably allowable to such a person as this."[18]

In urging SCOTUS to proceed deferentially – in contending for what Alexander Bickel would later call "the rule of the clear mistake"[19] – Thayer's argument was not that lawmakers are generally better than judges at addressing contested constitutional questions. His argument was simply that because in the United States, a democracy, the citizens are supposed to be the ultimate political sovereign, they, not the judiciary, should have the principal responsibility for addressing, typically through their elected and electorally accountable lawmakers, contested constitutional questions, and the lawmakers' answers to such questions, if reasonable, should prevail. Otherwise "the people cease to function as the popular sovereign."[20]

What Stephen Gardbaum described, in the passage quoted above, as "the essential argument" in support of weak-form over strong-form

---

[18]   Thayer, "The Origin and Scope of the American Doctrine of Constitutional Law," 149.

[19]   See Bickel, *The Least Dangerous Branch*, 34–6.

[20]   Kahn, *Legitimacy and History*, 87. For Kahn's commentary on Thayer's argument, see pp. 85–9.

Thayer also argued that by proceeding *nondeferentially*, SCOTUS subverts the capacity of the people and their representatives to deliberate about contested constitutional questions as responsibly as they should. Thayer elaborated the point in his book on John Marshall, who served as Chief Justice of the United States from 1801 to 1835:

> [T]he exercise of [judicial review], even when unavoidable, is always attended with a serious evil, namely, that the correction of legislative mistakes comes from the outside, and the people thus lose the political experience, and the moral education and stimulus that comes from fighting the question out in the ordinary way, and correcting their own errors . . . The tendency of a common and easy resort to this great function, now lamentably too common, is to dwarf the political capacity of the people, and to deaden its sense of moral responsibility . . . [B]y adhering rigidly to its own duty, the court will help, as nothing else can, to fix the spot where responsibility lies, and . . . to bring the people and their representatives to a sense of their own responsibility.

James Bradley Thayer, *John Marshall* 106–10 (1901). See also Thayer, "The Origin and Scope of the American Doctrine of Constitutional Law," 155–6. Keith Whittington reports:

judicial review – that it "produces a better, more democratically defensible balance of power between courts and legislatures with respect to rights" – also lends support to the claim that SCOTUS, in exercising strong-form judicial review, should "not step into the shoes of the law-maker" but, instead, should proceed in the deferential way Thayer urged. If we assume that for a democracy that takes human rights seriously, weak-form judicial review is preferable to strong-form judicial review, does it follow that strong-form judicial review exercised in the deferential way Thayer urged is preferable to strong-form judicial review exercised nondeferentially?

SCOTUS addresses constitutional questions of different sorts. The principal sorts are these:

- *federalism* questions, of two sorts:
  - questions about whether a federal law (or other federal policy) unconstitutionally intrudes on state authority;
  - questions about whether a state law (or other state policy) unconstitutionally intrudes on federal – in particular, congressional – authority;
- *separation-of-powers* questions, of two sorts:
  - questions about whether Congress is unconstitutionally intruding on presidential authority;
  - questions about whether the President is unconstitutionally intruding on congressional authority;
- *rights* questions: questions about whether a law (or other public policy) violates a constitutional right.

As the Supreme Court became increasingly activist in the late nineteenth century, James Bradley Thayer complained that this development "has tended to bereave our legislatures of their feeling or responsibility and their sense of honor . . . It is a common saying in our legislative bodies when any constitutional point is raised, 'Oh, the courts will set that right.'" The courts "have often assumed a tone that tended to encourage these views," but Thayer warned that such complacency overlooked "how great is legislative power, and how limited is judicial power."

Keith E. Whittington, *Political Foundations of Judicial Supremacy* 138 (2007) (quoting James Bradley Thayer, "Constitutionality of Legislation: The Precise Question for a Court," *The Nation*, April 10, 1884, 315).

Many modern students of American judicial review have echoed Thayer's concern. Alexander Bickel, for example, wrote that "[t]he search must be for a [judicial] function . . . whose discharge by the courts will not lower the quality of the other departments' performance by denuding them of the dignity and burden of their own responsibility." Bickel, *The Least Dangerous Branch*, 24.

That SCOTUS should proceed deferentially in addressing constitutional questions of one sort does not entail that SCOTUS should proceed deferentially in addressing constitutional questions of every sort. An argument I made over thirty years ago, in my first book, supports the position that although SCOTUS should proceed deferentially in addressing federalism questions about whether a *federal* law unconstitutionally intrudes on *state* authority, SCOTUS need not proceed deferentially in addressing federalism questions about whether a *state* law unconstitutionally intrudes on *federal* authority.[21]

In any event, I am concerned in this book only with rights questions. Rights questions, however, are of different sorts, and just as we should distinguish, in thinking about Thayerian deference, between federalism questions concerning the constitutionality of a federal law and federalism questions concerning the constitutionality of a state law, perhaps we should distinguish among different sorts of rights questions. Perhaps Thayerian deference, even if appropriate with respect to rights questions of some sorts, is inappropriate with respect to rights questions of other sorts. There is no good reason to exclude that possibility without considering it. I have suggested elsewhere that although Thayerian deference is, on balance, appropriate with respect to most sorts of rights questions, it is not appropriate with respect to questions about

---

[21] What I argued in *The Constitution, the Courts, and Human Rights* (1982), 37–60, supports the following positions:

- In addressing questions about whether a federal law (or other federal policy) unconstitutionally intrudes on state authority, SCOTUS should proceed deferentially.
- In addressing questions about whether a state law (or other state policy) unconstitutionally intrudes on federal – in particular, congressional – authority, SCOTUS need not proceed deferentially.
- In addressing questions about whether Congress is unconstitutionally intruding on presidential authority, or whether the President is unconstitutionally intruding on congressional authority, SCOTUS should proceed deferentially if with respect to the challenged government action, there is concord – or at least no discord – between Congress and the President.
- But if there is discord between Congress and the president with respect to the challenged government action, SCOTUS cannot proceed deferentially without also proceeding nondeferentially: To proceed deferentially with respect to Congress is to proceed nondeferentially with respect to the president, and to proceed deferentially with respect to the president is to proceed nondeferentially with respect to Congress. In cases of interbranch discord, however, SCOTUS does have this option: abstaining and thereby letting the legislative and executive branches resolve the conflict – or thereby forcing them to resolve it – by themselves. Cf. Josh Chafetz, "Congress's Constitution," 160 *University of Pennsylvania Law Review* 715 (2012).

whether a law (or other public policy) violates one of these rights: the right to seek, receive, and share information and ideas; the right to vote; and the right to run for and hold office.[22] However, none of the three constitutional controversies I address in this book – capital punishment, same-sex marriage, and abortion – implicates any of those rights.

AS I CONCLUDED IN THE PRECEDING CHAPTER, capital punishment violates the Cruel and Unusual Punishments Clause of the Eighth Amendment: No matter what the crime, punishing a criminal, even a mentally competent adult, by killing him is excessive – it crosses the line – and is evidenced as such by the fact that capital punishment has become demonstrably unusual. Is the lawmakers' contrary judgment – that not all capital punishment is "cruel and unusual" – a reasonable judgment, such that SCOTUS, proceeding deferentially, should refrain from ruling that capital punishment is unconstitutional? The reasons I gave in the preceding chapter support more than the conclusion that punishing a criminal by killing him is "cruel and unusual"; they support the further conclusion that the contrary judgment is not reasonable.

Predictably, however, not everyone – perhaps not even everyone who agrees that capital punishment is "cruel and unusual" – will concur that the lawmakers' contrary judgment is unreasonable. Disagreement about whether a constitutional judgment by lawmakers is reasonable serves to illustrate an important point about Thayerian deference: *Not every judge sincerely trying to proceed deferentially will draw the line between the "reasonable" and the "unreasonable" in precisely the same place.* We mustn't confuse Thayerian deference with a programmer's algorithm. One of Thayer's interpreters, Sanford Gabin, explained:

> Thayer's rule, like all guideposts, is not self-applying. Even limited by the rule of administration, judges, like criminal juries, might differ over what constitutes a reasonable doubt; the possibilities, the stuff of which reasonable doubts are made, do not always strike all men, however reasonable, alike. Even under Thayer's rule of administration, then, the freedom and the burden of decision making remain.[23]

---

[22] See Michael J. Perry, *The Political Morality of Liberal Democracy* 171–3 (2010).
[23] Gabin, *Judicial Review and the Reasonable Doubt Test*, 45–6.

Nonetheless, "that freedom is narrowed, and that was Thayer's aim. He sought to reduce the scope of judicial freedom without diminishing the judicial duty and burden of judging."[24]

Emphasizing what Gabin called, in the preceding passage, "the freedom and burden of judging," Thayer wrote: "The ultimate arbiter of what is rational and permissible is indeed always the courts, so far as litigated cases bring the question before them. This leaves to our courts a great and stately jurisdiction." But, warned Thayer, "[i]t will only imperil the whole of it if it is sought to give them more. They must not step into the shoes of the law-maker."[25]

---

[24]   Ibid., 46.

[25]   Thayer, "The Origin and Scope of the American Doctrine of Constitutional Law," 152. According to Mark Tushnet:

> We should distinguish between what I call pseudo-Thayerian review and true Thayerian review. Pseudo-Thayerian review occurs when the courts ask, "Did the legislature make a clear error in determining – if it did – that the legislation was consistent with the Constitution as *we* interpret it?" In this version, the courts make an independent judgment about what the Constitution means, and then ask whether a rational legislature could believe that the statute at issue was consistent with the Constitution so interpreted. In pseudo-Thayerian review, that is, the courts have the final (or only) say on what the Constitution means. True Thayerian review, in contrast, give the (rational) legislature a role in constitutional interpretation. The truly Thayerian court asks, "Putting aside our own views about what the Constitution means, could a rational legislature believe that the statute in question is consistent with some reasonable interpretation of the Constitution – again, even if that interpretation is not one that we ourselves would adopt?"

> Mark Tushnet, "The Supreme Court and Contemporary Constitutionalism: The Implications of the Development of Alternative Forms of Judicial Review," in Steven Kurtz et al., eds, *The Supreme Court and the Idea of Constitutionalism* 115–16 (2009).

> What Tushnet calls "true Thayerian review" is one possible version of Thayerian review. The version I have discussed in this chapter, however, is the version Tushnet tendentiously dubs "pseudo-Thayerian review." I am inclined to think that the latter version is more consistent than the former version with the classic view that "[i]t is emphatically the province and duty of the Judicial Department to say what the law is." *Marbury* v. *Madison*, 5 U.S. (1 Cranch) 137 (1803). Although according to the version of Thayerian review I discuss in this chapter it is "the province and duty" of SCOTUS "to say what the [constitutional] law is," it is not "the province and duty" of SCOTUS to favor its own judgment about the implications of a constitutional norm over the lawmakers' *reasonable* judgment about the implications of the norm. (Cf. Mitchell N. Berman, "Constitutional Decision Rules," 90 *Virginia Law Review* 1, 102–4 (2004): "[Thayerian deference,] if it is to exist, will find a more hospitable home at the level of applying constitutional meaning, not deriving it.") In any event, with respect to the specific question at issue in this chapter – SCOTUS's proper role *in protecting the constitutional morality of the United States* – I suppose it would be fair to say that I am a moderate rather than extreme Thayerian, and that my not embracing what Tushnet calls "true Thayerian review" reflects that fact.

6   THE RIGHT TO MORAL EQUALITY

Later in this book, I address two of the largest constitutional controversies in the United States today, one concerning same-sex marriage,
the other concerning abortion. The two rights that bear most directly
on those two controversies are the right to moral equality and the right
to religious and moral freedom, each of which fits this profile and is
therefore part of the constitutional morality of the United States: internationally recognized as a human right and entrenched in the constitutional law of the United States.[1] In the next chapter, I elaborate the
right to religious and moral freedom. In this chapter, I elaborate on the
right to moral equality: the right of every human being to be treated
by his or her government – indeed, by every government – as morally
equal to every other human being; or, put another way, the right not
to be treated as morally inferior to any other human being.[2]

The Universal Declaration of Human Rights refers, in the Preamble, to "the inherent dignity . . . of *all members of the human family*"
(emphasis added) and then states, in Article 1, that "[a]ll human
beings . . . should act towards one another in a spirit of brotherhood."
The right to moral equality follows naturally from – indeed, it is entailed
by – the normative ground of human rights: the imperative that every
government act toward every human being – toward "all members of
the human family" – "in a spirit of brotherhood." No government is
acting consistently with the normative ground of human rights to the

---

[1] In my previous book, *The Political Morality of Liberal Democracy* (2010), I argued that the
right to moral equality and the right to religious and moral freedom are the two principal
constituents of *liberal* democracy. More recently, Joyce Maclure and Charles Taylor have
argued that "respect for the moral equality of individuals and the protection of freedom
of conscience and of religion constitute the two major aims of secularism today." Joyce
Maclure and Charles Taylor, *Secularism and Freedom of Conscience* 4 (2011).

[2] The right, that is, of every *born* human being. See Chapter 9.

extent it is treating some human beings as morally inferior to some other human beings, in this sense:

> *not worthy of being treated "in a spirit of brotherhood," or less worthy than some other human beings of being so treated;*

or, put another way,

> *not worthy of being treated with respect and concern, or worthy only (like, say, some higher mammals) of being treated with less respect and concern than that due some other human beings.*

For government to disadvantage anyone, by doing something to her or by not doing something for her, on the basis of the demeaning view that she, or someone with whom she is associated – someone, say, to whom she is married – is morally inferior, in the sense just indicated, is for government to violate the imperative to act toward every human being as a member of the human family who, as such, is no less worthy than any other human being of being treated "in a spirit of brotherhood"; who, as such, is worthy of being treated with the same respect and concern due every human being. Government is disadvantaging to a human being on the basis of the demeaning view that she, or someone with whom she is associated, is morally inferior if but for that view, if in the absence of that view, government would not be disadvantaging her; if, in other words, that view is a "but for" predicate of government's disadvantaging her. The most common grounds for imputing moral inferiority to some human beings have been, as listed in Article 26 of the International Covenant on Civil and Political Rights, "race, colour, sex, language, religion, political or other opinion, national or social origin, property, birth or other status."[3]

The right to moral equality is often articulated as the right to "the equal protection of the law." Some examples:

- Article 26 of the International Covenant on Civil and Political Rights: "All persons are equal before the law and are entitled without any discrimination to the equal protection of the law. In this respect, the law shall prohibit any discrimination and guarantee to all persons

---

[3] See David Livingstone Smith, *Less Than Human: Why We Demean, Enslave and Exterminate Others* (2011); Richard Rorty, "Human Rights, Rationality, and Sentimentality," in Susan Hurley and Stephen Shute, eds., *On Human Rights: The 1993 Oxford Amnesty Lectures* 111, 112–14 (1993).

equal and effective protection against discrimination on any ground such as race, colour, sex, language, religion, political or other opinion, national or social origin, property, birth or other status." As of December 2012, 167 of the 195 countries that are members of the United Nations were parties to the ICCPR, including, as of 1992, the United States.

- The African Charter on Human and People's Rights states, in Article 2, that "[e]very individual shall be entitled to the enjoyment of the rights and freedoms recognized and guaranteed in the present Charter without distinction of any kind such as race, ethnic group, color, sex, language, religion, political or any other opinion, national and social origin, fortune, birth or other status"; the Charter then states, in Article 3: "1. Every individual shall be equal before the law. 2. Every individual shall be entitled to equal protection of the law."
- Article 15(1) of the Canadian Charter of Rights and Freedoms: "Every individual is equal before and under the law and has the right to the equal protection and equal benefit of the law without discrimination and, in particular, without discrimination based on race, national or ethnic origin, colour, religion, sex, age or mental or physical disability."
- Article 9 of the South African Constitution: "1. Everyone is equal before the law and has the right to equal protection and benefit of the law ... 3. The state may not unfairly discriminate directly or indirectly against anyone on one or more grounds, including race, gender, sex, pregnancy, marital status, ethnic or social origin, colour, sexual orientation, age, disability, religion, conscience, belief, culture, language and birth."

The right to moral equality entails the right to equal citizenship: Government may not disadvantage any of its citizens relative to any other of its citizens on the basis of the view that the disadvantaged citizens are morally inferior.

The right to moral equality does not require – no sensible right requires – government to treat all human beings the same. For example, government may deny a driver's license to those who are not yet sixteen years old. But government may not disadvantage any human being on the basis of the view that some human beings are morally inferior, in the sense indicated above.

Sometimes it is not open to serious question whether government is acting on the basis of the illicit view that some human beings are morally inferior. Sometimes it is obvious that government *is* acting – that it *is* disadvantaging some human beings – on that basis. For example, the laws struck down by the Supreme Court of the United States in *Brown* v. *Board of Education* (1954)[4] (de jure racial segregation) and the law struck down by the Court in *Loving* v. *Virginia* (1967)[5] (antimiscegenation law) – laws that were aspects of a (dying) system of racial apartheid – were obviously all enacted on that basis.[6] Sometimes it is obvious that government is *not* acting on the basis of the illicit view – as, for example, when it denies a driver's licenses to those who are not yet sixteen years old.

Sometimes, however, it *is* open to serious question whether government is acting on the basis of the illicit view. Consider, for example, a policy that disproportionately disadvantages persons who are members of a racial minority. Such as policy was at issue – and, controversially, was upheld by the Supreme Court – in *Washington* v. *Davis* (1976):[7] a test used by a municipal police department as a hiring criterion disproportionately disadvantaged job candidates who were members a racial minority. There may be good reason to suspect that – and therefore to inquire whether – the policy is based on what Paul Brest has aptly described as "racially selective sympathy and indifference," which is a variation on the view that "they" – the members of a racial group – are

---

[4]   347 U.S. 483. For a compelling essay on the importance of the Supreme Court's decision in *Brown*, see Paul Finkelman, "Civil Rights in Historical Context: In Defense of Brown," 118 *Harvard Law Review* 973 (2005).

[5]   388 U.S. 1.

[6]   In response to "a now-discredited argument in defense of antimiscegenation laws" – namely, "that whites can marry only within their race; nonwhites can marry only within their race; therefore, antimiscegenation laws do not deny 'equal options'" – John Corvino has written:

> Putting aside the problematic assumption of two and only two racial groups – whites and nonwhites – the argument does have a kind of formal parity to it. The reason that we regard its conclusion as objectionable nevertheless is that we recognize that the very point of antimiscegenation laws is to signify and maintain the false and pernicious belief that nonwhites are morally inferior to whites (that is, unequal).

John Corvino, "Homosexuality and the PIB Argument," 115 *Ethics* 501, 509 (2005).

[7]   426 U.S. 229.

morally inferior to "us."[8] Racially selective sympathy and indifference – "the failure to extend to a [racial] minority the same recognition of humanity, and hence the same sympathy and care, given as a matter of course to one's own group"[9] – obviously need not be conscious to be operative.

That the internationally recognized human right to moral equality is constitutionally entrenched is clear: It has long been a bedrock feature of the constitutional law of the United States – and, indeed, of the constitutional law of every state in the United States – that government may not disadvantage anyone on the basis of the demeaning view that some human beings are morally inferior. No court – neither any federal court, including the Supreme Court, nor any state court – would dream of ruling that the applicable constitutional law, federal or state, leaves legislators or other policymakers free to discriminate against or otherwise disadvantage anyone on the basis of that view. The serious question for a court, in a case in which it is argued that government is disadvantaging someone on that basis, is not whether government may do so – under the right to moral equality, it may not – but whether government is in fact doing so.

Consider, in that regard, the infamous *Plessy* v. *Ferguson* (1898),[10] in which the Supreme Court rejected a constitutional challenge to Louisiana's requirement "that all railway companies carrying passengers in their coaches in this State shall provide equal but separate accommodations for the white and colored races by providing two or more passenger coaches for each passenger train, or by dividing the passenger coaches by a partition so as to secure separate accommodations." The Court did not say that Louisiana was constitutionally free to discriminate on the basis of the view that the "colored race" is morally inferior to the "white race." Rather, the Court denied, ridiculously, that Louisiana was in fact discriminating on that basis: "We consider the underlying fallacy of the plaintiff's argument to consist in the assumption that the enforced separation of the two

---

[8] See Paul Brest, "Foreword: In Defense of the Antidiscrimination Principle," 90 *Harvard Law Review* 1 (1976). See also Michael J. Perry, "The Disproportionate Impact Theory of Racial Discrimination," 125 *University of Pennsylvania Law Review* 540 (1977).

[9] See Brest, "Foreword," 7–8.

[10] 163 U.S. 537.

races stamps the colored race with a badge of inferiority. If this be so, it is not by reason of anything found in the act, but solely because the colored race chooses to put that construction upon it."[11]

The question has been and remains contested whether constitutional enactors entrenched the right to moral equality – or, as it has been variously called, "the anticaste principle," "the anticaste rule," and "the no-caste rule"[12] – in the constitutional law of the United States.[13] However, because, as I noted above, the right to moral equality is undeniably constitutional bedrock, the right is entrenched in the constitutional law of the United States even if enactors did not entrench the right. Moreover, the right to moral equality that is constitutional bedrock is a right against government generally; it is a right against the federal government no less than against state government. This is as befits a right internationally recognized as a human right: What sense would it make for state government to be prohibited, but the federal government permitted, to treat some persons as morally inferior? As the Supreme Court unanimously declared in *Bolling* v. *Sharpe* (1954), in which it ruled that racially segregated public schooling in a federal enclave – the District of Columbia – was unconstitutional: "In view of our decision [in *Brown* v. *Board of Education*] that the Constitution prohibits the states from maintaining racially segregated public schools, it would be unthinkable that the same Constitution would impose a lesser duty on the Federal Government."[14]

I said that the right to moral equality is often articulated as the right to equal protection, and I gave examples from international human rights instruments and the constitutions of other countries; the example closest to home, however, is American constitutional discourse, in which the right to moral equality is called the right to equal protection. According to the Supreme Court, although it applies to state government in virtue of the Equal Protection Clause of the Fourteenth Amendment, the right to equal protection applies to the federal government, as the Court emphasized in *Bolling* v. *Sharpe*, in virtue of the Due Process Clause of the Fifth Amendment.

---

[11] Ibid., 551.
[12] See, e.g., Steven G. Calabresi and Julia T. Rickert, "Originalism and Sex Discrimination," 90 *Texas Law Review* 1 (2011).
[13] See ibid.
[14] 347 U.S. 497, 500.

The Court's reliance on the Fifth Amendment Due Process Clause in applying the right to equal protection to the federal government is problematic. In adding the Bill of Rights, including the Fifth Amendment, to the Constitution – the Bill of Rights entered into force in 1791 – the enactors of the Bill of Rights were entrenching several rights against the federal government in the constitutional law of the United States, but it is highly doubtful – indeed, if recent scholarship is to be believed, the claim is false – that they were entrenching, against the federal government, anything like the right to equal protection.[15] On the other hand, although section 1 of the Fourteenth Amendment states, in part, that "No state shall . . . deny to any person within its jurisdiction the equal protection of the laws," there is no warrant for thinking that the Fourteenth Amendment's enactors – who in the aftermath of the Civil War were understandably focused principally on state government, to which they explicitly referred in section 1 – were thereby leaving the federal government constitutionally free to deny to persons within *its* jurisdiction the equal protection of the laws. That is, whatever the enactors of the Fourteenth Amendment understood "the equal protection of the laws" to mean – precisely what they understood it to mean remains a disputed question[16] – there is no warrant for thinking that the right to equal protection they entrenched in the constitutional law of the United States applies just to state government.[17]

In any event, the important point for present purposes is that it has become constitutional bedrock – it is now constitutional bedrock – that, as befits a right internationally recognized as a human right, the right to moral equality – which, again, is articulated in American constitutional discourse as the right to equal protection – is a right not just against state government but against government generally, including the federal government. The federal government, no less than state government, is constitutionally forbidden to disadvantage any human being on the basis of the demeaning view that he or she, or someone with whom he or she is associated, is morally inferior.

---

[15] See Nathan S. Chapman and Michael W. McConnell, "Due Process as Separation of Powers," 121 *Yale Law Journal* 1672 (2012).

[16] See Calabresi and Rickert, "Originalism and Sex Discrimination." Cf. Ryan C. Williams, "Originalism and the Other Desegregation Decision." 99 *Virginia Law Review* – (2013).

[17] For my own effort to uncover the norms – the rights – that were entrenched in the constitutional law of the United States by the Fourteenth Amendment's enactors, see Michael J. Perry, *We the People: The Fourteenth Amendment and the Supreme Court* 48–87 (1999).

7 THE RIGHT TO RELIGIOUS AND MORAL FREEDOM

Religious diversity must be seen as an aspect of the phenomenon of "moral pluralism" with which contemporary democracies have to come to terms... Although the history of the West serves to explain the fixation on religion... the state of contemporary societies requires that we move beyond that fixation and consider how to manage fairly the moral diversity that now characterizes them. The field of application for secular governance has broadened to include all moral, spiritual, and religious options.

– Jocelyn Maclure and Charles Taylor[1]

Again, the two rights that bear most directly on the two large constitutional controversies that are the focus of the next two chapters – same-sex marriage and abortion – are the right to moral equality, which

---

[1] Jocelyn Maclure and Charles Taylor, *Secularism and Freedom of Conscience* 20, 106 (2011). ("'Moral pluralism' refers to the phenomenon of individuals adopting different and sometimes incompatible value systems and conceptions of the good." 20) In the conclusion to their book, Maclure and Taylor write: "There do not seem to be any principled reasons to isolate religion and place it in a class apart from the other conceptions of the world and of the good" 105. Brian Leiter reaches the same conclusion. See Brian Leiter, *Why Tolerate Religion?* (2012). (Although Leiter's rationale for reaching the same conclusion is vulnerable. See John Gray, "Giant Leaps for Mankind: Most of Our Beliefs Are Unwarranted, Even Absurd," *New Statesman*, Nov. 29, 2012.) Others who reach the same conclusion include: Gidon Sapir and Daniel Statman, "Why Freedom of Religion Does Not Include Freedom from Religion," 24 *Law and Philosophy* 467, 487 (2005) ("[W]hether we understand freedom of religion as a branch of freedom of conscience or as a branch of the right to culture, there is no justification for granting it special status within the framework of these rights."); Howard Kislowicz, Richard Haigh, and Adrienne Ng, "Calculations of Conscience: The Costs and Benefits of Religious and Conscientious Freedom," 48 *Alberta Law Review* 679, 681 (2011) ("arguing that there is no principled reason that matters of conscience should be treated differently from matters of religious belief and practice."); Gemma Cornelissen, "Religion-Based Exemptions: Are Religious Beliefs Special?," 25 *Ratio Juris* 85 (2012) (answering "no").

I elaborated in the preceding chapter, and the right to religious and moral freedom, which I elaborate in this chapter.

Jocelyn Maclure and Charles Taylor begin their recent book, *Secularism and Freedom of Conscience*, by stating that "[o]ne of the most important challenges facing contemporary societies is how to manage moral and religious diversity."[2] As I am about to explain, establishing and protecting the right to religious and moral freedom – Maclure and Taylor prefer the term "freedom of conscience" – is one of the most important ways for a society to "manage moral and religious diversity."

The articulation of the right to religious and moral freedom that we find in the International Covenant on Civil and Political Rights (ICCPR) is canonical in this sense: The great majority of the countries of the world – about 87% – are parties to the ICCPR, including, as of 1992, the United States.[3] Article 18 of the ICCPR declares:[4]

1. Everyone shall have the right to freedom of thought, conscience and religion. This right shall include freedom to have or to adopt a

---

[2] Maclure and Taylor, *Secularism and Freedom of Conscience*, 1. Maclure and Taylor conclude their book on the same note. See pp. 105–10.

[3] As of December 2012, 167 of the 193 member states of the United Nations were parties to the ICCPR.

[4] Article 9 of the European Convention for the Protection of Human Rights and Fundamental Freedoms is substantially identical:

1. Everyone has the right to freedom of thought, conscience and religion; this right includes freedom to change his religion or belief and freedom, either alone or in community with others and in public or private, to manifest his religion or belief, in worship, teaching, practice and observance.
2. Freedom to manifest one's religion or beliefs shall be subject only to such limitations as are prescribed by law and are necessary in a democratic society in the interests of public safety, for the protection of public order, health or morals, or for the protection of the rights and freedoms of others.

Article 12 of the American Convention on Human Rights is also substantially identical:

1. Everyone has the right to freedom of conscience and of religion. This right includes freedom to maintain or to change one's religion or beliefs, and freedom to profess or disseminate one's religion or beliefs, either individually or together with others, in public or in private.
2. No one shall be subject to restrictions that might impair his freedom to maintain or to change his religion or beliefs.
3. Freedom to manifest one's religion and beliefs may be subject only to the limitations prescribed by law that are necessary to protect public safety, order, health, or morals, or the rights or freedoms of others.
4. Parents or guardians, as the case may be, have the right to provide for the religious and moral education of their children or wards that is in accord with their own convictions.

religion or belief of his choice, and freedom, either individually or in community with others and in public or private, to manifest his religion or belief in worship, observance, practice, and teaching.

2. No one shall be subject to coercion which would impair his freedom to have or to adopt a religion or belief of his choice.

3. Freedom to manifest one's religion or beliefs may be subject only to such limitations as are prescribed by law and are necessary to protect public safety, order, health, or morals or the fundamental rights and freedoms of others.

4. The States Parties to the present Covenant undertake to have respect for the liberty of parents and, when applicable, legal guardians to ensure the religious and moral education of their children in conformity with their own convictions.[5]

The United Nations Human Rights Committee – the body that monitors compliance with the ICCPR and, under the First Optional Protocol to the ICCPR, adjudicates cases brought by individuals alleging that a state party is in violation of the ICCPR – has stated that "[t]he right to freedom of thought, conscience and religion . . . in article 18.1 is far-reaching and profound."[6] How "far-reaching and profound"? Note the breadth of the right that according to Article 18 "[e]veryone shall have": the right to freedom not just of "religion" but also of "conscience." The "right shall include freedom to have or adopt a religion *or belief* of his choice, and freedom, either individually or in community with others and in public or private, to manifest his religion *or belief* in worship, observance, practice and teaching" (emphasis added). Article

---

[5] Article 18 of the ICCPR is an elaboration of Article 18 of the Universal Declaration of Human Rights: "Everyone has the right to freedom of thought, conscience and religion; this right includes freedom to change his religion or belief, and freedom, either alone or in community with others and in public or private, to manifest his religion or belief in teaching, practice, worship and observance." Another international document merits mention: The Declaration on the Elimination of All Forms of Intolerance and of Discrimination Based on Religion or Belief, adopted by the UN General Assembly on Nov. 25, 1981. See Symposium, "The Foundations and Frontiers of Religious Liberty: A 25th Anniversary Celebration of the 1981 U.N. Declaration on Religious Tolerance," 21 *Emory International Law Review* 1–275 (2007).

[6] Human Rights Committee, General Comment 22, Article 18 (Forty-eighth session, 1993), in Compilation of General Comments and General Recommendations Adopted by Human Rights Treaty Bodies, U.N. Doc. HRI/GEN/1/Rev.1 at 35 (1994), http://www.unhchr.ch/tbs/doc.nsf/%28Symbol%29/9a30112c27d1167cc12563ed004d8f15?Opendocument.

18 explicitly indicates that the right concerns moral as well as religious freedom – Article 18 explicitly identifies the "belief" that is protected as moral belief – when it states that "[t]he State parties to the [ICCPR] undertake to have respect for the liberty of parents and, when applicable, legal guardians to assure the religious *and moral* education of their children in conformity with their own convictions" (emphasis added).[7] So, the right we are considering in this chapter protects not only freedom to practice one's religion, including, of course, one's religiously based morality; it also protects freedom to practice one's morality – freedom to "to manifest his . . . belief in . . . practice" – even if one's morality is not embedded in a religious tradition, *even if, that is, one's morality is embedded not in a transcendent worldview but in a worldview that is not transcendent.* (By a "transcendent" worldview, I mean a worldview that affirms, rather than denies or is agnostic about, the existence of a "transcendent" reality, as distinct from the reality that is or could be the object of natural-scientific inquiry.[8]) As the Human Rights Committee has put the point:

> The Committee draws the attention of States parties to the fact that the freedom of thought and the freedom of conscience are protected equally with the freedom of religion and belief . . . Article 18 protects theistic, non-theistic and atheistic beliefs, as well as the right not to profess any religion or belief. The terms "belief" and "religion" are to be broadly construed. Article 18 is not limited in its application to traditional religions or to religions and beliefs with institutional characteristics or practices analogous to those of traditional religions.[9]

In deriving a right to conscientious objection from Article 18, the Human Rights Committee explained that "the [legal] obligation to

---

[7] Cf. Barbara Bennett Woodhouse, "Religion and Children's Rights," in John Witte, Jr., and M. Christian Green, eds., *Religion and Human Rights* 299 (2012).

[8] On the idea of the "transcendent," see Charles Taylor, *A Secular Age* (2007); Michael Warner, Jonathan VanAntwerpen, and Craig Calhoun, eds., *Varieties of Secularism in a Secular Age* (2010).

[9] Human Rights Committee, General Comment 22. Cf. Maclure and Taylor, *Secularism and Freedom of Conscience*, 20: "The democratic state must . . . treat equally citizens who act on religious beliefs and those who do not; it must, in other words, be neutral in relation to the different worldviews and conceptions of the good – secular, spiritual, and religious – with which citizens identify."

use lethal force may seriously conflict with the freedom of conscience and the right to manifest one's religion or belief" and emphasized that "there shall be no differentiation among conscientious objectors on the basis of the nature of their particular beliefs."[10]

It is misleading, though common, to describe the human right we are considering in this chapter as the right to *religious* freedom.[11] Given the breadth of the right – the "far-reaching and profound" right of which the ICCPR's Article 18 is the canonical articulation – the right is accurately described as the right to *religious and moral* freedom.

The Supreme Court of Canada has emphasized that the right to religious and moral freedom is a broad right that protects freedom to practice one's morality without regard to whether one's morality is religiously based. Referring to section 2(a) of Canada's Charter of Rights and Freedoms, which states that "[e]veryone has ... freedom of conscience and religion," the Court has explained: "The purpose of s. 2(a) is to ensure that society does not interfere with profoundly personal beliefs that govern one's perception of oneself, humankind, nature, and, in some cases, a higher or different order of being. These beliefs, in turn, govern one's conduct and practices."[12] Section 2(a) "means that, subject to [certain limitations], no one is to be forced to act in a way contrary to his beliefs or his conscience."[13]

Religious and moral freedom – as both the UN Human Rights Committee and the Canadian Supreme Court have emphasized – is the freedom to live one's life in accord with one's religious and/or moral convictions and commitments – at least some of which are, for

---

[10] Human Rights Committee, General Comment 22. See *Yoon and Choi* v. *Republic of Korea*, CCPR/C/88/D/1321–22/2004 (2006), http://www.wri-irg.org/node/6221 (ruling that Article 18 requires that parties to the ICCPR provide for conscientious objection to military service). For relevant discussion, see Maclure and Taylor, *Secularism and Freedom of Conscience*, 89–91.

[11] For a recent example of such a description, see Christopher McCrudden, "Catholicism, Human Rights and the Public Sphere," 5 *International Journal of Public Theology* 331 (2011).

[12] *R.* v. *Edwards Books and Art Ltd.*, [1986] 2 S.C.R. 713, 759.

[13] *R.* v. *Big M Drug Mart Ltd.*, [1985] 1 S.C.R. 295, 337. See Kislowicz, Haigh, and Ng, "Calculations of Conscience," 707–13.

many, the yield of one's grappling with what are sometimes called "ultimate" questions, such as: Who are we? Where did we come from; what is our origin, our beginning? Where are we going; what is our destiny, our end?[14] What is the meaning of suffering? Of evil? Of death? And there is the cardinal such question, the question that comprises many of the others: Is human life ultimately meaningful or, instead, ultimately bereft of meaning, meaningless, absurd?[15] If any questions are fundamental, these questions – what Catholic theologian David Tracy has memorably called "religious or limit questions"[16] – are fundamental. Such questions – "naive" questions, "questions with no answers," "barriers that cannot be breached"[17] – are

---

[14] "In an old rabbinic text three other questions are suggested: 'Whence did you come?' 'Whither are you going?' 'Before whom are you destined to give account?'" Abraham J. Heschel, *Who Is Man?* 28 (1965). "All people by nature desire to know the mystery from which they come and to which they go." Denise Lardner Carmody and John Tully Carmody, *Western Ways to the Center: An Introduction to Religions of the West* 198–99 (1983). "The questions Tolstoy asked, and Gauguin in, say, his great Tahiti triptych, completed just before he died ('Where Do We Come From? What Are We? Where Are We Going?'), are the eternal questions children ask more intensely, unremittingly, and subtly than we sometimes imagine." Robert Coles, *The Spiritual Life of Children* 37 (1990).

[15] For the person deep in the grip of, the person claimed by, the problem of meaning, "[t]he cry for meaning is a cry for ultimate relationship, for ultimate belonging," wrote Rabbi Heschel. "It is a cry in which all pretensions are abandoned. Are we alone in the wilderness of time, alone in the dreadfully marvelous universe, of which we are a part and where we feel forever like strangers? Is there a Presence to live by? A Presence worth living for, worth dying for? Is there a way of living in the Presence? Is there a way of living compatible with the Presence?" Heschel, *Who Is Man?*, 75. Cf. W.D. Joske, "Philosophy and the Meaning of Life," in E.D. Klemke, ed., *The Meaning of Life* 248, 250 (1981) ("If, as Kurt Vonnegut speculates in The Sirens of Titan, the ultimate end of human activity is the delivery of a small piece of steel to a wrecked space ship wanting to continue a journey of no importance whatsoever, the end would be too trivial to justify the means."); Robert Nozick, *Philosophical Explanations* 586 (1981) ("If the cosmic role of human beings was to provide a negative lesson to some others ('don't act like them') or to provide needed food to passing intergalactic travelers who were important, this would not suit our aspirations – not even if afterwards the intergalactic travelers smacked their lips and said that we tasted good.").

[16] David Tracy, *Plurality and Ambiguity: Religion, Hermeneutics, Hope* 86 (1987).

[17] In Milan Kundera's *The Unbearable Lightness of Being*, the narrator, referring to "the questions that had been going through Tereza's head since she was a child," says that "the only truly serious questions are ones that even a child can formulate. Only the most naive of questions are truly serious. They are the questions with no answers. A question with no answer is a barrier than cannot be breached. In other words, it is questions with no answers that set the limits of human possibilities, describe the boundaries of human existence." Milan Kundera, *The Unbearable Lightness of Being* 139 (1984).

"the most serious and difficult ... that any human being or society must face."[18] Historically, extended communities – "traditions" – are principal matrices of answers to all such "religious or limit questions."[19]

Of course, not all who address such questions end up giving answers that constitute a transcendent worldview. To the contrary, many end up giving answers that constitute a thoroughgoing rejection of any transcendent worldview.[20] Nonetheless, John Paul II was surely right

---

[18] David Tracy, *The Analogical Imagination* 4 (1981). Tracy adds: "To formulate such questions honestly and well, to respond to them with passion and rigor, is the work of all theology ... Religions ask and respond to such fundamental questions ... Theologians, by definition, risk an intellectual life on the wager that religious traditions can be studied as authentic responses to just such questions."

[19] "Not the individual man nor a single generation by its own power, can erect the bridge that leads to God. Faith is the achievement of many generations, an effort accumulated over centuries. Many of its ideas are as the light of the star that left its source a long time ago. Many enigmatic songs, unfathomable today, are the resonance of voices of bygone times. There is a collective memory of God in the human spirit, and it is this memory which is the main source of our faith." From Abraham Heschel's two-part essay "Faith," first published in volume 10 of *The Reconstructionist*, Nov. 3 and 17, 1944. For a later statement on faith, incorporating some of the original essay, see Abraham J. Heschel, *Man is Not Alone* 159–76 (1951).

[20] Consider, for example, Bertrand Russell's worldview:

> That man is the product of causes which had no prevision of the end they were achieving; that his origin, his growth, his hopes and fears, his loves and his beliefs, are but the outcome of accidental collocations of atoms; that no fire, no heroism, no intensity of thought and feeling, can preserve an individual life beyond the grave; that all the labor of the ages, all the devotion, all the inspiration, all the noonday brightness of human genius, are destined to extinction in the vast death of the solar system, and that the whole temple of man's achievement must inevitably be buried beneath the debris of a universe in ruins – all these things, if not quite beyond dispute, are yet so certain that no philosophy which rejects them can hope to stand. Only within the scaffolding of these truths, only on the firm foundation of unyielding despair, can the soul's habitation henceforth be safely built.

> Bertrand Russell, *Mysticism and Logic* 47–8 (1917). Consider too Clarence Darrow's similarly bleak vision, as recounted by Paul Edwards:

> Darrow, one of the most compassionate men who ever lived, ... concluded that life was an "awful joke." ... Darrow offered as one of his reasons the apparent aimlessness of all that happens. "This weary old world goes on, begetting, with birth and with living and with death," he remarked in his moving plea for the boy-murderers Loeb and Leopold, "and all of it is blind from the beginning to the end." Elsewhere he wrote: "Life is like a ship on the sea, tossed by every wave and by every wind; a ship headed for no port and no harbor, with no rudder, no compass, no pilot; simply floating for a time, then lost in the waves." In addition

in his encyclical *Fides et Ratio* that such questions "have their common source in the quest for meaning which has always compelled the human heart" and that "the answer given to these questions decides the direction which people seek to give to their lives."[21]

Two clarifications are in order. First: The practices protected by the right to religious and moral freedom include not just practices one believes oneself religiously and/or morally obligated to engage in. As the Canadian Supreme Court explained, in a case involving a religious practice:

> to the aimlessness of life and the universe, there is the fact of death. "I love my friends," wrote Darrow, "but they all must come to a tragic end." Death is more terrible the more one is attached to things in the world. Life, he concludes, is "not worthwhile," and he adds . . . that "it is an unpleasant interruption of nothing, and the best thing you can say of it is that it does not last long."

Paul Edwards, "Life, Meaning and Value of," 4 *Encyclopedia of Philosophy* 467, 470 (Paul Edwards, ed., 1967). Whether Clarence Darrow was in fact "one of the most compassionate men who ever lived" is open to question. See Gary Wills, *Under God: Religion and American Politics*, chs. 8–9 (1990).

[21] John Paul II, *On the Relation Between Faith and Reason (Fides et Ratio)*, issued on Sept. 14, 1998. In the introduction to *Fides et Ratio*, John Paul II wrote:

> Moreover, a cursory glance at ancient history shows clearly how in different parts of the world, with their different cultures, there arise at the same time the fundamental questions which pervade human life: Who am I? Where have I come from and where am I going? Why is there evil? What is there after this life? These are the questions which we find in the sacred writings of Israel and also in the Veda and the Avesta; we find them in the writings of Confucius and Lao-Tze, and in the preaching of Tirthankara and Buddha; they appear in the poetry of Homer and in the tragedies of Euripides and Sophocles as they do in the philosophical writings of Plato and Aristotle. They are questions which have their common source in the quest for meaning which has always compelled the human heart. In fact, the answer given to these questions decides the direction which people seek to give to their lives.

Introduction, pt. 1. See also chapter 3, pt. 26. (*Fides et Ratio* would more accurately be named *Fides et Philosophia*.) We find a similar statement in the Second Vatican Council's *Declaration on the Relation of the Church to Non-Christian Religions* (Nostra Aetate, 1):

> People look to their different religions for an answer to the unsolved riddles of human existence. The problems that weigh heavily on people's hearts are the same today as in ages past. What is humanity? What is the meaning and purpose of life? Where does suffering originate, and what end does it serve? How can genuine happiness be found? What happens at death? What is judgement? What reward follows death? And finally, what is the ultimate mystery, beyond human explanation, which embraces our entire existence, from which we take our origin and toward which we tend?

[T]o frame the right either in terms of objective religious "obligation" or even as the sincere subjective belief that an obligation exists and that the practice is required . . . would disregard the value of non-obligatory religious experiences by excluding those experiences from protection. Jewish women, for example, strictly speaking, do not have a biblically mandated "obligation" to dwell in a succah during the Succot holiday. If a woman, however, nonetheless sincerely believes that sitting and eating in a succah brings her closer to her Maker, is that somehow less deserving of recognition simply because she has no strict "obligation" to do so? Is the Jewish yarmulke or Sikh turban worthy of less recognition simply because it may be borne out of religious custom, not obligation? Should an individual Jew, who may personally deny the modern relevance of literal biblical "obligation" or "commandment," be precluded from making a freedom of religion argument despite the fact that for some reason he or she sincerely derives a closeness to his or her God by sitting in a succah? Surely not.[22]

The second clarification: The practices protected by the right to religious and moral freedom are those that are animated by what Maclure and Taylor call a person's "core or meaning-giving beliefs and commitments" as distinct from those that are animated by "the legitimate but less fundamental 'preferences' we display as individuals."[23]

[T]he beliefs that engage my conscience and the values with which I most identify, and those that allow me to find my way in a plural moral space, must be distinguished from my desires, tastes, and other personal preferences, that is, from all things liable to contribute to my well-being but which I could forgo without feeling as if I were betraying myself or straying from the path I have chosen. The nonfulfillment of a desire may upset me, but it generally does not impinge on the bedrock values and beliefs that define me in the most fundamental way; it does not inflict "moral harm."[24]

---

[22] *Syndicat Northcrest v. Amselem,* [2004] 2 R.C.S. 551, 588. "It is the religious or spiritual essence of an action, not any mandatory or perceived-as-mandatory nature of its observance, that attracts protection" (553).

[23] Maclure and Taylor, *Secularism and Freedom of Conscience,* 12–13. For discussion of the distinction, see pp. 76–7, 89–93, 97.

[24] Ibid., 77. Maclure and Taylor are well aware that there will be cases where it is difficult to administer the distinction between "core or meaning-giving beliefs and commitments" and "the legitimate but less fundamental 'preferences' we display as individuals," see

SOME ICCPR RIGHTS – such as the Article 7 right not to "be subjected to torture or to cruel, inhuman or degrading treatment or punishment" – are unconditional (absolute): they forbid (or require) government to do something, *period.*[25] Some other ICCPR rights, by contrast, are conditional: they forbid (or require) government to do something *unless certain conditions are satisfied.* As Article 18 makes clear, the right to religious and moral freedom is conditional;[26] under

pp. 91–7. But there will also be many cases where the distinction is relatively easy to administer. For example:

> [A] Muslim nurse's decision to wear a scarf cannot be placed on the same footing as a colleague's choice to wear a baseball cap. In the first case the woman feels an obligation – to deviate from it would go against a practice that contributes toward defining her, she would be betraying herself, and her sense of integrity would be violated – which is not normally the case for her colleague (77).

[25] Article 7 states: "No one shall be subjected to torture or to cruel, inhuman or degrading treatment or punishment. In particular, no one shall be subjected without his free consent to medical or scientific experimentation."

[26] Similarly, the right to the free exercise of religion entrenched in the constitutional law of the United States is conditional; it permits government to prohibit some religious practices. See, e.g., *Reynolds* v. *United States*, 98 U.S. 145, 166 (1879) (upholding the constitutionality of a law banning polygamy):

> Laws are made for the government of actions, and while they cannot interfere with mere religious belief and opinions, they may with practices. Suppose one believed that human sacrifices were a necessary part of religious worship, would it be seriously contended that the civil government under which he lived could not interfere to prevent a sacrifice? Or if a wife religiously believed it was her duty to burn herself upon the funeral pile of her dead husband, would it be beyond the power of the civil government to prevent her carrying her belief into practice?

By its very terms, the free exercise right forbids government to prohibit, not the exercise of religion, but the "free" exercise of religion – that is, the freedom of religious exercise. (The First Amendment states, in part: "Congress shall make no law respecting an establishment of religion, or prohibiting the free exercise thereof . . . ") Just as government may not abridge "the freedom of speech" or "the freedom of the press," so too it may not prohibit the freedom of religious exercise. The right to freedom of religious exercise is not an unconditional right to do, on the basis of religious belief or for religious reasons, whatever one wants. One need not concoct outdated hypotheticals about human sacrifice to dramatize the point. One need only point, for example, to the refusal of some Christian Science parents to seek readily available lifesaving medical care for their gravely ill child. See, e.g., *Lundman* v. *McKown*, 530 N.W.2d 807 (Minnesota 1995). See also Caroline Frasier, "Suffering Children and the Christian Science Church," *Atlantic Monthly*, April 1995, 105. Just as the right to freedom of speech does not privilege one to say, and right to the freedom of the press does not privilege one to publish, whatever one wants wherever one wants whenever one wants, the right to freedom of religious exercise does

the right, government may not ban or otherwise impede a practice protected by the right, unless each of three conditions is satisfied:

- **The legitimacy condition:** The ban or other policy must serve a legitimate government objective.[27]
- **The least burdensome alternative condition:** The policy must be necessary to serve the legitimate government objective, in the sense that the policy serves the objective significantly better than would any less burdensome (to the protected practice) policy.[28]
- **The proportionality condition:** The good the policy achieves must be sufficiently weighty to warrant the burden the policy imposes on those who want to act in a way the policy bans or otherwise impedes.[29]

not – because it cannot – privilege one to do, on the basis of religious belief or for religious reasons, whatever one wants wherever one wants whenever one wants.

[27] The Siracusa Principles state: "10. Whenever a limitation is required in the terms of the Covenant to be 'necessary,' this term implies that the limitation: (a) is based on one of the grounds justifying limitations recognized by the relevant article of the covenant, . . . [and] (c) pursues a legitimate aim."

For the Siracusa Principles, see United Nations, Economic and Social Council, U.N. Sub-Commission on Prevention of Discrimination and Protection of Minorities, Siracusa Principles on the Limitation and Derogation of Provisions in the International Covenant on Civil and Political Rights, Annex, UN Doc E/CN.4/1984/4 (1984), reprinted at 7 *Human Rights Quarterly* 3 (1985).

[28] The Siracusa Principles state: "11. In applying a limitation, a state shall use no more restrictive means than are required for the achievement of the purpose of the limitation."

[29] The Siracusa Principles state: "10. Whenever a limitation is required in the terms of the Covenant to be "necessary," this term implies that the limitation: . . . (b) responds to a pressing public or social need, . . . and (d) is proportionate to that aim." The right to religious and moral freedom obviously would provide no meaningful protection for practices covered by the right if the consistency of a ban or other policy with the right was to be determined without regard to whether the benefit of the policy was proportionate to the cost of the policy. And, indeed, Article 18 is authoritatively understood to require that the benefit of the policy be proportionate to the cost of the policy.

For an explication and defense of proportionality inquiry, see Matthias Klatt and Moritz Meister, "Proportionality – A Benefit to Human Rights? Remarks on the I*CON Controversy," 10 *International Journal of Constitutional Law* 687 (2012); Kai Möller, "Proportionality: Challenging the Critics," 10 *International Journal of Constitutional Law* 709 (2012). See also, with particular reference to proportionality inquiry under the right to religious and moral freedom, T. Jeremy Gunn, "Permissible Limitations on the Freedom of Religion or Belief," in John Witte, Jr., and M. Christian Green, eds., *Religion and Human Rights* 254, 263–6 (2012); Kislowicz, Haigh, and Ng, "Calculations of Conscience," 686–93.

The relationship between the normative ground of human rights (NGHR) – the fundamental imperative, articulated in Article 1 of the Universal Declaration of Human Rights, to "act towards one another in a spirit of brotherhood" – and the right we considered in Chapter 4 is clear: To subject a human being to "cruel, inhuman or degrading" punishment is obviously not to treat him or her "in a spirit of brotherhood." The relationship between the NGHR and the right we considered in Chapter 6 is also clear: The right to moral equality is the right to be treated in accord with the "in a spirit of brotherhood" imperative. What is the relationship between the NGHR and the right we are considering in this chapter: Why should we think that government, if it is to act toward its citizens and all other human beings with whom it deals "in a spirit of brotherhood," must respect and protect the right to religious and moral freedom?

To prevent someone from living his or her life in accord with his or her religious and/or moral convictions and commitments, or to make it significantly more difficult for him or her to do so, is hurtful to him or her, sometimes greatly hurtful. As philosopher Mark Wicclair puts the point in his important book, *Conscientious Objection in Health Care: An Ethical Analysis*: "[Even] one instance of acting against one's conscience – an act of self-betrayal – can be devastating and unbearable."[30] Wicclair elaborates:

> [A] loss of moral integrity can be devastating. It can result in strong feelings of guilt, remorse, and shame as well as loss of self-respect. Moral integrity can be of central importance to people whose core beliefs are secular as well as those whose core beliefs are religious. [Martha] Nussbaum cites a powerful image that Roger Williams used to defend liberty of conscience: "To impose an orthodoxy upon the conscience is nothing less than what Williams, in a memorable and oft-repeated image, called 'Soule rape.'" The reference to rape of the *soul* suggests that this statement was meant primarily as a defense of religious tolerance. Nevertheless, when a failure to

---

[30] Mark R. Wicclair, *Conscientious Objection in Health Care: An Ethical Analysis* 11 (2011). See also Sapir and Statman, "Why Freedom of Religion," 474: "[C]oercing people to act against their deepest normative beliefs presents a severe threat to their integrity and makes them experience strong feelings of self-alienation and loss of identity; therefore, it should be avoided as far as possible."

accommodate secular core beliefs results in a loss of moral integrity, it can be experienced as an assault on one's self or identity.[31]

The countries of the world – the great majority of them – agree that for a government to cause anyone such hurt is for the government to fail to act towards him or her "in a spirit of brotherhood," *unless* the law or other policy that is the source of the hurt satisfies each of the three conditions: legitimacy, least burdensome alternative, and proportionality. Again, the right to religious and moral freedom is not – as a practical matter it cannot be – unconditional.

ARTICLE 18 SENSIBLY AND EXPLICITLY allows government to act for the purpose of protecting "public safety, order, health, or morals or the fundamental rights and freedoms of others." Given, however, that the right we are considering in this chapter – the right of which Article 18 is the canonical articulation – is the right to religious *and moral* freedom – this question is especially important: What morals count as *public* morals, under the right to religious and moral freedom?

The Siracusa Principles on the Limitation and Derogation Provisions in the International Covenant on Civil and Political Rights[32] state:

2. The scope of a limitation referred to in the Covenant shall not be interpreted so as to jeopardize the essence of the right concerned.
3. All limitation clauses shall be interpreted strictly and in favor of the rights at issue.
4. All limitations shall be interpreted in the light and context of the particular right concerned.

Therefore, with respect to "public morals," the Human Rights Committee has emphasized:

> [T]he concept of morals derives from many social, philosophical and religious traditions; consequently, limitations on the freedom to manifest a religion or belief for the purpose of protecting morals

---

[31] Ibid., 26 (quoting Martha C. Nussbaum, *Liberty of Conscience: In Defense of America's Defense of Religious Equality* 37 (2008)). For Wicclair's full response to the question "why [is] the exercise of conscience is valuable and worth protecting," see pp. 25–31.

[32] For the Siracusa Principles, see n. 27.

must be based on principles not deriving exclusively from a single tradition . . . If a set of beliefs is treated as official ideology in constitutions, statutes, proclamations of ruling parties, etc., or in actual practice, this shall not result in any impairment of the freedoms under article 18 or any other rights recognized under the Covenant nor in any discrimination against persons who do not accept the official ideology or who oppose it.[33]

As the editors of a casebook on the ICCPR have put the point, in summarizing several statements by the Human Rights Committee concerning protection of "public morals" under the right to religious and moral freedom: "'[P]ublic morals' measures should reflect a pluralistic view of society, rather than a single religious culture."[34]

"Protecting public morals" is undeniably a legitimate government objective under the right to religious and moral freedom: Again, the canonical articulation of the right – Article 18 of the ICCPR – explicitly says so. However, if in banning or otherwise regulating (impeding) conduct *purportedly* in pursuit of that objective, government is acting based on – "based on" in the sense that government would not be regulating the conduct "but for" – either a religious belief that the conduct is immoral or a sectarian nonreligious belief that the conduct is immoral, government is not truly acting to protect *public* morals. It is, instead, acting to protect *sectarian* morals, *and protecting sectarian morals is not a legitimate government objective under the right to religious and moral freedom*. Again, "[o]ne of the most important challenges facing contemporary societies is how to manage moral and religious diversity;"[35] establishing and protecting the right to religious and moral freedom is a principal way for a society to "manage moral and religious diversity."

When is a nonreligious belief that X (a type of conduct) is immoral a sectarian belief? Consider what the celebrated American Jesuit John Courtney Murray wrote, in the mid-1960s, in his "Memo to [Boston's] Cardinal Cushing on Contraception Legislation":

---

[33] Human Rights Committee, General Comment 22.
[34] Sarah Joseph, Jenny Schultz and Melissa Castan, eds., *The International Covenant on Civil and Political Rights* 510 (2004).
[35] See n. 2.

[T]he practice [contraception], undertaken in the interests of "responsible parenthood," has received official sanction by many religious groups within the community. It is difficult to see how the state can forbid, as contrary to public morality, a practice that numerous religious leaders approve as morally right. The stand taken by these religious groups may be lamentable from the Catholic moral point of view. But it is decisive from the point of view of law and jurisprudence.[36]

Murray's insight can be generalized: A belief, including a nonreligious belief, that X is immoral is sectarian if the claim that X is immoral is one that is widely contested – and in that sense sectarian – among the citizens of a religiously and morally pluralistic democracy. The right to religious and moral freedom leaves no room for the political-powers-that-be to ban or otherwise regulate conduct based on sectarian belief that the conduct is immoral.

Of course, it will not always be obvious which side of the line a particular moral belief falls on – sectarian or nonsectarian – but often it will be obvious. As Murray understood and emphasized to Cardinal Cushing, the belief that contraception is immoral had clearly become sectarian. By contrast, certain moral beliefs – certain moral norms – are now clearly ecumenical, rather than sectarian, in religiously and morally pluralistic democracies. Consider, in that regard, what Maclure and Taylor have said about "popular sovereignty" and "basic human rights":

[They] are the *constitutive* values of liberal and democratic political systems; they provide these systems with their foundation and aims.

---

[36] "Memo to Cardinal Cushing on Contraception Legislation" (n.d., mid-1960s), http://woodstock.georgetown.edu/library/murray/1965f.htm. See also John Courtney Murray, SJ, Toledo Talk [delivered in Toledo on May 5, 1967), http://woodstock.georgetown.edu/library/murray/1965f.htm. Murray's influence on Boston's Archbishop, Cardinal Richard Cushing, and Cushing's influence on the repeal of the Massachusetts ban on the sale of contraceptives, is discussed in Seth Meehan, "Legal Aid," *Boston College Magazine*, Spring 2011, and in Seth Meehan, "Catholics and Contraception: Boston, 1965," *New York Times*, March 15, 2012. See also Joshua J. McElwee, "A Cardinal's Role in the End of a State's Ban on Contraception," *National Catholic Reporter*, Mar. 2–15, 2012. For the larger context within which Father Murray wrote and spoke, see Leslie Woodcock Tentler, *Catholics and Contraception: An American History* (2004). For a recent reflection on Murray's work by one of his foremost intellectual heirs, see David Hollenbach, SJ, "Religious Freedom and Law: John Courtney Murray Today," 1 *Journal of Moral Theology* 69, 75 (2012).

Although these values are not neutral, they are legitimate, because it is they that allow citizens espousing very different conceptions of the good to live together in peace. They allow individuals to be sovereign in their choices of conscience and to define their own life plan while respecting others' right to do the same. That is why people with very diverse religious, metaphysical, and secular convictions can share and affirm these constitutive values. They often arrive at them by very different paths, but they come together to defend them.[37]

Again, to prevent someone from living his or her life in accord with his or her religious and/or moral convictions and commitments, or to make it significantly more difficult for him or her to do so, is hurtful to the person, sometimes greatly hurtful. Moreover, the hurtful imposition of sectarian moral belief is likely to be profoundly divisive in a religiously and morally pluralistic society. A society that takes seriously the right to religious and moral freedom understands not only that "its unity does not lie in unanimity about the meaning and goals of existence but also that any efforts in the direction of such a uniformization would have devastating consequences for social peace."[38] It is fitting, then, that the great majority of the countries of the world have converged on the right to religious and moral freedom, under which, according to the legitimacy condition, government may not regulate conduct on the basis of sectarian moral belief. It is fitting, that is, that the great majority of the countries of the world, in recognizing the right to religious and moral freedom as a human right, agree that for a government to prevent someone from living his or her life in accord with his religious and/or moral convictions and commitments, or to make it significantly

---

[37] Maclure and Taylor, *Secularism and Freedom of Conscience*, 11.

Kent Greenawalt has written that "[a] vast array of laws and policies . . . imply the incorrectness of particular religious views." Kent Greenawalt, "Five Questions about Religion Judges Are Afraid to Ask," in Nancy L. Rosenblum, ed., *Obligations of Citizenship and Demands of Faith* 196, 199 (2000). He gives three examples: a law that educational funds be "made available equally to men and women[,]" a decision to go to war, and a judicial order that a state desegregate its schools. I disagree. The proposition that a law banning racial segregation (for example) is warranted on the basis of certain premises – *premises that are admissible under the right to religious and moral freedom* – does not entail that it is incorrect to conclude on the basis of certain other premises – *premises that are not admissible under the right* – that the law is contrary to God's will.

[38] Maclure and Taylor, *Secularism and Freedom of Conscience*, 18.

more difficult for him or her to do so, is for the government to fail to act consistently with the NGHR – it is for the government to fail to act toward the person "in a spirit of brotherhood" – unless the law or other policy that is the source of the hurt satisfies all three conditions: legitimacy, least burdensome alternative, and proportionality.[39]

IN THE PRECEDING CHAPTER, I explained why we are warranted in saying that the internationally recognized human right to moral equality is entrenched in the constitutional law of the United States. Let me now explain why we are warranted in saying that the internationally recognized human right to religious and moral freedom, like the right to moral equality, is constitutionally entrenched – and is therefore, like the right to moral equality, part of the constitutional morality of the United States.

It is a bedrock feature of the constitutional law of the United States that neither the federal government nor state government may, in the words of the First Amendment, "prohibit[] the free exercise [of religion]." As interpreted by a majority of the justices now sitting on the

---

[39] The rationale for the right to religious and moral freedom that I have just sketched is a nonsectarian rationale. Cf. Douglas Laycock, "Reviews of a Lifetime," 89 *Texas Law Review* 949, 985 (2011):

> The only reasons that can justify religious liberty to a broad audience in a religiously diverse society are reasons that do not require acceptance or rejection of any propositions of religious faith. Of course such a scheme will not persuade everybody, and perhaps in the end will not persuade anybody. But that is what I was trying to do. I am happy to supplement the argument with religious reasons when speaking to audiences that might be persuaded by them.

Some citizens have a religious reason (or reasons) for affirming the right to religious and moral freedom, and for them, the religious reason may be the dominant reason. On religious reasons for religious liberty, see Daniel O. Conkle, "Religious Truth, Pluralism, and Secularization: The Shaking Foundations of American Religious Liberty," 32 *Cardozo Law Review* 1755, 1763–7 (2011).

That the coercive imposition of sectarian moral belief violates the right to religious and moral freedom does not entail that the noncoercive affirmation of religious belief does so. Examples of the latter, from the United States: the phrase "under God" in the Pledge of Allegiance, "In God We Trust" as the national motto, and "God save this honorable court" intoned at the beginning of judicial proceedings. I have addressed elsewhere the question whether the noncoercive affirmation of religious belief violates the Establishment Clause of the U.S. Constitution: Perry, *The Political Morality of Liberal Democracy* 100–19 (2010) (Chapter 6: "Religion as a Basis of Lawmaking"), also available, in an earlier version, at http://ssrn.com/abstract=1057721.

Supreme Court of the United States, the right to the free exercise of religion is not the same as – it is not congruent with – the internationally recognized human right to religious and moral freedom. There is no need here to explicate the free exercise right as interpreted by a majority of the sitting justices: Religious liberty scholar Daniel Conkle has done just that in his admirably concise and accessible book *Constitutional Law: The Religion Clauses* (2008) (see pages 81–108). For present purposes, it suffices to say that, in my judgment, those religious liberty scholars are persuasive who contend – as distinguished religious liberty scholars Douglas Laycock and Michael McConnell contend[40] – that the present Court's interpretation of the free exercise right is too narrow and that the better interpretation of the right is one according to which the right protects (conditionally, not unconditionally) this comprehensive religious freedom: freedom to practice, and otherwise live one's life in accord with, one's own religion; freedom from laws and other public policies that coerce one to practice, or otherwise live one's life in accord with, a religion not one's own, a religion one rejects; and freedom from laws that discriminate against one on the ground that one does not practice, or otherwise live one's life in accord with, a particular religion or group of religions.

I noted earlier in this chapter that those who struggle with "religious or limit questions" – such as the question "Does God exist?" – do not invariably end up giving answers that constitute a theistic or otherwise transcendent worldview. As I said, many end up giving answers that constitute a thoroughgoing rejection of any transcendent worldview. Nonetheless, wrote John Paul II in his encyclical *Fides et Ratio*, such questions "have their common source in the quest for meaning which has always compelled the human heart" and "the answer given to these questions decides the direction which people seek to give to their lives."[41] What sense does it make, then, to interpret "religion" in the free exercise right so narrowly – why think that the enactors

---

[40] See Douglas Laycock, *Religious Liberty, Volume Two: The Free Exercise Clause* 47–230 (2011); Michael W. McConnell, "The Origins and Historical Understanding of Free Exercise of religion," 103 *Harvard Law Review* 1409 (1990); Michael W. McConnell, "Free Exercise Revisionism and the Smith decision," 57 *University of Chicago Law Review* 1109 (1990).

[41] See n. 21.

of the free exercise provision understood "religion" so narrowly, even though the particular instances of "religion" with which they (most of them) were familiar and on which they were focused were theistic – that the provision ends up protecting only conduct embedded in a theistic worldview? Is Buddhism, which in the main is nontheistic, to be excluded from coverage under the free exercise right? And if not – if Buddhism is to be included – why not other nontheistic worldviews too? Douglas Laycock, speaking of the free exercise right, is surely correct to insist that "we have to understand religion broadly, so that nonbelievers are protected when they do things that are analogous to the exercise of religion . . . Nonbelievers have consciences, and occasionally, their deeply held conscientious beliefs conflict with government regulation."[42]

The appeal of a broad rather than miserly understanding of "religion" is reflected in the breadth of Article 18 of the ICCPR, which, again, as the Human Rights Committee has emphasized, protects

> the freedom of thought and the freedom of conscience . . . equally with the freedom of religion and belief . . . Article 18 protects theistic, non-theistic and atheistic beliefs, as well as the right not to profess any religion or belief. The terms "belief" and "religion" are to be broadly construed. Article 18 is not limited in its application to traditional religions or to religions and beliefs with institutional characteristics or practices analogous to those of traditional religions.[43]

The appeal of a broad understanding of "religion" is also reflected in what the Canadian Supreme Court has said about the religious freedom provision of the Canadian Constitution: that it "ensure[s] that society does not interfere with profoundly personal beliefs that govern one's perception of oneself, humankind, nature, and, in some cases, a higher or different order of being. These beliefs, in turn, govern one's conduct and practices."[44] According to the Canadian

---

[42] Douglas Laycock, "McElroy Lecture: Sex, Atheism, and the Free Exercise of Religion," *University of Detroit Mercy Law Review* 407, 431 (2011). See also Douglas Laycock, "Religious Liberty as Liberty," 7 *Journal of Contemporary Legal Issues* 313, 336–7 (1996).

[43] See n. 9.

[44] See n. 12.

Supreme Court, the provision "means that, subject to [certain limitations], no one is to be forced to act in a way contrary to his beliefs or his conscience."[45]

This, then, is why we are warranted in saying that the internationally recognized human right to religious and moral freedom is entrenched in the constitutional law of the United States – and is therefore part of the constitutional morality of the United States: The right to the free exercise of religion is entrenched in the constitutional law of the United States, and that right, *correctly interpreted*, is congruent with the right to religious and moral freedom. That is, the free exercise right, correctly interpreted, protects (conditionally, not unconditionally) freedom to live one's life in accord with one's own worldview, whether that worldview is theistic or nontheistic; freedom from laws (and other public policies) that coerce one to live one's life in accord with someone else's worldview – a worldview one rejects – whether that worldview is theistic or nontheistic; and freedom from laws that discriminate against one on the ground that one does not live one's life in accord with a particular worldview or group of worldviews, whether that worldview(s) is theistic or nontheistic.[46]

---

[45] See n. 13.

[46] Law professor George Wright has said to me, in correspondence:

> If the Framers had consensually concluded that religious conscience is somehow distinctive, and to be constitutionally distinguished from a more general, or a purely secular, conscience, I would have lodged no serious objection at the time. But as today's culture, or at least key segments thereof, rejects the idea of any relevant distinctiveness of religious conscience, my Hobbesian approach urges that we simply accept the *equality* of religious and secular consciences, lest we find ourselves seeking, imprudently, to build a stable society on the basis of an apparent principle that persons of exclusively secular conscience are, by loose implication, somehow not operating at the same level of moral depth, seriousness, sustained motivational force, or profundity as are some persons of religious conscience.

E-mail from George Wright to Michael Perry, Jan. 14, 2013.
   I have heard it suggested – though I am not arguing here – that to interpret the right to the free exercise of religion to protect religious but not secular conscience is to interpret the right such that it is in tension with the constitutional requirement that government not "establish" religion or with the right to the equal protection of the laws – or with both. It bears mention, in that regard, that in *Welsh v. United States*, 398 U.S. 333 (1970), Justice Harlan, concurring in the result, argued that for Congress to grant conscientious objector status to those whose pacifism is based on theistic religious belief – or, more broadly, on theistic or nontheistic religious belief – while denying such status to those whose

Even though as interpreted by a majority of the sitting justices of the Supreme Court, the free exercise right is not congruent with the right to religious and moral freedom, a version of the right to religious and moral freedom – a version that the Supreme Court has sometimes called "the right of privacy" – has been protected by the Court as a constitutional right for almost fifty years. Consider the following rulings by the Supreme Court in the period since the mid-1960s:

- A 1965 ruling and a 1972 ruling, read in conjunction with one another, establish that government may ban neither the use nor the distribution of contraceptive devices or drugs.[47] In the 1972 ruling, the Supreme Court declared: "If the right of privacy means anything, it is the right of the *individual*, married or single, to be free from unwarranted governmental intrusion into matters so fundamentally affecting a person as the decision whether to bear or beget a child."[48]
- In 1973, the Supreme Court ruled that restrictive abortion legislation implicated, and that some such legislation violated, "the right of privacy."[49] In 1992, in reaffirming the 1973 ruling, the Court explained:

> Men and women of good conscience can disagree, and we suppose some always shall disagree, about the profound moral and spiritual implications of terminating a pregnancy, even in its earliest stage. Some of us as individuals find abortion offensive to our most basic principles of morality, but that cannot control our decision. Our obligation is to define the liberty of all, not to mandate our own moral code. The underlying constitutional issue is whether the State can resolve these philosophic questions in such a definitive way that a woman lacks all choice in the matter, except perhaps [where] the pregnancy is itself a danger to her own life or health, or is the result of rape or incest . . .

---

pacifism is based on nonreligious belief is to violate the First Amendment requirement that "Congress . . . make no law respecting an establishment of religion" (356).

[47] See *Griswold* v. *Connecticut*, 381 U.S. 479 (1965); *Eisenstadt* v. *Baird*, 405 U.S. 438 (1972).

[48] Ibid., 453 (emphasis in original).

[49] See *Roe* v. *Wade*, 410 U.S. 113 (1973).

Our law affords constitutional protection to personal decisions relating to marriage, procreation, contraception, family relationships, child rearing, and education . . . These matters, involving the most intimate and personal choices a person may make in a lifetime, choices central to personal dignity and autonomy, are central to the liberty protected by the Fourteenth Amendment. At the heart of liberty is the right to define one's own concept of existence, of meaning, of the universe, and of the mystery of human life. Beliefs about these matters could not define the attributes of personhood were they formed under compulsion of the State.[50]

• In 1978, in ruling that "the decision to marry [is] among the personal decisions protected by the right of privacy," the Supreme Court stated:

It is not surprising that the decision to marry has been placed on the same level of importance as decisions relating to procreation, childbirth, child rearing, and family relationships . . . [I]t would make little sense to recognize a right of privacy with respect to other matters of family life and not with respect to the decision to enter the relationship that is the foundation of the family in our society . . .

By reaffirming the fundamental character of the right to marry, we do not mean to suggest that every state regulation which relates in any way to the incidents of or prerequisites for marriage must be subjected to rigorous scrutiny. To the contrary, reasonable regulations that do not significantly interfere with decisions to enter into the marital relationship may legitimately be imposed . . . [However, w]hen a statutory classification significantly interferes with the exercise of a fundamental right, it cannot be upheld unless it is supported by sufficiently important state interests and is closely tailored to effectuate only those interests.[51]

• In 2003, the Supreme Court ruled that government may not criminalize adult, consensual sexual intimacy and that therefore a criminal ban on same-sex sexual intimacy was unconstitutional:

[50] *Planned Parenthood of Southeastern Pennsylvania* v. *Casey*, 505 U.S. 833, 850–1 (1992).
[51] *Zablocki* v. *Redhail*, 434 U.S. 374, 386, 388 (1978). See also *Turner* v. *Safley*, 482 U.S. 78 (1987).

Liberty presumes an autonomy of self that includes freedom of... certain intimate conduct... [Government should be wary about attempting] to define the meaning of [an adult, consensual] relationship or to set its boundaries absent injury to a person or abuse of an institution the law protects... [A]dults may choose to enter upon this relationship... and still retain their dignity as free persons. When sexuality finds overt expression in intimate conduct with another person, the conduct can be but one element in a personal bond that is more enduring. The liberty protected by the Constitution allows homosexual persons to make this choice...

[F]or centuries, there have been powerful voices to condemn homosexual conduct as immoral. [This does not] answer the question before us, however. The issue is whether the majority may use the power of the State to enforce these views on the whole society through operation of the criminal law. "Our obligation is to define the liberty of all, not to mandate our own moral code."... "[T]hat the governing majority in a State has traditionally viewed a particular practice as immoral is not a sufficient reason for upholding a law prohibiting the practice... [I]ndividual decisions by married persons, concerning the intimacies of their physical relationship, even when not intended to produce offspring, are a form of 'liberty' protected by the Due Process Clause of the Fourteenth Amendment. Moreover, this protection extends to intimate choices by unmarried as well as married persons."[52]

---

[52]   *Lawrence v. Texas*, 539 U.S. 558, 562, 567, 571, 577–8 (2003) (quoting, at 571, *Planned Parenthood of Southeastern Pennsylvania v. Casey*, 505 U.S. 833, 850 (1992), and quoting, at 577–8, *Bowers v. Hardwick*, 478 U.S. 186, 216 (1986) (Stevens, J., dissenting)).

   Legal historian William Novak has noted that "[b]y the standards of late twentieth-century law, the public regulation of morality [in the United States] is increasingly suspect." William J. Novak, *The People's Welfare: Law and Regulation in Nineteenth-Century America* 149 (1996). Novak explains:

   The burgeoning public/private distinction, the jurisprudential separation of law and morality, and the expansion of constitutionally protected rights of expression and privacy have yielded a polity whose legitimacy theoretically rests on its ability to keep out of the private moral affairs of its citizens. As the American Law Institute declared in the 1955 Model Penal Code, "We deem it inappropriate for the government to attempt to control behavior that has no substantial significance except as to the morality of the actor."

   Novak goes on to illustrate that "[t]he relationship between laws and morals in the nineteenth century could not have been more different. Of all the contests over public power in that period, morals regulation was the easy case." See ibid., 149–89.

The Supreme Court sought to justify its rulings in the foregoing cases on the basis of "the right to privacy" and/or the right not to have government "deprive" one of "liberty . . . without due process of law."[53] As a matter of defensible constitutional interpretation, however, the Court would have been on much less controversial ground had it sought to justify its rulings on the basis of the right – the right *correctly interpreted* – not to have government "prohibit" one from engaging in "the free exercise of religion."[54] This is not to say, however, that all of the Court's rulings in the foregoing and related cases are in the end justifiable on that basis. I conclude in Chapter 9 that the Court's ruling in one of the two 1973 Abortion Cases – *Doe* v. *Bolton*[55] – is not justifiable on the basis of the right to religious and moral freedom.

[53] The Due Process Clause of the Fourteenth Amendment, which is a limit on state government, provides: "[N]or shall any State deprive any person of life, liberty, or property, without due process of law." The Due Process Clause of the Fifth Amendment, which, like the rest of the Fifth Amendment, is a limit on the federal government, provides: "[N]or shall any person . . . be deprived of life, liberty, or property, without due process of law."

[54] For an impressive argument that we should reject the position "that [under the due process clauses] courts may identify certain liberties with no source in positive law and protect them even against general and prospective legislation enforced with all proper procedure," see Nathan S. Chapman and Michael W. McConnell, "Due Process as Separation of Powers," 121 *Yale Law Journal* 1672, 1792–1801 (2012).

[55] 410 U.S. 179 (1973).

8   SAME-SEX MARRIAGE

The two rights that bear most directly on the constitutional controversy addressed in this chapter are the two rights elaborated in the preceding two chapters: right to moral equality and the right to religious and moral freedom. Does what we may call "the exclusion policy" – excluding same-sex couples from civil marriage – violate either right?

WHAT IS MARRIAGE?

In their essay, "What Is Marriage?,"[1] Sherif Girgis, Robert George, and Ryan Anderson argue that we should adhere in our law to a particular understanding of "marriage," which, following the authors, we may call the "conjugal" understanding. According to the conjugal understanding, as the authors explain:

1. A couple is accurately described as "married" if and only if their relationship satisfies certain conditions, one of which is procreative – biologically procreative – complementarity.
2. The relationship of no same-sex couple satisfies the procreative complementarity condition.
3. Therefore, no same-sex couple is accurately described as "married" (according to the conjugal understanding).

However, others argue that we should accept in our law what a growing number are accepting outside our law, namely, a different

---

[1] Sherif Girgis, Robert George, and Ryan Anderson, "What Is Marriage?," 34 *Harvard Journal of Law and Public Policy* 245, 260–3 (2010). The essay has been expanded into a book: Sherif Girgis, Ryan Anderson, and Robert P. George, *What is Marriage? Man and Woman: A Defense* (2013). My citations in this chapter are to the essay.

understanding of "marriage" – a revised understanding – according to which:

1. A couple is accurately described as "married" if and only if their relationship satisfies certain conditions: the same conditions that are part of the conjugal understanding, except for procreative complementarity.
2. The relationship of some same-sex couples – like that of some opposite-sex couples – satisfies all of the specified conditions.
3. Therefore, some same-sex couples – and some opposite-sex couples – are accurately described as "married" (according to the revised understanding).

So, two different understandings – two different conceptions – of "marriage."[2] What is there to say in support of the proposition that we should not accept in our law the revised understanding of "marriage" but should instead adhere to the conjugal understanding, according to which no same-sex couple is accurately described as "married"? These are the principal things that have been said in support of that proposition:

1. Same-sex sexual conduct is immoral.
2. Admitting same-sex couples to civil marriage would imperil the welfare of children.
3. Admitting same-sex couples to civil marriage would imperil the health of the institution of traditional (i.e., opposite-sex) marriage, an institution that benefits society in various important ways.

---

[2] Cf. Mark Strasser, *Notre Dame Philosophical Reviews* 2012.07.41, http://ndpr.nd.edu/news/32246-debating-same-sex-marriage/:

> The American family has undergone a transformation because of the availability of assisted reproductive technologies, the acceptance of adoption, the number of children born to unmarried parents, and the number of married couples who are intentionally childless. In part because of the frequency of divorce and in part because of the increased number of children living with only one or perhaps neither of their biological parents, we now have a much more complicated and diverse array of families that simply cannot be captured by the pictures of marriage and family that [Maggie] Gallagher paints.

The "picture of marriage and family" Maggie Gallagher paints is the same picture the authors of "What is Marriage?" paint. See John Corvino and Maggie Gallagher, *Debating Same-Sex Marriage* (2012).

In "What Is Marriage?" the authors say – among the other things they say – both 2 and 3. (They studiously avoid saying 1.) The principal point the authors press, however, in response to the question that is the title of their essay, is that it is of the very nature of "marriage" that it is a relationship between one man and one woman. In her book, *Ministers of the Law: A Natural Law Theory of Legal Authority*, Jean Porter, a Catholic theologian on the faculty of the University of Notre Dame and a scholar of natural law, has explained and contended, contra the kind of argument mounted by Robert George and his co-authors:

> Marriage is always expressed through some set of conventional practices which will inevitably serve a range of other purposes proper to the kinship structures and personal interactions of the complex social primates that we are. This being the case, I think we should be very hesitant to rule out unconventional forms of marriage too quickly on the grounds that these are contrary to the natural purposes of the institution. What seems from one perspective to be contrary to natural purposes might appear on longer experience as a legitimate expansion of those purposes, which does not undermine, and may well strengthen, the central purposes which the institution must serve if society is to continue at all. For this reason, I would support the legal recognition of same-sex unions as marriages.[3]

In a growing number of countries, the state of affairs endorsed by Porter – "the legal recognition of same-sex unions as marriages" – is supported by a growing number of persons. One such country is our neighbor to the north, Canada, where in 2005 the Parliament enacted legislation granting same-sex couples access to civil marriage. This is not to say that Canadians are now all of one mind; of course, they are not. This statement by Martin Cauchon, made in 2002 when he was the Minister of Justice and Attorney General of Canada, remains accurate:

[3] Jean Porter, *Ministers of the Law: A Natural Law Theory of Legal Authority* 286–7 (2010). Porter adds, where I have put the ellipsis: "and I would grant legal recognition to some forms of plural marriages as well."

Not just in Canada but around the world, individuals and their governments have debated whether marriage has a continuing value to society, and if so whether and how the state should recognize married relationships in law. The Canadian public, like those in many other countries, are divided on this question. Some feel strongly that governments should continue to support marriage as an opposite-sex institution, since married couples and their children are the principal social unit on which our society is based. Others believe that, for reasons of equality, governments should treat all conjugal relationships – opposite-sex and same-sex – identically. Still others believe that in a modern society, governments should cease to recognize any one form of relationship over another and that marriage should be removed from the law and left to individuals and their religious institutions.[4]

As Cauchon's statement indicates, some have suggested that it would be better if government were to get out of the business of awarding the title "marriage" and instead create civil unions for couples, both opposite-sex couples and same-sex, who satisfy certain conditions. For example, Martha Nussbaum has written that it would be preferable, "as a matter of both political theory and public policy, if the state withdrew from the marrying business, leaving the expressive domain to religions and to other private groups, and offering civil unions to both same- and opposite-sex couples."[5]

In this chapter, I explain why so long as government remains in the business of awarding the title "marriage" to opposite-sex couples, the

[4] Martin Cauchon, Department of Justice of Canada, Marriage And Legal Recognition of Same Sex Unions, http://www.justice.gc.ca/eng/dept-min/pub/mar/mar.pdf.

[5] Martha C. Nussbaum, "A Right to Marry?," 98 *California Law Review* 667, 672 (2010). See also p. 695; Martha Albertson Fineman, "Why Marriage?," 9 *Virginia Journal of Social Policy and the Law* 239 (2001); Tamara Metz, *Untying the Knot: Marriage, the State, and the Case for Their Divorce* (2010); Charles J. Reid, Jr., "Book Review," 53 *Journal of Church and State* 132 (2011) (reviewing Tamara Metz, *Untying the Knot: Marriage, the State, and the Case for Their Divorce* (2010)); Elizabeth Brake, *Minimizing Marriage: Marriage, Morality, and the Law* (2012); Carolyn McConnell, "What's in a Name? The Case for the Disestablishment of Marriage" (2012), http://ssrn.com/abstract=2006785. For a skeptical view, see Laurie Shrage, "The End of 'Marriage,'" *New York Times*, Nov. 4, 2012. Cf. Pamela S. Karlan, "Let's Call the Whole Thing Off: Can States Abolish the Institution of Marriage?," 98 *California Law Review* 697 (2010); Martha C. Nussbaum, "Reply," 98 *California Law Review* 731–4 (2010) (responding to Karlan).

exclusion policy – excluding same-sex couples from civil marriage – violates the right I elaborated in the preceding chapter: the right to religious and moral freedom.[6]

But, first, let us inquire whether, as many believe, the exclusion policy violates the right I elaborated in Chapter 6: the right to moral equality.

THE RIGHT TO MORAL EQUALITY

The exclusion policy obviously disadvantages gays and lesbians, and the more extreme versions of the policy obviously disadvantage gays and lesbians more severely. The most extreme version: refusing to grant to same-sex unions any of the legal benefits granted to opposite-sex marriages. A less extreme version: granting to same-sex unions some but not all of the legal benefits granted to opposite-sex marriages. The least extreme version: granting to same-sex unions all of the legal benefits granted to opposite-sex marriages, but refusing to call such unions – refusing to "dignify" such unions with the honorific name – "marriage."

However, that the exclusion policy disadvantages gays and lesbians does not entail that the policy violates the right to moral equality. The policy violates the right to moral equality if, and only if, the policy is based on the view that gays and lesbians are morally inferior human beings – "morally inferior" in the sense specified in Chapter 6. Is the exclusion policy based on that view? Is that view a "but for" predicate of the policy?

The view that gays and lesbians are morally inferior human beings is sadly familiar. Richard Posner, writing about the "irrational fear and loathing of" homosexuals, has observed that homosexuals, like the Jews with whom they "were frequently bracketed in medieval persecutions[,] . . . are despised more for who they are than for what they

---

[6] On the importance of gaining access to civil *marriage*, see Mathew S. Nosanchuk, "Response: No Substitutions, Please," 100 *Georgetown Law Journal* 1989, 2004–13 (2012).

do."[7] The Connecticut Supreme Court has echoed that observation, noting that homosexuals are often "'ridiculed, ostracized, despised, demonized and condemned' merely for being who they are."[8] Andrew Koppelman has rehearsed some grim examples: "the judge's famous speech at Oscar Wilde's sentencing for sodomy, one of the most prominent legal texts in the history of homosexuality, [which] 'treats the prisoners as objects of disgust, vile contaminants who are not really people, and who therefore need not be addressed as if they were people.'" Koppelman continues: "From this it is not very far to Heinrich Himmler's speech to his SS generals, in which he explained that the medieval German practice of drowning gay men in bogs 'was no punishment, merely the extermination of an abnormal life. It had to be removed just as we [now] pull up stinging nettles, toss them on a heap, and burn them.'"[9]

So we should not discount the possibility that some policies that disadvantage gays and lesbians do indeed violate the right to moral equality. An ugly example remains on the books in Florida: "No person eligible to adopt under this statute [the Florida Adoption Act] may adopt if that person is a homosexual."[10] Under the Florida law, which is fairly described as homophobic, ex-felons of all sorts may adopt a child; even a convicted child abuser may adopt a child. But no homosexual may do so. The Florida courts were right to rule that the statute

---

[7] Richard Posner, *Sex and Reason* 346 (1992). Cf. Louis Crompton, *Homosexuality and Civilization* (2003). Crompton's book is discussed in Edward Rothstein, "Annals of Homosexuality: From Greek to Grim to Gay," *New York Times*, Dec. 13, 2003.
As history teaches, an "irrational fear and loathing" of any group often has tragic consequences. The irrational fear and loathing of homosexuals is no exception. There is, for example, the horrible phenomenon of "gay bashing." "The coordinator of one hospital's victim assistance program reported that 'attacks against gay men were the most heinous and brutal I encountered.' A physician reported that injuries suffered by the victims of homophobic violence he had treated were so 'vicious' as to make clear that 'the intent is to kill and maim.'" Andrew Koppelman, *Antidiscrimination Law and Social Equality* 165 (1996). As "[a] federal task force on youth suicide noted[,] because 'gay youth face a hostile and condemning environment, verbal and phyical abuse, and rejection and isolation from family and peers,' young gays are two to three times more likely than other young people to attempt and to commit suicide" (149).
[8] *Kerrigan* v. *Commissioner of Public Health*, 957 A.2d 407, 445–6 (Connecticut 2008).
[9] Andrew Koppelman, "Are the Boy Scouts Being as Bad as Racists? Judging the Scouts' Antigay Policy," 18 *Public Affairs Quarterly* 363, 372 (2004).
[10] § 63.042(3), Fla. Stat. (2006).

violates Florida's version of the right to moral equality: the right that "[u]nder the Florida Constitution, each individual person has . . . to equal protection of the laws."[11]

But that some policies that disadvantage gays and lesbians violate the right to moral equality does not entail that every law and policy that disadvantages gays and lesbians violates the right to moral equality. And, as it happens, it is problematic to insist that in contemporary liberal democracies, such as the United States, the view that gays and lesbians are morally inferior human beings is a "but for" predicate of the exclusion policy.

In the United States and other liberal democracies, this is the dominant and, for many, sufficient rationale for the exclusion policy: *Admitting same-sex couples to civil marriage would tend to legitimize – "normalize" – and thereby incentivize same-sex sexual conduct. This we must not do: Same-sex sexual conduct is immoral.* However, the claim that same-sex sexual conduct is immoral does not assert, imply, or presuppose that those who engage in the conduct are morally inferior human beings, any more than the claim that theft is immoral asserts, implies, or presupposes that those who steal are morally inferior human beings. By contrast, "the very point" of laws that criminalized interracial marriage was "to signify and maintain the false and pernicious belief that nonwhites are morally inferior to whites."[12]

This is not to deny that some "of the antigay animus that exists in the United States is just like racism, in the virulence of the rage it bespeaks and the hatred it directs towards those who are its objects."[13] Again, some policies that disadvantage gays and lesbians violate the right to moral equality. But "[n]ot all antigay views . . . deny the personhood

---

[11] Florida Department of Children and Families v. In re: Matter of Adoption of X.X.G. and N.R.G., Third District Court of Appeal, No. 3D08–3044 (Sept. 22, 2010). Article 1, section 2 of the Florida Constitution states:

> SECTION 2. Basic rights. – All natural persons, female and male alike, are equal before the law and have inalienable rights, among which are the right to enjoy and defend life and liberty, to pursue happiness, to be rewarded for industry, and to acquire, possess and protect property.

[12] John Corvino, "Homosexuality and the PIB Argument," 115 *Ethics* 501, 509 (2005).

[13] Andrew Koppelman, "You Can't Hurry Love: Why Antidiscrimination Protections for Gay People Should Have Religious Exemptions," 72 *Brooklyn Law Review* 125, 145 (2006).

and equal citizenship of gay people."[14] As Robert Nagel has emphasized, "[t]here is the obvious but important possibility that one can
'hate' an individual's behavior without hating the individual."[15] The
pope and bishops of the Catholic Church insist that same-sex sexual
conduct is immoral and are prominent – indeed, leading – opponents
of "legislative and judicial attempts, both at state and federal levels, to
grant same-sex unions the equivalent status and rights of marriage – by
naming them marriage, civil unions or by other means."[16] Nonetheless, the pope and bishops also insist that all human beings, gays and
lesbians no less than others, are equally beloved children of God. "[Our
teaching] about the dignity of homosexual persons is clear. They must
be accepted with respect, compassion, and sensitivity. Our respect for
them means that we condemn all forms of unjust discrimination, har-
rassment or abuse."[17]

[14] Ibid.

[15] See Robert F. Nagel, "Playing Defense in Colorado," *First Things*, May 1998, 34, 35.

[16] United States Conference of Catholic Bishops Administrative Committee, "Promote,
Protect, Preserve Marriage: Statement on Marriage and Homosexual Unions," 33 *Origins*
257, 259 (2003).

[17] Ibid. See William N. Eskridge Jr., "Noah's Curse: How Religion Often Conflates Status,
Belief, and Conduct to Resist Antidiscrimination Norms," 45 *Georgia Law Review* 657,
697, 704 (2011):

> The Vatican's 1975 Declaration *Persona Humana* announced that "homosexual
> acts" are "disordered," but also acknowledged the modern distinction between
> sexual orientation and sexual acts. The next year, the National Conference of
> Catholic Bishops responded with a more gay-tolerant document, "To Live in
> Christ Jesus," which said this: Homosexuals, like everyone else, should not suf-
> fer from prejudice against their basic human rights. They have a right to respect,
> friendship and justice. They should have an active role in the Christian commu-
> nity." Different dioceses adopted slightly different readings of these documents.
> For example, the Church in the state of Washington interpreted the pronounce-
> ments to support the conclusion that *"prejudice against homosexuals is a greater
> infringement of the norm of Christian morality than is homosexual orientation or
> activity."* . . .
>
> [R]eflecting a strong turn in public opinion toward toleration for gay people, the
> American Catholic Church was subtly readjusting its doctrinal stance toward
> homosexuality. According to the Vatican, men and women with homosexual
> tendencies "must be accepted with respect, compassion, and sensitivity. Every
> sign of unjust discrimination in their regard should be avoided." After fighting
> the antidiscrimination law in Massachusetts through the 1980s, Catholic dio-
> ceses acquiesced in similar laws adopted by Catholic Connecticut in 1991 and
> Catholic Rhode Island in 1995. Archbishop John Francis Whealon of Hartford,
> Connecticut said this in 1991: "The Church clearly teaches that homosexual

Predictably, many will be quick to claim that government may not adjudge – that it is no part of government's legitimate business to adjudge – same-sex sexual conduct to be immoral. However, if it is true that government may not adjudge same-sex sexual conduct to be immoral, it is not because government's doing so violates the right to moral equality: Again, adjudging same-sex sexual conduct to be immoral does not assert, imply, or presuppose that those who engage in the conduct are morally inferior human beings. If government may not adjudge same-sex sexual conduct to be immoral – more precisely, if government may not exclude same-sex couples from civil marriage based on the view that same-sex sexual conduct is immoral – it is because government's doing so violates a right other than the right to moral equality.

THE RIGHT TO RELIGIOUS AND MORAL FREEDOM

Legal scholar Kenji Yoshino has emphasized "how much human flourishing is enabled by the [marriage] right and how much it is impeded by its denial." So, for "many gay rights advocates," writes Yoshino, "the issue is less one of gay equality than of individual liberty."[18] A friendly amendment to Yoshino's statement: The issue is (as I have just argued) not one of moral equality; at least, it is less one of moral equality than (as I am about to argue) of religious and moral freedom.

Something philosopher James Griffin wrote in his book *On Human Rights* helps us to see that the issue is more one of freedom – or, to use the word Griffin (like Yoshino) uses, liberty – than of equality: It is often unnecessary for government to make it possible for everyone to

men and women should not suffer prejudice on the basis of their sexual orientation. Such discrimination is contrary to the Gospel of Jesus Christ and is always morally wrong." Many Connecticut legislators took the Archbishop's statement as tacit approval of the antidiscrimination measure (adorned with religious liberty-protective exemptions). The Roman Catholic shift in emphasis – not necessarily a shift in precise doctrine – was representative of organized religion in America, as public opinion shifted strongly toward toleration of gay Americans and same-sex couples.

[18] Kenji Yoshino, "Marriage Partners," *New York Times Magazine*, June 1, 2008.

live precisely the life one "has settled on. Most individual conceptions of a worthwhile life have alternatives, as good or nearly as good, and a person may reasonably be asked to find an alternative, if the form first chosen is costly or reduces options for others." Nonetheless, "if there are same-sex couples who want to form some sort of union and raise children – who want, that is, to have the rich, stable, recognized, respected relations that are at the heart of most people's conceptions of a worthwhile life – and, because of our ethical traditions, there are no social institutions to allow it, then we should create one or another form of them." Then, echoing Yoshino, Griffin continues: "This too, I believe, is an issue of liberty." He explains:

> No matter how many options there are already, this one, because of its centrality to characteristic human conceptions of a worthwhile life, must be added... What is at stake for same-sex couples are several of the most important components of a good life available to human beings... Some persons do not want deep personal relations or to raise children. But the great majority of us do, and the [exclusion policy denies to] same-sex couples some of the greatest, most widely distributed, and most deeply embedded – sometimes even genetically embedded – least easily substituted ends of human life there are.[19]

THE ARGUMENT THAT THE EXCLUSION POLICY violates the right to moral equality is, as I explained in the preceding part of this chapter, problematic. But even if one concludes that the moral-equality argument against the exclusion policy is persuasive – some readers will so conclude[20] – the following question, to which we now turn, persists and is important: Does the exclusion policy violate the right to religious and moral freedom?

A core part of the freedom to live one's life in accord with one's religious and/or moral convictions and commitments – which is the freedom protected by the right to religious and moral freedom – is

---

[19] James Griffin, *On Human Rights* 163–4, 168 (2008) (passages rearranged).

[20] See Michael C. Dorf, "Same-Sex Marriage, Second-Class Citizenship, and Law's Social Meanings," 97 *Virginia Law Review* 1267, 1310–15 (2011); Douglas NeJaime, "Marriage Inequality: Same-Sex relationships, Religious Exemptions, and the Production of Sexual Orientation Discrimination," 100 *California Law Review* 1169 (2012).

the freedom to live one's life in a marriage of one's choosing (if one chooses to live one's life in a marriage). So the exclusion policy clearly implicates the right to religious and moral freedom. But that the exclusion policy *implicates* the right to religious and moral freedom does not entail that the policy *violates* the right. The right to religious and moral freedom is not absolute, but conditional: A policy that implicates the right violates the right if, and only if, the policy fails to satisfy the legitimacy condition, the least burdensome alternative condition, or the proportionality condition. As it happens, and as I am about to explain, the exclusion policy fails to satisfy the legitimacy condition – the policy fails to serve a legitimate government objective – and therefore violates the right to religious and moral freedom.

The government objectives that have been asserted in defense of the exclusion policy are of two sorts: *morality-based* objectives, which are objectives whose pursuit by government presupposes that same-sex sexual conduct is immoral, and *non-morality-based* objectives, which are objectives whose pursuit by government does not presuppose that same-sex sexual conduct is immoral.

The principal non-morality-based government objectives that have been asserted in defense of the exclusion policy are (1) protecting the welfare of children and (2) protecting the health of the institution of traditional (i.e., opposite-sex) marriage. Although both are undeniably legitimate (and weighty) government objectives, a substantial literature now supports the proposition that excluding same-sex couples from civil marriage serves neither objective. Indeed, no credible argument supports the claim that all the several states in the United States and all the several countries in the world that have thus far admitted same-sex couples to civil marriage[21] have thereby disserved – imperiled – either the welfare of children or the health of the institution of traditional

---

[21] In the United States, as of December 2012, nine states and the District of Columbia (2010) grant access to civil marriage to same-sex couples: Massachusetts (2003), Connecticut (2008), Iowa (2009), New Hampshire (2009), Vermont (2009), New York (2011), Maine (2012), Maryland (2012), and Washington (2012). Many more states, as of December 2012, grant to same-sex unions all or some of the legal benefits granted to opposite-sex marriages, but without calling the unions "marriage": California, Colorado, Delaware, Hawaii, Illinois, Nevada, New Jersey, Oregon, Rhode Island, and Wisconsin.

As of December 2012, a dozen countries grant access to civil marriage to same-sex couples: the Netherlands (since 2000), Belgium (2003), Canada (2005), Spain

marriage or both.[22] Indeed, excluding same-sex couples from civil marriage disserves – and admitting them to civil marriage serves – the welfare of those many children now being raised by same-sex couples.[23]

In any event, the dominant rationale for the exclusion policy – as is well known – involves a morality-based government objective: *Admitting same-sex couples to civil marriage would tend to legitimize –*

(2005), South Africa (2006), Norway (2009), Sweden (2009), Argentina (2010), Portugal (2010), Iceland (2010), Denmark (2012), and New Zealand (2013). In December 2009, Mexico City granted access to civil marriage to same-sex couples. In January 2012, the judiciary in Alagoas (Brazil) announced that same-sex marriages would be performed there. Many more countries – or parts of countries – grant to same-sex unions all or some of the legal benefits granted to opposite-sex marriages, but without calling the unions "marriage": Andorra, Australia, Austria, Brazil, Colombia, Croatia, the Czech Republic, Ecuador, Finland, France, Germany, Greenland, Hungary, Ireland, Isle of Man, Israel, Lichtenstein, Luxembourg, parts of Mexico (Coahuila and the Federal District), Slovenia, Switzerland, the United Kingdom, and Uruguay. I may have overlooked one or more countries.

22 If you are skeptical about my "no credible argument" claim, I recommend that you read this to-and-fro: Maggie Gallagher, "Prepared Statement of Maggie Gallagher," 58 *Drake Law Review* 889 (2010); Andrew Koppelman, "Prepared Statement of Andrew Koppelman," 58 *Drake Law Review* 905 (2010); Discussion [among Maggie Gallagher, Andrew Koppelman, and others], 58 *Drake Law Review* 913 (2010). See also Tobias Barrington Wolff, "Collegiality and Individual Dignity," 81 *Fordham Law Review* 829, 831, n. 2 (2012).

In his letter "to Congress on Litigation Involving the Defense of Marriage Act," Feb. 23, 2011, U.S. Attorney General Eric Holder stated: "As the [U.S.] Department [of Justice] has explained in numerous filings, since the enactment of DOMA, many leading medical, psychological, and social welfare organizations have concluded, based on numerous studies, that children raised by gay and lesbian parents are as likely to be well-adjusted as children raised by heterosexual parents." http://www.justice.gov/opa/pr/2011/February/11-ag-223.html. See also Carlos A. Ball, "Social Science Studies and the Children of Lesbians and Gay Men: The Rational Basis Perspective" (2012), http://ssrn.com/abstract=2079991.

For a strenuous but unavailing attempt to provide a credible argument that granting access to civil marriage to same-sex couples imperils both the institution of opposite-sex marriage and the welfare of children, see Girgis, George, and Anderson, "What is Marriage?," 260–3.

This useful book was published after this chapter was drafted: John Corvino and Maggie Gallagher, *Debating Same-Sex Marriage* (2012). For excellent commentary on the book, see Strasser, *Notre Dame Philosophilca Reviews*.

23 "[A]ccording to the 2010 census, one-quarter of same-sex households are raising children." Kenji Yoshino, "For Obama, It's About the Children," *New York Times*, May 12, 2012. See Sabrina Tavernise, "Adoptions Rise by Same-Sex Couples, Despite Legal Barriers," *New York Times*, June 13, 2011; Frank Bruni, "2 Dads, 2 Daughters, 1 Big Day," *New York Times*, June 21, 2011.

"normalize" – *and thereby incentivize same-sex sexual conduct. This we must not do: Same-sex sexual conduct is immoral.*[24] For example, in 2003, the Vatican – specifically, the Congregation for the Doctrine of the Faith, whose Prefect at the time, Joseph Cardinal Ratzinger, became Pope Benedict XVI – argued that admitting same-sex couples to civil marriage would signal "the approval of deviant behavior, with the consequences of making it a model in present-day society."[25]

Excluding same-sex couples from civil marriage obviously serves the government objective of not taking a step that would tend to legitimize conduct believed by many to be immoral: same-sex sexual conduct. The serious question is whether that government objective – that *morality-based* government objective – qualifies as a *legitimate* government objective under the right to religious and moral freedom. The answer depends on the reason or reasons lawmakers have for believing that same-sex sexual conduct is immoral. If the only reason the lawmakers have is a religious reason – for example, and in the words of one evangelical minister, "[same-sex sexual conduct] is in direct

---

[24] In his letter "to Congress on Litigation Involving the Defense of Marriage Act," Feb. 23, 2011, U.S. Attorney General Eric Holder stated: "[T]he legislative record underlying DOMA's passage contains . . . numerous expressions reflecting moral disapproval of gays and lesbians and their intimate and family relationships." In a note attached to that sentence – note vii – the letter states:

> *See, e.g.*, H.R. Rep. at 15–16 (judgment [opposing same-sex marriage] entails both moral disapproval of homosexuality and a moral conviction that heterosexuality better comports with traditional (especially Judeo-Christian) morality"); *id.* at 16 (same-sex marriage "legitimates a public union, a legal status that most people . . . feel ought to be illegitimate" and "put[s] a stamp of approval . . . on a union that many people . . . think is immoral"); *id.* at 15 ("Civil laws that permit only heterosexual marriage reflect and honor a collective moral judgment about human sexuality"); *id.* (reasons behind heterosexual marriage – procreation and child-rearing – are "in accord with nature and hence have a moral component"); *id.* at 31 (favorably citing the holding [of the U.S. Supreme Court in *Bowers* v. *Hardwick*, 478 U.S. 186 (1986)] that an "anti-sodomy law served the rational purpose of expressing the presumed belief . . . that homosexual sodomy is immoral and unacceptable"); *id.* at 17 n.56 (favorably citing statement in dissenting opinion in *Romer* [v. *Evans*, 517 U.S. 620 (1996)] that "[t]his Court has no business . . . pronouncing that 'animosity' toward homosexuality is evil").

http://www.justice.gov/opa/pr/2011/February/11-ag-223.html.

[25] Congregation for the Doctrine of the Faith, *Considerations Regarding Proposals to Give Legal Recognition to Unions Between Homosexual Persons* (2003), http://www.vatican .va/roman_curia/congregations/cfaith/documents/rc_con_cfaith_doc_20030731_homosexual-unions_en.html.

opposition to God's truth as He has revealed it in the Scriptures"[26] – then the government objective is clearly not legitimate. As I explained in the preceding chapter, although government's acting to protect *public* morals is undeniably a legitimate government objective under the right to religious and moral freedom, government's acting to protect *sectarian* morals is not a legitimate government objective. *The right to religious and moral freedom leaves no room for the political-powers-that-be to ban or otherwise regulate conduct based on sectarian belief that the conduct is immoral.*

However, a religious reason is not the only reason lawmakers have for believing that that same-sex sexual conduct is immoral. Indeed, the path of reasoning runs in the opposite direction for many religious believers, whose position is not that because it is contrary to the will of God, same-sex sexual conduct is immoral, but that because it is immoral, same-sex sexual conduct is contrary to the will of God.[27]

The pope and bishops of the Roman Catholic Church – the "magisterium" of the Church – are leading opponents of "legislative and judicial attempts, both at state and federal levels, to grant same-sex unions the equivalent status and rights of marriage – by naming them marriage,

---

[26] So said the Rev. Ron Johnson, Jr., on Sept. 28, 2008. See Peter Slevin, "33 Pastors Flout Tax Law With Political Sermons," *Washington Post*, Sept. 29, 2008. See also John Frank, "Churches Speak Up on Gay Marriage," [Charlotte, NC] *News and Observer*, Sept. 18, 2011.

For many Christians, even many evangelical Christians, the belief that same-sex sexual conduct is contrary to the will of God is no longer credible. See, e.g., David G. Meyers and Letha Dawson Scanzoni, *What God Has Joined Together? A Christian Case for Gay Marriage* (2005).

I have explained elsewhere why Christians, as Christians, have good reason to be wary about relying on the biblically based argument that same-sex sexual conduct is contrary to the will of God as a ground for supporting the exclusion policy. See Michael J. Perry, *Under God? Religious Faith and Liberal Democracy* 55–80 (2003). Cf. Nicholas D. Kristof, "Lovers Under the Skin," *New York Times*, Dec. 3, 2003: "A 1958 poll found that 96 percent of whites disapproved of marriages between blacks and whites . . . In 1959 a judge justified Virginia's ban on interracial marriage by declaring that 'Almighty God . . . did not intend for the races to mix.'"

[27] It is not always clear which of two different positions one is espousing when one says that X is contrary to the will of God: (1) X is contrary to the will of God and *therefore* immoral. (2) X is contrary to the will of God *because* X is immoral. According to the first position, the reason for concluding that X is immoral is theological: "X is contrary to the will of God." But according to the second position, the reason for concluding that X is immoral is unstated and not necessarily theological, even though the "therefore" – "X is immoral and therefore contrary to the will of God" – is a theological claim.

civil unions or by other means."[28] The magisterium's reason – its ratio-nale – for believing that same-sex sexual conduct is immoral is a non-religious reason: a reason that does not assert, imply, or presuppose any religious premise, even the premise that God exists.

According to the magisterium, it is immoral not just for same-sex couples but for anyone and everyone – even a man and a woman who are married to one another – to engage in (i.e., pursuant to a knowing, uncoerced choice to engage in) any sexual conduct that is "inherently nonprocreative," and same-sex sexual conduct – like con-tracepted male-female sexual intercourse[29] and every act of mastur-bation, oral sex, and anal sex – is inherently nonprocreative. Because "[w]hat are called 'homosexual unions' . . . are inherently nonprocre-ative," declared the Administrative Committee of the U.S. Conference of Catholic Bishops, they "cannot be given the status of marriage."[30]

---

[28] See United States Conference of Catholic Bishops, "Promote, Protect, Preserve Mar-riage." It bears repetition that the pope and bishops also insist that all human beings, gays and lesbians no less than others, are equally beloved children of God. See n. 17.

[29] See Leslie Woodcock Tentler, *Catholics and Contraception: An American History* (2004).

[30] Statement of the Administrative Committee, United States Conference of Catholic Bish-ops, "Preserve, Protect, Promote Marriage," Sept. 9, 2003, http://old.usccb.org/comm/archives/2006/06-052.shtml. See also Congregation for the Doctrine of the Faith, "Con-siderations Regarding Proposals to Give Legal Recognition to Unions Between Homo-sexual Persons," http://www.vatican.va/roman_curia/congregations/cfaith/documents/rc_con_cfaith_doc_20030731_homosexual-unions_en.html.

For anyone who rejects the Church's argument about the immorality of engaging in "inherently nonprocreative" sexual conduct,

> it is no longer possible to argue that sex/love between two persons of the same sex cannot be a valid embrace of bodily selves expressing love. If sex/love is centered primarily on communion between two selves rather than on biologistic concepts of procreative complementarity, then the love of two persons of the same sex need be no less than that of two persons of the opposite sex. Nor need their experience of ecstatic bodily communion be less valuable.

Rosemary Ruether, "The Personalization of Sexuality," in Eugene Bianchi and Rosemary Ruether, eds., *From Machismo to Mutuality: Essays on Sexism and Woman-Man Liberation* 70, 83 (1976). Cf. Edward Collins Vacek, SJ, "The Meaning of Marriage: Of Two Minds," *Commonweal*, Oct. 24, 2003, 17, 18–19: "When, after Vatican II, Catholics began to connect sexual activity more strongly with expressing love than with making babies, it became harder to see how homosexual acts are completely different from heterosexual acts."

However, to reject the Church's argument about the immorality of "inherently non-procreative" sexual conduct does not entail acceptance of the proposition that when it comes to sexual conduct, anything goes. As Margaret Farley, a Catholic sister and formerly Stark Professor of Christian Ethics at Yale University, has explained:

As Joseph Cardinal Ratzinger stated in 2003, speaking for the Congregation for the Doctrine of the Faith: Because they "close the sexual act to the gift of life," "homosexual acts go against the natural moral law."[31]

The pope and bishops' position that inherently nonprocreative sexual conduct is, as such – as inherently nonprocreative – immoral is a sectarian moral position; indeed, it is a conspicuously sectarian moral position. It bears mention, in that regard, that the position is extremely controversial *even just among Catholic moral theologians*,[32] not to

> My answer [to the question of what norms should govern same-sex relations and activities] has been: the norms of justice – the norms which govern all human relationships and those which are particular to the intimacy of sexual relations. Most generally, the norms are respect for persons through respect for autonomy and rationality; respect for relationality through requirements of mutuality, equality, commitment, and fruitfulness. More specifically one might say things like: sex between two persons of the same sex (just as two persons of the opposite sex) should not be used in a way that exploits, objectifies, or dominates; homosexual (like heterosexual) rape, violence, or any harmful use of power against unwilling victims (or those incapacitated by reason of age, etc.) is never justified; freedom, integrity, privacy are values to be affirmed in every homosexual (as heterosexual) relationship; all in all, individuals are not to be harmed, and the common good is to be promoted.

Margaret A. Farley, "An Ethic for Same-Sex Relations," in Robert Nugent, ed., *A Challenge to Love: Gay and Lesbian Catholics in the Church* 93, 105 (1983). Farley then adds that "[t]he Christian community will want and need to add those norms of faithfulness, forgiveness, of patience and hope, which are essential to any relationships between persons in the Church." See also Margaret A. Farley, *Just Love: A Framework for Christian Sexual Ethics* 293–4 (2006).

[31] See Congregation for the Doctrine of the Faith, *Considerations Regarding Proposals*. See also David Hollenbach, SJ, "Religious Freedom and Law: John Courtney Murray Today," 1 *Journal of Moral Theology* 69, 75 (2012):

> The United States Catholic Bishops have adopted particularly pointed public advocacy positions on . . . resistance to gay marriage and public acceptance of the legitimacy of same sex relationships. The Bishops' 2007 statement *Forming Consciences for Faithful Citizenship* was a formal instruction by the U.S. hierarchy covering the full range of the public dimensions of the Church's moral concerns. In this document, . . . echoing the affirmation by the Catechism of the Catholic Church that homosexual acts "are contrary to the natural law" and that "under no circumstances can they be approved," the bishops oppose[d] "same-sex unions or other distortions of marriage."

[32] See, e.g., Stephen J. Pope, "The Magisterium's Arguments against 'Same-Sex Marriage': An Ethical Analysis and Critique," 65 *Theological Studies* 530 (2004); Todd A. Salzman and Michael G. Lawler, "Catholic Sexual Ethics: Complementarity and the Truly Human," 67 *Theological Studies* 625 (2006); Patrick Lee and Robert P. George, "What Male-Female Complementarity Makes Possible: Marriage as a Two-in-One-Flesh

mention among the larger community of religious ethicists. Therefore, whether government's pursuit of the objective of not taking a step that would tend to legitimize immoral conduct is based on a biblical rationale or on the bishops' nonreligious rationale – or on both – the objective is not a legitimate government objective: Again, the right to religious and moral freedom leaves no room for the political-powers-that-be to ban or otherwise regulate conduct based on sectarian moral belief.

Consider again what John Courtney Murray wrote, in the mid-1960s, in his "Memo to [Boston's] Cardinal Cushing on Contraception Legislation":

> [T]he practice [contraception], undertaken in the interests of "responsible parenthood," has received official sanction by many religious groups within the community. It is difficult to see how the state can forbid, as contrary to public morality, a practice that numerous religious leaders approve as morally right. The stand taken by these religious groups may be lamentable from the Catholic moral point of view. But it is decisive from the point of view of law and jurisprudence.[33]

Father Murray did not explain in his memo what he meant by "the point of view of law and jurisprudence." Nonetheless, what Murray said was "decisive from the point of view of law and jurisprudence" *is* decisive from the point of view of *the right to religious and moral freedom*: Given

Union," 69 *Theological Studies* 641 (2008); Todd A. Salzman and Michael G. Lawler, "Truly Human Sexual Acts: A Response to Patrick Lee and Robert George," 69 *Theological Studies* 663 (2008). See also n. 30.

Moreover, "[a] report by Washington-based Public Religion Research Institute found that 74 percent of Catholics favor legal recognition for same-sex relationships, either through civil unions (31 percent) or civil marriage (43 percent). That figure is higher than the 64 percent of all Americans, 67 percent of mainline Protestants, 48 percent of black Protestants and 40 percent of evangelicals." *National Catholic Reporter*, April 1, 2011, 16. "What's more, even among Catholics who attend services weekly or more, only about one-third (31%) say there should be no legal recognition for a gay couple's relationship, a vew held by just 13% of those who attend once or twice a month and 16% of those who attend less often." "New Poll: Nuance on Same-Sex Unions Drives Up Catholic Support," http://blog.faithinpubliclife.org/2011/03/new_poll_highlights_catholic_s.html, Mar. 22, 2011.

[33] "Memo to Cardinal Cushing on Contraception Legislation" (n.d., mid-1960s), http://woodstock.georgetown.edu/library/murray/1965f.htm. See Chapter 7, n. 36.

the sectarian nature of the Catholic magisterium's moral teaching that the use of contraceptives is immoral, no government objective that is legitimate under the right to religious and moral freedom warrants a government ban on the use of contraceptives.

Moreover, we may say about the policy of excluding same-sex couples from civil marriage much the same thing Father Murray said to Cardinal Cushing about Massachusetts' anti-contraceptive policy: *Same-sex marriage has received official approval by various religious groups within the community.*[34] *It is difficult to see how the state can refuse to countenance, as contrary to public morality, a relationship that numerous religious leaders and other morally upright people approve as morally good. The stand taken by these religious groups and others may be lamentable from the Catholic moral point of view. But it is decisive from the point of view of the right to religious and moral freedom.*

ASSUMING THAT IT SHOULD PROCEED IN A THAYERIAN MODE, how should the Supreme Court of the United States rule on the question whether excluding same-sex couples from civil marriage violates the right to religious and moral freedom? In particular, how should the Court rule on the question whether the exclusion policy satisfies the legitimacy condition? Given the principal arguments that have been advanced in defense of the exclusion policy, one's answer depends on whether one concludes that any of these four judgments is reasonable:

- The exclusion policy serves this government objective, which is a legitimate government objective – legitimate, that is, under the right to religious and moral freedom: not legitimizing – "normalizing" – conduct that, because contrary to the will of God, is immoral.

---

[34] See Eskridge, "Noah's Curse," 707–8; Laurie Goodstein, "Unions That Divide: Churches Split over Gay Marriage," *New York Times*, May 13, 2012; Maggie Astor, "Illinois Clergy Members Support Same-Sex Marriage in Letter Signed by 260," *New York Times*, Dec. 23, 2012. Cf. Samuel G. Freedman, "How Clergy Helped a Same-Sex Marriage Law Pass," *New York Times*, June 16, 2011.

- The exclusion policy serves this government objective, which is a legitimate government objective: not legitimizing conduct that, because inherently nonprocreative, is immoral.
- The exclusion policy serves this government objective, which is a legitimate government objective: protecting the welfare of children.
- The exclusion policy serves this government objective, which is a legitimate government objective: protecting the health of the institution of traditional marriage.

Both of the first two objectives are clearly out of bounds under the right to religious and moral freedom: Government's pursuit of each of the two objectives is based on sectarian moral belief. The third and fourth objectives, by contrast, are both undeniably legitimate (and important) government objectives. The serious question, for the judge proceeding in the Thayerian mode, is whether the judgment that the exclusion policy serves the third objective, or the fourth, or both, is reasonable. It would not be surprising if some judges, proceeding in a Thayerian mode, answered yes while others answered no: As I emphasized in Chapter 5, we mustn't confuse Thayerian deference with a programmer's algorithm. My own answer is clear from what I said earlier in this chapter:

> No credible argument supports the claim that all the several states in the United States and all the several countries in the world that have thus far admitted same-sex couples to civil marriage have thereby disserved – imperiled – either the welfare of children or the health of the institution of traditional marriage or both. Indeed, excluding same-sex couples from civil marriage disserves – and admitting them to civil marriage serves – the welfare of those many children now being raised by same-sex couples.[35]

---

[35] Speaking of countries that have admitted same-sex couples to civil marriage: Canada has done so. However, Canada does not recognize – indeed, Canada bans – polygamous unions. Recently, the Supreme Court of British Columbia ruled that the Canadian ban on polygamous unions does not violate the right to religious and moral freedom. See *Reference re: Section 293 of the Criminal Code of Canada*, 2011 BCSC 1588 (Nov. 23, 2011). The court's opinion in the case serves as a persuasive rejoinder to the suggestion, made by some who oppose the legal recognition of same-sex marriage, that if it were true that government must recognize same-sex marriage, then it would be true too that government must recognize polygamous marriage. Cf. Rose McDermott, "Polygamy:

APPENDIX

Religion as a Basis of Lawmaking under the Right to Religious and Moral Freedom

As I explained in the preceding chapter and emphasized in this chapter, the right to religious and moral freedom leaves no room for the political-powers-that-be to ban or otherwise regulate conduct based on – "based on" in the sense that government would not be regulating the conduct "but for" – sectarian moral belief, such as "this conduct is contrary to the will of God." Consider, in that regard, the following passages from *Varnum* v. *Brien* (2009), in which the Iowa Supreme Court ruled that the state constitution requires Iowa to admit same-sex couples to civil marriage:

> Now that we have addressed and rejected each specific interest advanced by the County to justify the classification drawn under the statute, we consider the reason for the exclusion of gay and lesbian couples from civil marriage left unspoken by the County: religious opposition to same-sex marriage. The County's silence reflects, we believe, its understanding this reason cannot, under our Iowa Constitution, be used to justify a ban on same-sex marriage.

> While unexpressed, religious sentiment most likely motivates many, if not most, opponents of same-sex civil marriage and perhaps even shapes the views of those people who may accept gay and lesbian unions but find the notion of same-sex marriage unsettling. Consequently, we address the religious undercurrent propelling the same-sex marriage debate as a means to fully explain our rationale for rejecting the dual-gender requirement of the marriage statute.

> It is quite understandable that religiously motivated opposition to same-sex civil marriage shapes the basis for legal opposition to same-sex marriage, even if only indirectly. Religious objections to same-sex marriage are supported by thousands of years of tradition and biblical interpretation. The belief that the "sanctity of

More Common than You Think," *Wall Street Journal*, April 11, 2011 (arguing that the "data shows that plural marriage is a disaster for women's rights").

marriage" would be undermined by the inclusion of gay and lesbian couples bears a striking conceptual resemblance to the expressed secular rationale for maintaining the tradition of marriage as a union between dual-gender couples, but better identifies the source of the opposition. Whether expressly or impliedly, much of society rejects same-sex marriage due to sincere, deeply ingrained – even fundamental – religious belief.

Yet, such views are not the only religious views of marriage. As demonstrated by amicus groups, other equally sincere groups and people in Iowa and around the nation have strong religious views that yield the opposite conclusion.

This contrast of opinions in our society largely explains the absence of any religion-based rationale to test the constitutionality of Iowa's same-sex marriage ban. Our constitution does not permit any branch of government to resolve these types of religious debates and entrusts to courts the task of ensuring government *avoids* them. (See Iowa Const. art. I, § 3: "The general assembly shall make no law respecting an establishment of religion.") The statute at issue in this case does not prescribe a definition of marriage for religious institutions. Instead, the statute declares, "Marriage is a civil contract" and then regulates that civil contract (Iowa Code § 595A.1). Thus, in pursuing our task in this case, we proceed as civil judges, far removed from the theological debate of religious clerics, and focus only on the concept of civil marriage and the state licensing system that identifies a limited class of persons entitled to secular rights and benefits associated with civil marriage.

We, of course, have a constitutional mandate to protect the free exercise of religion in Iowa, which includes the freedom of a religious organization to define marriages it solemnizes as unions between a man and a woman. (See Iowa Const. art. I, § 3: "The general assembly shall make no law . . . prohibiting the free exercise [of religion].") This mission to protect religious freedom is consistent with our task to prevent government from endorsing any religious view. State government can have no religious views, either directly or indirectly, expressed through its legislation. This proposition is the essence of the separation of church and state.

As a result, civil marriage must [not] be judged . . . under religious doctrines or the religious views of individuals. This approach does not disrespect or denigrate the religious views of many Iowans who may strongly believe in marriage as a dual-gender union, but considers, as we must, only the constitutional rights of all people, as expressed by the promise of equal protection for all. We are not permitted to do less and would damage our constitution immeasurably by trying to do more.

> The only legitimate inquiry we can make is whether [the statute] is constitutional. If it is not, its virtues . . . cannot save it; if it is, its faults cannot be invoked to accomplish its destruction. If the provisions of the Constitution be not upheld when they pinch as well as when they comfort, they may as well be abandoned.

In the final analysis, we give respect to the views of all Iowans on the issue of same-sex marriage – religious or otherwise – by giving respect to our constitutional principles. These principles require that the state recognize both opposite-sex and same-sex civil marriage. Religious doctrine and views contrary to this principle of law are unaffected, and people can continue to associate with the religions that best reflect their views. A religious denomination can still define marriage as a union between a man and a woman, and a marriage ceremony performed by a minister, priest, rabbi, or other person ordained or designated as a leader of the person's religious faith does not lose its meaning as a sacrament or other religious institution. The sanctity of all religious marriages celebrated in the future will have the same meaning as those celebrated in the past. The only difference is *civil* marriage will now take on a new meaning that reflects a more complete understanding of equal protection of the law. This result is what our constitution requires.[36]

---

[36] 763 N.W.2d 862, 904–6 (Iowa 2009).

9 ABORTION

In this, the final chapter, we address what has been, for us in the United States, one of the most intractable and divisive constitutional controversies since the end of the Second World War – if not the most intractable and divisive constitutional controversy.

Let us begin with this question, which, as I explained in the appendix to Chapter 3, is the third of three fundamental questions about the normative ground of human rights (NGHR): In the NGHR – according to which governments are to "act towards all human beings in a spirit of brotherhood" – does "all" human beings mean *all* human beings, *even unborn human beings*?

Even though "many describe the status of the embryo imprecisely by asking when human life begins or whether the embryo is a human being . . . no one seriously denies that the human zygote is a human life. The zygote is not dead. It is also not simian, porcine, or canine."[1] Philosopher Peter Singer, who is famously pro-choice, has acknowledged that "the early embryo is a 'human life.' Embryos formed from the sperm and eggs of human beings are certainly human, no matter how early in their development they may be. They are of the species Homo sapiens, and not of any other species. We can tell when they are alive, and when they have died. So long as they are alive, they are human life."[2] Similarly, constitutional scholar Laurence Tribe, a staunch pro-choice advocate, has written that "the fetus is alive. It

---

[1] H. Tristram Engelhardt, Jr., "Moral Knowledge: Some Reflections on Moral Controversies, Incompatible Moral Epistemologies, and the Culture Wars," 10 *Christian Bioethics* 79, 84 (2004).

[2] Peter Singer, *The President of Good and Evil: The Ethics of George W. Bush* 37 (2004).

belongs to the human species. It elicits sympathy and even love, in part because it is so dependent and helpless."[3] It is beyond serious debate that an unborn human being *is* a human being: a member of the human species, not of some other species.

Nonetheless, in the NGHR, "all" human beings is widely understood to mean only all *born* human beings. At the beginning of the era of international human rights, the Universal Declaration of Human Rights (1948) stated, in Article 1: "All human beings are *born* free and equal in dignity and rights. They are endowed with reason and conscience and should act towards one another in a spirit of brotherhood" (emphasis added). Forty years later – well after abortion had emerged as a greatly controversial issue in the United States and elsewhere – the drafters of the Convention on the Rights of the Child, which was adopted by the UN General Assembly in 1989 and entered into force in 1990, implicitly affirmed that "all" human beings means only all *born* human beings when they specifically declined to use language that would have required parties to the Convention to ban abortion.[4]

Notwithstanding that in the NGHR "all" human beings is widely understood to mean only all *born* human beings, many believe that even all unborn human beings are bearers of the right to life – and that the law should recognize and protect every unborn human being's right to life. The American Convention on Human Rights, which was adopted by the Organization of American States in 1969 and entered into force in 1978, states, in Article 1(2), that "[f]or the purposes of this Convention, 'person' means every human being," and, in Article 4(1), that "[e]very person has the right to have his life respected [and

---

[3] Laurence H. Tribe, "Will the Abortion Fight Ever End: A Nation Held Hostage," *New York Times*, July 2, 1990.

[4] See Cynthia Price Cohen, "United Nations Convention on the Rights of the Child: Introductory Note," 44 *International Commission of Jurists Review* 36, 39 (1990); Dominic McGoldrick, "The United Nations Convention on the Rights of the Child," 5 *International Journal of Law and Family* 132, 133–4 (1991). Cf. Rebecca J. Cook and Bernard M. Dickens, "Human Rights Dynamics of Abortion Law Reform," 25 *Human Rights Quarterly* 1 (2003). As of December 2012, there are more parties to the Convention on the Rights of the Child – 193 – than to any other UN-sponsored human rights treaty. Only the United States and Somalia are not parties.

this] right shall be protected by law and, in general, from the moment of conception."[5]

Should the law provide that that all unborn human beings have a right to life, which is articulated in the American Convention as "the right to have one's life respected"? The Protocol on the Rights of Women in Africa, which was added to the African Charter on Human and People's Rights in 2003 and entered into force in 2005, gives a starkly different answer from that given by the American Convention: Article 14(2)(c) of the former instrument instructs state parties to "take all appropriate measures to... protect the reproductive rights of women by authorising medical abortion in cases of sexual assault, rape, incest, and where continued pregnancy endangers the mental and physical health of the mother or the life of the mother or the foetus."[6]

Again, should the law provide that all unborn human beings have a right to life? The answer one gives depends in part on why one affirms – on the reason or reasons one has for affirming – the NGHR in the first place, if one does affirm it. (The reader may find it useful at this point to review the discussion in Chapter 3.) If one's rationale for affirming the NGHR is the first of the three rationales considered in Chapter 3 – the twofold "every human being has inherent dignity and is inviolable" rationale – and, further, if one bases that rationale on a religious worldview, then perhaps one will insist that because all unborn human beings no less than all born human beings are created in the "image of God," all unborn human beings have a God-given right to life, which the law should respect and protect. Not every religious believer will give that answer, however: Religious believers are not all of one mind on the question of whether all unborn human beings, even those at an early stage of gestational development, are bearers of a right to life.[7]

---

[5] As of December 2012, there were 23 parties to the American Convention, which entered into force in 1978. (Venezuela's denunciation of the Convention, in 2012, will be effective in 2013.) The United States is not a party.

[6] As of December 2012, a majority of the 53 countries that are members of the African Union were parties to the protocol, although a handful of that majority had expressed a reservation with respect to Article 14. For a discussion of the protocol's position on abortion, see Charles G. Ngwena, "Inscribing Abortion as a Human Right: Significance of the Protocol on the Rights of Women in Africa," 32 *Human Rights Quarterly* 783 (2010).

[7] See, e.g., Daniel Maguire, *Sacred Rights: The Case for Contraception and Abortion in Word Religions* (2003); Jean Porter, "Is the Embryo a Person? Arguing with the Catholic Traditions," *Commonweal*, Feb. 8, 2002.

If one's rationale for affirming the NGHR is the twofold "every human being has inherent dignity and is inviolable" rationale but one bases that rationale solely on a secular worldview, then perhaps one will conclude, as has James Griffin in his book *On Human Rights*, that neither unborn human beings nor even infants are bearers of human rights because what is true of some human beings is not true either of unborn human beings or even of infants: "We human beings have a conception of ourselves and of our past and future. We reflect and assess. We form pictures of what a good life would be – often, it is true, only on a small scale, but occasionally also on a large scale. And we try to realize these pictures. This is what we mean by a distinctively *human* existence – distinctive so far as we know . . . Human rights can be seen as protections of our human standing or . . . our personhood."[8] Or perhaps one will conclude, as has Princeton scholar Robert George on the basis of purely secular reasoning, that all unborn human beings no less than all born human beings are bearers of a right to life, which the law should recognize and protect.[9] As with religious believers, so too with those who deploy secular reasoning: They are not all of one mind.

If one's rationale for affirming the NGHR is solely of the third sort considered in Chapter 3 – self-interest – it is difficult to see why one would answer that the law should provide that all unborn human beings have a right to life: Permissive abortion policies – unlike, for example, torture, racial discrimination, the denial of religious freedom, and severe, unrelenting poverty – are not hostile to the "conditions of stability and well-being which are necessary for peaceful and friendly relations among nations." (The quoted language appears both in Article 55(3) of the UN Charter and in paragraph 6 of the Vienna Declaration and Programme of Action.)

Finally, if one's rationale for affirming the NGHR is solely of the second sort considered in Chapter 3 – the altruistic perspective, without any theological or philosophical (secular-philosophical) backing – how will one likely answer the question whether the law should provide that all unborn human beings have a right to life? It depends.

The altruism of many persons extends beyond all born human beings to all unborn human beings – and even, perhaps, to nonhuman

---

[8] James Griffin, *On Human Rights* 32–3 (2008).
[9] See Robert P. George and Christopher Tollefsen, *Embryo: A Defense of Human Life* (2008).

but sentient creatures. Nonetheless, the altruistic concern that one has for the welfare, including the life, of an unborn human being – at least, an unborn human being at an early gestational stage, say, prior to the emergence of "organized cortical brain activity"[10] – may well not dominate one's altruistic concern for the welfare of a woman who is constrained by her circumstances to choose to terminate an unwanted pregnancy. In my experience, this describes many persons: their altruistic concern for the welfare of unborn human beings at an early gestational stage, although quite real, does not dominate their altruistic concern for the welfare of women constrained to choose to have an abortion.[11] Such persons understandably oppose laws banning abortion at an early gestational stage.

To recapitulate: In the NGHR, "all" human beings is widely understood to mean only all *born* human beings; whether one who affirms the NGHR believes that the law should provide that all unborn human beings have what the American Convention on Human Rights calls "the right to have one's life respected" depends in part on the reason or reasons one has for affirming (if one affirms) the NGHR in the first place.

GIVEN THAT "ALL" HUMAN BEINGS MEANS, in the NGHR, only all *born* human beings, it is not surprising that governments are free, insofar as internationally recognized human rights are concerned, *not* to ban abortion.[12] Are governments also free, insofar as internationally recognized human rights are concerned, *to* ban abortion? As I report in the appendix to this chapter, one of the most important human rights NGOs in the world – Human Rights Watch – insists that the criminalization of abortion is a human rights violation. Is it?

---

[10] Cf. David Boonin, *A Defense of Abortion* (2003).

[11] Cf. Jon A. Shields, "Abortion and the Limits of Philosophy" (2012), http://www.thepublic discourse.com/2012/06/5516.

[12] Readers with a special interest in abortion as a human rights issue would do well to read Tania Penovic, "Book Review," 33 *Human Rights Quarterly* 229 (2011) (reviewing Rita Joseph, *Human Rights and the Unborn Child* (2009)). Penovic concludes her review with this comment: "While Joseph's philosophical position is expressed with passion and at times eloquence, she errs in co-opting international human rights law as an embodiment of her views. The resulting amalgam of lax legal reasoning, vitriol and ill-disciplined name-calling marks a lost opportunity to advance legal scholarship."

In the preceding chapter, I pursued the implications of two rights – the right to moral equality and the right to religious and moral freedom – for the exclusion of same-sex couples from civil marriage. Both rights, again, are part of the constitutional morality of the United States: internationally recognized as human rights and, as I have explained, entrenched in the constitutional law of the United States. In the remainder of this chapter, I pursue the implications of the same two rights for the criminalization of abortion. In particular, I inquire how the Supreme Court of the United States should have answered the question with which it was presented in 1973: What sorts of criminal bans on abortion, if any, are constitutional? By bans on abortion, I mean bans on *pre-viability* abortion,[13] which are much more controversial than bans on post-viability abortion: Post-viability abortion is widely regarded as uncomfortably close to infanticide.

Of all the constitutional rulings by the Supreme Court since the end of the Second World War, none have been more persistently controversial than its rulings, in 1973, in the abortion cases: *Roe* v. *Wade*[14] and *Doe* v. *Bolton*.[15] In *Roe*, the Court invalidated a Texas law that banned all abortions except those necessary to save the life of the mother. The Georgia law at issue in *Doe* was more permissive; it exempted abortions necessary "because (1) a continuation of the pregnancy would endanger the life of the pregnant woman or would seriously and permanently injure her health; or (2) the fetus would very likely be born with a grave, permanent, and irremediable mental or physical defect; or (3) the pregnancy resulted from forcible or statutory rape." Nonetheless, the Court invalidated the Georgia law. In 1992, four Supreme Court justices voted to overrule the abortion cases; a bare majority of the Court – five justices – refused to go along.[16] In 2013, forty years after the Court's rulings in the abortion cases, four justices, given the opportunity, would almost certainly vote to overrule the abortion cases: Chief

---

[13] In 1998, the *New York Times* reported that because of advances "in neonatology, most experts place the point of fetal viability at 23 or 24 weeks." Sheryl Gay Stolberg, "Shifting Certainties in the Abortion War," *New York Times*, Jan. 11, 1998.

[14] 410 U.S. 113 (1973).

[15] 410 U.S. 179 (1973).

[16] *Planned Parenthood of Southeastern Pennsylvania* v. *Casey*, 505 U.S. 833 (1992). The four were Chief Justice William Rehnquist and Justices Byron White, Antonin Scalia, and Clarence Thomas.

Justice John Roberts and Justices Antonin Scalia, Clarence Thomas, and Samuel Alito.

As the laws that were at issue in *Roe* v. *Wade* and *Doe* v. *Bolton* illustrate, not all criminal bans on (pre-viability) abortion are identical: The Texas law was much more restrictive than the Georgia law. (Like the Texas law, the Irish law discussed in the appendix to this chapter bans all abortions not necessary to save the mother's life.) That bans of one sort are unconstitutional does not entail that bans of every sort are unconstitutional. I want to begin by considering bans on abortion that, unlike the Texas law, are *relatively* permissive: bans that exempt, in addition to abortions necessary to save the mother's life, abortions of the following sorts: (1) abortions necessary to protect the mother's physical health from a serious threat of grave and irreparable harm; (2) abortions to terminate a pregnancy that began with rape; and (3) abortions to terminate a pregnancy that will end with a child who, because of a grave defect, is "born into what is certain to be a brief life of grievous suffering"[17] – or with a child who, because of the congenital brain disorder known as anencephaly, is missing a major portion of its brain and is destined to die within hours or days of its birth.[18] (Note that the third exemption is narrower than the exemption in the Georgia law, which governed pregnancies in which "the fetus would very likely be born with a grave, permanent, and irremediable mental or physical defect.")

---

[17] John Schwartz, "When Torment is Baby's Destiny, Euthanasia Is Defended," *New York Times*, March 10, 2005. Cf. Associated Press, "Study: Newborn Euthanasia Often Unreported," *New York Times*, March 10, 2005.

[18] Cf. Global Legal Monitor (Law Library of Congress), "Brazil: Criminalization of Some Abortions Ruled Unconstitutional," http://www.loc.gov/lawweb/servlet/lloc_news?disp3_l205403096_text.

> Anencephaly, often diagnosed when the fetus is in utero, is a neural tube defect in which a major portion of the brain, skull, and scalp fail to develop. An infant born with this disorder lacks a cerebrum, and will usually be born blind, deaf, and unconscious. If an anencephalic infant is not stillborn, the baby will often die within hours or days. In a rare case, the infant may survive longer, as in the well-known case in Brazil of Marcela Ferreira, who lived for 20 months. But infants with anencephaly do not gain consciousness and cannot survive infancy.

> Human Rights Watch, "Brazil: Supreme Court Abortion Ruling a Positive Step," http://www.hrw.org/news/2012/04/19/brazil-supreme-court-abortion-ruling-positive-step.

Does a ban that fits the foregoing profile violate the right to religious and moral freedom? Such a ban undeniably implicates the right
to religious and moral freedom,[19] but to *implicate* is not necessarily to
violate. Recall from Chapter 7 that a ban does not violate the right to
religious and moral freedom unless the ban fails to satisfy the legitimacy condition, the least burdensome alternative condition, or the
proportionality condition.

That an abortion ban of the sort we are now considering satisfies the
legitimacy condition – that it serves a legitimate government objective –
is clear: Protecting the life of a human being is a legitimate – indeed,
a paramount – government objective, and that the life is that of an
unborn human being, even an unborn human being at an early stage
of gestational development, doesn't make the government objective
illegitimate. (It is noteworthy that U.S. law makes it a crime to injure or
kill a "child in utero" – defined as "a member of the species *Homo sapiens*, at any stage of development, who is carried in the womb" – while
committing one or more of over sixty different federal crimes.[20]) Recall

---

[19] See *Planned Parenthood of Southeastern Pennsylvania* v. *Casey*, 505 U.S. 833, 850–1 (1992):

> Men and women of good conscience can disagree, and we suppose some always
> shall disagree, about the profound moral and spiritual implications of terminating
> a pregnancy, even in its earliest stage. Some of us as individuals find abortion
> offensive to our most basic principles of morality, but that cannot control our
> decision. Our obligation is to define the liberty of all, not to mandate our own
> moral code. The underlying constitutional issue is whether the State can resolve
> these philosophic questions in such a definitive way that a woman lacks all choice
> in the matter, except perhaps [where] the pregnancy is itself a danger to her own
> life or health, or is the result of rape or incest....

> Our law affords constitutional protection to personal decisions relating to mar-
> riage, procreation, contraception, family relationships, child rearing, and edu-
> cation.... These matters, involving the most intimate and personal choices a
> person may make in a lifetime, choices central to personal dignity and auton-
> omy, are central to the liberty protected by the Fourteenth Amendment. At
> the heart of liberty is the right to define one's own concept of existence, of
> meaning, of the universe, and of the mystery of human life. Beliefs about these
> matters could not define the attributes of personhood were they formed under
> compulsion of the State.

[20] The law is codified in two sections of the United States Code: Title 18, Chapter 1
(Crimes) §1841 (18 USC 1841), and Title 10, Chapter 22 (*Uniform Code of Military
Justice*) §919a (Article 119a). Cf. Rod Norland, "Unborn Afghan Child Said to be 17th
Victim of Killing Spree," *New York Times*, Mar. 26, 2012.

from Chapter 7 that no government objective is legitimate, under the right to religious and moral freedom, if government's pursuit of the objective based on – "based on" in the sense that government would not be pursuing the objective "but for" – sectarian moral belief. Government's pursuit of the objective of protecting the life of an unborn human being is based partly on the premise that an unborn human being *is* a human being, but that premise is neither a moral belief nor a sectarian belief: As I emphasized at the beginning of this chapter, that an unborn human being *is* a human being – a member of the human species, not of some other species – is an uncontested biological fact. Government's pursuit of the objective of protecting the life of an unborn human being is also based partly on the moral premise that the life of a human being is worthy of protection, but that premise is not sectarian.

It is also clear that a ban on abortion satisfies the least burdensome alternative condition: Just as there is no reason to doubt that there are fewer infanticides under a ban on infanticide than there would be if there were no ban on infanticide, there is no reason to doubt that there would be fewer abortions under a ban on abortion than there are in the absence of a ban on abortion.

The seriously contested, and difficult, question is whether a ban on abortion satisfies the proportionality condition – whether, that is, the good the policy achieves is sufficiently weighty to warrant the burden the policy imposes on those who want to act in a way the policy bans.

There is no denying that a ban on abortion – even a ban of the *relatively* permissive sort we are now considering – imposes a heavy burden on the women who, but for the policy, would choose to have an abortion:

> The detriment that the State would impose upon the pregnant woman by denying this choice altogether is apparent. Specific and direct harm medically diagnosable even in early pregnancy may be involved. Maternity, or additional offspring, may force upon the woman a distressful life and future. Psychological harm may be imminent. Mental and physical health may be taxed by child care. There is also the distress, for all concerned, associated with the unwanted child, and there is the problem of bringing a child into a family already unable, psychologically and otherwise, to care

for it. In other cases, as in this one, the additional difficulties and continuing stigma of unwed motherhood may be involved.[21]

In his justly famous critique of the Supreme Court's rulings in the abortion cases, John Hart Ely wrote that we must not "underestimate what is at stake: Having an unwanted child can go a long way toward ruining a woman's life."[22]

Notwithstanding the heavy burden it imposes on (some) women, many conclude that a ban on abortion – a ban of the sort we are now considering – satisfies the proportionality condition: in particular, those who discern no good reason to distinguish, along the dimension of importance, among (a) the welfare of newborns and infants, (b) the welfare of unborn human beings at a late gestational stage; and (c) the welfare of unborn human beings at an early gestational stage. "[N]o stage of nascent development ... is so significant that it points to a major qualitative change: not implantation, not quickening, not viability, not birth."[23]

---

[21] *Roe* v. *Wade*, 410 U.S. at 153. According to Richard Posner, the Court understated the weight of the burden:

> No effort is made to dramatize the hardships to a woman forced to carry her fetus to term against her will. The opinion does point out that "maternity, or additional offspring, may force upon the woman a distressful life and future," and it elaborates on the point for a few more sentences. But there is no mention of the woman who is raped, who is poor, or whose fetus is deformed. There is no reference to the death of women from illegal abortions.

Richard A. Posner, *Sex and Reason* 337 (1992).

[22] John Hart Ely, "The Wages of Crying Wolf: A Comment on *Roe* v. *Wade*," 82 *Yale Law Journal* 920, 923 (1973).

[23] Richard A. McCormick, SJ, *Corrective Vision: Explorations in Moral Theology* 183 (1994). Cf. Michael J. Wreen, "The Standing Is Slippery," 79 *Philosophy* 553, 571–2 (2004) (emphasis added):

> The Abortion Argument offers an indirect argument for its conclusion, one that simply piggybacks on the claim that a given being, a two-year-old, is a human being/person/etc. The fundamental grounds for, say, possession of a right to life are not mentioned, much less explored, in the argument. What this means is that it's a secondary, indirect argument, one that attempts to carry the day *without itself tackling any of the weightier issues, both metaphysical and moral, that surround humanity, personhood, moral status, and the right to life.* It could be that such an argument is the best that can be done as far as the issue of foetal status and the morality of abortion is concerned.

However, many others conclude that the heavy burden a ban on abortion of the sort we are now considering imposes on women is too great: in particular, those whose concern for the welfare of the women who bear, or would bear, the burden dominates their concern for the welfare of unborn human beings at an early gestational stage. Such persons typically believe that there *is* good reason to distinguish, along the dimension of importance, between welfare of newborns and infants and the welfare of unborn human beings at an early gestational stage – for example, at the stage at which what philosopher David Boonin has called "organized cortical brain activity" emerges, which, Boonin explains, is no earlier than approximately the twenty-fifth week of gestation.[24] Because for such persons a ban on abortion does not satisfy the proportionality condition, the ban – unlike a ban on infanticide – violates the right to religious and moral freedom. That conclusion is certainly not unreasonable.

But neither can the contrary conclusion fairly be said to be unreasonable: the conclusion that a ban of sort we are now considering satisfies the proportionality condition, notwithstanding the heavy burden such a ban imposes on women. Recall from Chapter 5 that the lawmakers' judgment is reasonable, according to Thayer, if rational, well-informed, and thoughtful persons could affirm the judgment: "The rationally permissible opinion of which we have been talking is the opinion reasonably allowable to . . . a competent and duly instructed person who has carefully applied his faculties to the question."[25] Because the disagreement about whether an abortion ban of the relatively permissive sort we are now considering satisfies the proportionality condition is a reasonable disagreement, the Supreme Court, if proceeding in a Thayerian mode, is not warranted in ruling that such a ban does not satisfy the proportionality condition.[26] Something Justice David Souter

---

[24] See Boonin, *A Defense of Abortion*, 115 et seq.

[25] See James Bradley Thayer, "The Origin and Scope of the American Doctrine of Constitutional Law," 7 *Harvard Law Review* 129, 149 (1893) (passages rearranged).

[26] Cf. Jeremy Waldron, "A Right-Based Critique of Constitutional Rights," 13 *Oxford Journal of Legal Studies* 18, 50–1 (1993):

> [T]hink what we might say to some public-spirited citizen who wishes to launch a campaign or lobby her [representative] on some issue of rights about which she feels strongly and on which she has done her best to arrive at a considered and

wrote, in his concurring opinion in a case in which the Supreme Court unanimously rejected a constitutional challenge to a ban on physician-assisted suicide, is relevant here:

> [This Court] has no warrant to substitute one reasonable resolution of the contending positions for another, but authority to supplant the balance already struck between the contenders only when it falls outside *the realm of the reasonable* . . . [We should] respect legislation within *the zone of reasonableness* . . . It is no justification for judicial intervention merely to identify a reasonable resolution of contending values that differs from the terms of the legislation under review. It is only when the legislation's justifying principle, critically valued, is so far from being commensurate with the individual interest as to be arbitrarily or pointlessly applied that the statute must give way.[27]

LET US NOW CONSIDER ABORTION BANS OF A DIFFERENT SORT: those, such as the Texas law that was invalidated in *Roe* v. *Wade* and the Irish law discussed in the appendix, that exempt only abortions necessary to save the life of the mother. Under an abortion ban of such an extreme sort, the burden imposed on (some) women is especially heavy: being forced to continue with (1) pregnancies the continuation of which are a serious threat of grave and

impartial view. She is not asking to be a dictator; she perfectly accepts that her voice should have no more power than that of anyone else who is prepared to participate in politics. But – like her suffragette forbears – she wants a vote; she wants her voice and her activity to count on matters of high political importance.

[I]magine ourselves saying to her: "You may write to the newspaper and get up a petition and organize a pressure group to lobby [the legislature]. But even if you succeed, beyond your wildest dreams, and orchestrate the support of a large number of like-minded men and women, and manage to prevail in the legislature, your measure may be challenged and struck down because your view . . . does not accord with the judges' view. When their votes differ from yours, theirs are the votes that will prevail." It is my submission that saying this does not comport with the respect and honor normally accorded to ordinary men and women in the context of a theory of rights.

[27] *Washington* v. *Glucksburg*, 521 U.S. at 764–5, 768 (Souter, J., concurring in judgment) (emphasis added). Here is a similar statement by the Canadian Supreme Court: "Parliament has enacted this legislation after a long consultation process that included a consideration of the constitutional standards outlined by this Court . . . While it is the role of the Court to specify such standards, there may be a range of permissible regimes that can meet these standards. It goes without saying that this range is not confined to the specific rule adopted by the Court pursuant to its competence in the common law." *Regina* v. *Mills*, 3 S.C.R. 668 at para. 59 (1999).

irreparable harm to the mother's physical health; (2) pregnancies that began with rape; and (3) pregnancies that will end with a child who is missing a major portion of its brain and is destined to die within hours or days of its birth or who is "born into what is certain to be a brief life of grievous suffering."[28]

Recall from Chapter 6 that according to the right to moral equality, government may not disadvantage anyone on the basis of the view that he or she is morally inferior, in this sense: *not worthy of being treated with respect and concern, or worthy only of being treated with less respect and concern than that due some other human beings.* So a law that disadvantages the members of a racial minority, for example, on the basis of such a view – on the basis of what Paul Brest has memorably called "racially selective sympathy and indifference"[29] – violates the right to moral equality. Similarly, a law that disadvantages women on the basis of what I have elsewhere called (with a bow to Paul Brest) "sex-selective sympathy and indifference" violates the right to moral equality.[30] Neither racially selective sympathy and indifference – "the failure to extend to a [racial] minority the same recognition of humanity, and hence the same sympathy and care, given as a matter of course to one's own group"[31] – nor sex-selective sympathy and indifference need be conscious to be operative.

I cannot resist the conclusion that extreme bans on abortion, such as the Texas law, are based on sex-selective sympathy and indifference: a failure to take seriously the well-being of women, a failure to take seriously, that is, the especially heavy burden such a ban imposes on women.[32]

---

[28] See n. 17–18.

[29] See Paul Brest, "Foreword: In Defense of the Antidiscrimination Principle," 90 *Harvard Law Review* 1 (1976).

[30] See Michael J. Perry, *We the People: The Fourteenth Amendment and the Supreme Court* 160–3 (1999).

[31] See Brest, "Foreword," 7–8.

[32] See ibid. Rosalind Dixon and Martha Nussbaum have noted that "Kenneth Karst, Ruth Bader Ginsburg, Cass Sunstein and Reva Siegel, among others, have further made powerful equality-based arguments in favor of recognizing a constitutional right of access to abortion." Rosalind Dixon and Martha Nussbaum, "Abortion, Dignity and a Capabilities Approach" (2011), http://ssrn.com/abstract=1799190 (citing, at pp. 13–14, work by Karst, Ginsburg, Sunstein, and Siegel). Erika Bachiochi cites the same and also other such equality-based arguments: Erika Bachiochi, "Embodied Equality: Debunking Equal

- Just as forcing a woman to continue with a pregnancy that will kill her is to demean the woman's well-being, so too forcing a woman to continue with a pregnancy the continuation of which is a serious threat of grave and irreparable harm to the her physical health is to demean her well-being.
- Forcing a woman to continue with a pregnancy that began with rape is to demean her well-being.
- Forcing a woman to continue with a pregnancy that will end with a child who is missing a major portion of its brain and is destined to die within hours or days of its birth or who is "born into what is certain to be a brief life of grievous suffering" is to demean her well-being.[33]

It is noteworthy that notwithstanding the provision of the American Convention on Human Rights quoted earlier in this chapter – Article 4(1), according to which "[e]very person has the right to have his life respected [and this] right shall be protected by law and, in general, from the moment of conception" – the Convention has not been construed to require state parties to adopt extreme abortion bans; to the contrary, the Convention has been construed by the Inter-American Commission on Human Rights to allow states parties to adopt nonextreme abortion policies.[34]

For the reasons stated in the preceding paragraph, extreme abortion bans violate not only the right to moral equality but also the right to religious and moral freedom: Such bans fail to satisfy – the resolution

---

Protection Arguments for Abortion Rights," 34 *Harvard Journal of Law and Public Policy* 889, 891 n. 3 (2011). For a recent article pressing what Dixon and Nussbaum call "equality-based arguments in favor of recognizing a constitutional right of access to abortion," see Priscilla J. Smith, "Give Justice Ginsburg What She Wants: Using Sex Equality Arguments to Demand Examination of the Legitimacy of State Interests in Abortion Regulation," 34 *Harvard Journal of Law and Gender* 377 (2011). Cf. Reva B. Siegel, "*Roe*'s Roots: The Women's Rights Claims That Engendered *Roe*," 90 *Boston University Law Review* 1875 (2010).

[33] That forcing a woman to continue with such a pregnancy is based on a failure to take seriously the especially heavy burden that such coercion imposes on the women is not belied by the fact that some women *choose* to continue with such a pregnancy.

[34] For a discussion and criticism of the Inter-American Commission's construal of the Convention, see Ligia M. De Jesus, "Post *Baby Boy v. United States* Developments in the Inter-American System of Human Rights: Inconsistent Application of the American Convention's Protection of the Right to Life from Conception," 17 *Law and Business Review of the Americas* 435 (2011).

of the competing interests represented by such bans fails to satisfy – the proportionality aspect of the right to religious and moral freedom. Indeed, for the reasons stated in the preceding paragraph, the conclusion is warranted even from a Thayerian perspective that extreme abortion bans violate the right to religious and moral freedom: The judgment that the resolution of the competing interests represented by such bans is proportionate is not a reasonable judgment; the judgment appears reasonable only if we fail to take seriously the especially heavy burden that such bans impose on women.

Do relatively permissive bans on abortion, like extreme bans, violate the right to moral equality? An affirmative answer is too tendentious, in my judgment, to warrant the Supreme Court's invalidation of the Georgia law at issue in *Doe v. Bolton*. That law, after all, was a reform measure, "patterned," as the Court reported in *Doe v. Bolton*,

> upon the American Law Institute's Model Penal Code, § 230.3 (Proposed Official Draft, 1962)... The ALI proposal has served [as of 1973] as the model for recent legislation in approximately one-fourth of our States. The new Georgia provisions replaced statutory law that had been in effect for more than 90 years... The predecessor statute paralleled the Texas legislation considered in *Roe v. Wade*... and made all abortions criminal except those necessary 'to preserve the life' of the pregnant woman.[35]

By contrast, the Supreme Court's invalidation of the Texas law that was at issue in *Roe v. Wade* was warranted, in my judgment. Indeed, the Court's ruling against the Texas law was warranted even if we assume that the Court should have proceeded in a Thayerian mode:

- The judgment that such a ban is constitutional – *a criminal ban that would not have been enacted but for a failure to take seriously the especially heavy burden the law imposes on women* – is not a reasonable constitutional judgment. To the contrary, it is an unreasonable – a clearly mistaken – constitutional judgment: a judgment that clearly misconceives the right to moral equality.
- Relatedly, the judgment that the resolution of the competing interests represented by an extreme ban satisfies the proportionality aspect of the right to religious and moral freedom is not a reasonable judgment;

---

[35]   410 U.S. at 182–3.

again, the judgment appears reasonable only if we fail to take seriously the especially heavy burden that such bans impose on women.

THE POSITION AT WHICH I HAVE ARRIVED – that the Supreme Court's ruling against the Texas law, but not its ruling against the Georgia law, was warranted – is, of course, controversial: Many insist that both rulings were warranted; many others, that neither ruling was warranted. Although controversial, the position at which I have arrived brings me into alignment – for me, comfortable alignment – with the position espoused by Justice Ruth Bader Ginsburg in 1985, when she was a judge of the United States Court of Appeals for the District of Columbia Circuit: In the abortion cases, then-Judge Ginsburg wrote, the Supreme Court should not have "gone beyond a ruling on the extreme [Texas] statute before the Court... Heavy-handed judicial intervention was difficult to justify and appears to have provoked, not resolved, conflict."[36]

My twofold response to the question whether governments – which are free, insofar as internationally recognized human rights are concerned, *not* to ban abortion – are also free *to* ban abortion, is this: From the perspective of the judiciary proceeding in the Thayerian mode, governments may enact relatively permissive bans of the sort considered in this chapter; extreme bans, however – including the Irish ban discussed in the appendix – violate both the right to moral equality and the right to religious and moral freedom.

APPENDIX

Abortion, Human Rights NGOs, and Ireland

Amnesty International (AI) and Human Rights Watch (HRW) are two of the world's most important human rights NGOs. Both AI and HRW have weighed in on the controversial question of whether banning abortion constitutes a human rights violation.

---

[36] Ruth Bader Ginsburg, "Some Thoughts on Equality and Autonomy in Relation to *Roe v. Wade*," 63 *North Carolina Law Review* 375, 385–6 (1985).

The stand AI took in 2007 was controversial among its membership, which includes many anti-abortion Catholics. In response to the controversy, AI issued a press release on June 14, 2007, which stated in part:

Amnesty International Defends Access to Abortion for Women at Risk

Amnesty International today firmly stood by the rights of women and girls to be free from threat, force or coercion as they exercise their sexual and reproductive rights . . .

"Millions of people around the world of many faiths and creeds donate to Amnesty International as individuals. Among them are welcome donations from members of the Catholic faith. We hope that Amnesty International's work against torture, against the death penalty and for the proper administration of justice including for women and girls will continue to draw active support from people of conviction the world over," said Kate Gilmore[, Executive Deputy Secretary General of Amnesty International].

Defending the right of women to sexual and reproductive integrity in the face of grave human rights violations, Amnesty International recently incorporated a focus on selected aspects of abortion into its broader policy on sexual and reproductive rights. These additions do not promote abortion as a universal right and Amnesty International remains silent on the rights and wrongs of abortion.

"Amnesty International's position is not for abortion as a right but for women's human rights to be free of fear, threat and coercion as they manage all consequences of rape and other grave human rights violations," clarified Kate Gilmore . . .

[AI's policy,] standing alongside its long-standing opposition to forced abortion, is to support the decriminalisation of abortion, to ensure women have access to health care when complications arise from abortion and to defend women's access to abortion, within reasonable gestational limits, when their health or human rights are in danger.

"Amnesty International stands alongside the victims and survivors of human rights violations. Our policy reflects our obligation of solidarity as a human rights movement with, for example, the rape survivor in Darfur who, because she is left pregnant as a result of the enemy, is further ostracized by her community," said Kate Gilmore.

AI's position, as reported in the press release, is guarded; it can be read as opposed to extreme bans on abortion but as agnostic with respect to relatively permissive bans of the sort considered in this chapter.

Like AI, HRW has weighed in on whether banning abortion constitutes a human rights violation. Consider, for example, this statement, issued by HRW on Jan. 28, 2010:

Ireland: Abortion Limits Violate Human Rights

The Irish government actively seeks to restrict access to abortion services and information both within Ireland and for its residents seeking care abroad, Human Rights Watch said in a report released today.

The 57-page report, "A State of Isolation: Access to Abortion for Women in Ireland," details how women struggle to overcome the financial, logistical, physical, and emotional burdens imposed by restrictive laws and policies that force them to seek care abroad, without support from the state. Every year thousands of women and girls travel from Ireland to other European countries for abortions.

"Women in need of abortion services should, as a matter of international law and – frankly – human decency, be able to count on support from their government as they face a difficult situation," said Marianne Mollmann, women's rights advocacy director at Human Rights Watch. "But in Ireland they are actively stonewalled, stigmatized, and written out."

In Ireland, abortion is legally restricted in almost all circumstances, with potential penalties of penal servitude for life for both patients and service providers, except where the pregnant woman's life is in danger, but there is little legal and policy guidance on when, specifically, an abortion might be legally performed within Ireland. As a result, some doctors are reluctant even to provide pre-natal screening for severe fetal abnormalities, and very few – if any – women have access to legal abortions at home. The government has indicated that it has no current plans to clarify the possible reach of the criminal penalties. The government does not keep figures on legal and illegal abortions carried out in Ireland, or on the number of women traveling abroad for services.

"Irish law on abortion is in and of itself an affront to human rights," Mollmann said. "But it is made worse by the fact that even those who may qualify for a legal abortion in Ireland cannot get one due to deliberately murky policies that carry an implied threat of prosecution."

But women also face more active sabotaging of their health decisions by the state. Throughout the last two decades, the Irish government has used injunctions to prevent individuals from traveling abroad for abortion. As recently as 2007, a 17-year-old girl in the custody of the Health Services Executive had to go to court to get permission to travel to the United Kingdom for an abortion.

Organizations that provide information on how to access abortion services abroad face restrictions on when and how this information can legally be conveyed, under threat of penalties. And the government does nothing to prevent "rogue" agencies that represent themselves as providers of information about abortion from circulating blatantly misleading and false information.

"Women should not have to make decisions about their health and lives based on lies," Mollmann said. "Yet the law leaves 'rogue' agencies unregulated and threatens honest service providers with fines or worse if they help a distressed woman make a phone call to a clinic abroad."[37]

Human Rights Watch has made it clear elsewhere that its position is not just that an extreme ban on abortion, such as Ireland's, but that any ban on abortion – even a relatively permissive ban of the sort considered in this chapter – is a violation of a women's human rights.[38]

In December 2010, almost a year after HRW issued its statement condemning Ireland's ban on abortion as a violation of human rights, the European Court of Human Rights decided *Case of A, B and C* v.

[37] See also Human Rights Watch, "Argentina: Guarantee Women's Access to Health Care" (2010), http://www.hrw.org/en/news/2010/08/10/argentina-guarantee-women-s-access-health-care; Human Rights Watch, "Illusions of Care: Lack of Accountability for Reproductive Rights in Argentina" (2010) http://www.hrw.org/node/92124.

[38] See Human Rights Watch, "Q&A: Human Rights Law and Access to Abortion" (2010), http://www.hrw.org/backgrounder/americas/argentina0605/.

Ireland, Application no. 25579/05, addressing the question whether Ireland's ban, among the most extreme in Europe, violates the European Convention for the Protection of Human Rights and Fundamental Freedoms.[39] The seventeen ECHR judges who participated in the case ruled unanimously that

> the [Irish] authorities had failed to comply with their positive obligation [under Article 8 of the European Convention[40]] to secure ... [the] effective respect for [one's] private life by reason of the absence of any implementing legislation or regulatory regime providing an accessible and effective procedure by which [a woman can establish] whether she qualifie[s] for a lawful abortion in Ireland in accordance with Article 40.3.3 of the [Irish] Constitution.[41] Accordingly, the Court finds that there has been a violation of Article 8 of the Convention.

[39] The ECHR's decision is available online.

[40] Article 8 states:

1. Everyone has the right to respect for his private and family life, his home and his correspondence.
2. There shall be no interference by a public authority with the exercise of this right except such as is in accordance with the law and is necessary in a democratic society in the interests of national security, public safety or the economic well-being of the country, for the prevention of disorder or crime, for the protection of health or morals, or for the protection of the rights and freedoms of others.

[41] Article 40.3 of the Irish Constitution states:

1. The State guarantees in its laws to respect, and, as far as practicable, by its laws to defend and vindicate the personal rights of the citizen.
2. The State shall, in particular, by its laws protect as best it may from unjust attack and, in the case of injustice done, vindicate the life, person, good name, and property rights of every citizen.
3. The State acknowledges the right to life of the unborn and, with due regard to the equal right to life of the mother, guarantees in its laws to respect, and, as far as practicable, by its laws to defend and vindicate that right.

This subsection shall not limit freedom to travel between the State and another state. This subsection shall not limit freedom to obtain or make available, in the State, subject to such conditions as may be laid down by law, information relating to services lawfully available in another state.

As interpreted by the Irish Supreme Court, Article 40.3.3 entitles a woman to terminate a pre-viability pregnancy if, and only if, the termination is necessary to save her life.

However, the seventeen judges were divided on a different issue. A majority of the Court – nine judges – ruled that Ireland's refusal to permit women to have an abortion in order to protect their "health or well-being" did not violate Article 8 of the European Convention, given that Ireland permitted women who wanted to have an abortion for health or well-being reasons to travel abroad to do so and also permitted access to information about abortion services abroad to be freely communicated in Ireland. Two judges concurred in the judgment of the Court, arguing that although Ireland, by refusing to permit abortions for health or well-being reasons, had not violated Article 8 in the particular circumstances of the case, "it cannot be excluded that in other cases, in which there are grave dangers to the health or well-being of the woman wishing to have an abortion, the State's prohibition on abortion could . . . result in a violation of Article 8 of the Convention, since [Article 8] protects the right to personal autonomy as well as to physical and psychological integrity." Six judges dissented, arguing that Ireland's refusal to permit abortions for health or well-being reasons violated Article 8.[42]

---

[42] Consider two lines of inquiry about the ECHR's decision in *Case of A, B and C v. Ireland*:

- Ireland, which may criminally ban – and, therefore, criminally punish – anyone's paying children for sex while in the territory of Ireland, may also, as a matter of settled international law, criminally ban its nationals' and residents' paying children for sex while in the territory of another country, even one where such activity is not criminal. Does it make sense, then, to rule, as the ECHR did, that Ireland may criminally ban anyone's having (or participating in) an abortion for health or well-being reasons while in the territory of Ireland, but that Ireland may not criminally ban its nationals' and residents' having such an abortion while in the territory of another country, such as England, where such an abortion is not criminal?
- What warrants – does Article 8 warrant – the ECHR's saying, in effect, that Ireland may not criminally ban anyone's having an abortion for health or well-being reasons while in the territory of Ireland *unless Ireland allows its nationals and residents to go next door (i.e., across the Irish Sea), to England, to have such an abortion?* If Ireland may not, consistently with Article 8, ban its nationals and residents from having an abortion for health or well-being reasons while abroad, why doesn't Article 8 also prevent Ireland from banning its nationals and residents from having such an abortion while at home in Ireland?

For a discussion of the case, see Elizabeth Wicks, "*A, B, C v. Ireland*: Abortion Law under the European Convention on Human Rights," 11 *Human Rights Law Review* 556 (2011). See also Federico Fabbrini, "The European Court of Human Rights, the EU Charter of Fundamental Rights, and the Right to Abortion: *Roe* v. *Wade* on the Other Side of the Atlantic?," 18 *Columbia Journal of European Law* 1 (2011).

CONCLUDING NOTE

I began this book by observing that in the period since the end of the Second World War, there has emerged what never before existed: a truly global political morality. That morality – the morality of human rights – consists both of a fundamental imperative, which is the normative ground of human rights, and of various rights recognized by the great majority of the countries of the world as human rights. Some of the morality of human rights is entrenched – some of the rights internationally recognized as human rights are entrenched – in the constitutional law of the United States. I have focused in this book on three such rights, and on three large constitutional controversies, each of which implicates at least one of the three rights.

These are the conclusions I have reached:

- Punishing a criminal by killing him violates the right not to be subjected to "cruel and unusual" punishment, and the Supreme Court of the United States should so rule – that is, even proceeding in a Thayerian mode the Court should so rule.
- Even if, as I have suggested, the exclusion policy – excluding same-sex couples from civil marriage – does not violate the right to moral equality, the policy *does* violate the right to religious and moral freedom, and the Court should so rule.
- Unlike a relatively permissive ban on abortion of the sort that was at issue in *Doe* v. *Bolton,* an extreme ban on abortion, such as the ban the Court struck down in *Roe* v. *Wade,* violates both the right to moral equality and the right to religious and moral freedom.

INDEX